THE ECONOMIC ROLE OF THE CROWN IN THE OLD BABYLONIAN PERIOD

UNDENA PUBLICATIONS
MALIBU 1977

Bibliotheca Mesopotamica

Primary sources and interpretive analyses for the study of Mesopotamian civilization and its influences from late prehistory to the end of the cuneiform tradition

Edited by Giorgio Buccellati

Volume Five

Undena Publications
Malibu 1977

The Economic Role of the Crown in the Old Babylonian Period

by Norman Yoffee

PUBLICATION OF THIS BOOK
HAS BEEN AIDED BY A GRANT FROM
THE DEPARTMENT OF ANTHROPOLOGY ALUMNI FUND,
UNIVERSITY OF ARIZONA

Library of Congress Card Number: 76-18605
ISBN: 0-89003-021-9 (hard cover)
0-89003-020-0 (paper cover)

TABLE OF CONTENTS

LIST OF TABLES

LIST OF ABBREVIATIONS

AASOR	*Annual of the American Schools of Oriental Research*
AbB	*Altbabylonische Briefe,* ed. F. R. Kraus
ABPh	*Altbabylonische Briefe aus dem Museum zu Philadelphia,* A. Ungnad
A-d	Ammi-ditana
AfO	*Archiv fuer Orientforschung*
Agricultura	*Agricultura Mesopotamica,* A. Salonen
AHw	*Akkadisches Handwoerterbuch,* W. von Soden
AJA	*American Journal of Archaeology*
AJSL	*American Journal of Semitic Languages and Literatures*
ANET	*Ancient Near Eastern Texts Relating to the Old Testament,* ed., J. Pritchard
AnOr	*Analecta Orientalia*
AOS	*American Oriental Series*
ARM	*Archives Royales de Mari*
ARN	*Altbabylonische Rechtsurkunden aus Nippur,* F. R. Kraus, M. Çığ, H. Kızılyay
ArOr	*Archiv Orientální*
A-ṣ	Ammi-ṣaduqa
AS	*Assyriological Studies* (Chicago)
BA	*Beitraege zur Assyriologie und semitischen Sprachwissenschaft*
BaghMitt	*Baghdader Mitteilungen*
BAP	*Beitraege zum altbabylonischen Privatrecht,* B. Meissner
BAW	*Beitraege zum assyrischen Woerterbuch,* B. Meissner
BB	*Babylonische Briefe aus der Zeit der Hammurapi-Dynastie,* A. Ungnad
BDHP	*Business Documents of the Hammurabi Period,* L. Waterman
BE	*The Babylonian Expedition of the University of Pennsylvania. Series A: Cuneiform Texts*
Beamtennamen	*Das Priester- und Beamtentum der altbabylonischen Kontrakte,* E. Lindl
BIN	*Babylonian Inscriptions in the Collection of James B. Nies*
BiOr	*Bibliotheca Orientalis*
CAD	*The Assyrian Dictionary of the University of Chicago*
CAH	*The Cambridge Ancient History*
CH	Code of Hammurapi
CT	*Cuneiform Texts from Babylonian Tablets . . . in the British Museum*
Date Palm	*The Date Palm and its By-products according to the Cuneiform Sources,* B. Landsberger

Eames	*Catalogue of the Cuneiform Tablets of the Wilberforce Eames Babylonian Collection in the New York Public Library*, A. L. Oppenheim
ed-Dēr	*Altbabylonische Rechts- und Wirtschaftsurkunden aus Tell ed-Dēr im Iraq Museum*, D. O. Edzard
Edikt	*Ein Edikt des Koenigs Ammiṣaduqa von Babylon*, F. R. Kraus
Festschrift Boehl	*Symbolae biblicae et mesopotamicae F. M. Th. de Liagre Boehl dedicatae*, ed. A. Kampman
Festschrift David	*Symbolae iuridicae et historicae Martino David dedicatae* vol II, eds., Ankum, Fernstra, Leemans
Festschrift Koschaker	*Symbolae ad iura Orientis Antiqui pertinentes P. Koschaker dedicatae*
GAG	*Grundriss der akkadischen Grammatik*, W. von Soden
Gerichtswesen	*Das altbabylonische Gerichtswesen*, A. Walther
Heidelberger Studien	*Heidelberger Studien zum alten Orient*, ed. D. O. Edzard
HG	*Hammurabi's Gesetz*, J. Kohler, P. Koschaker, A. Ungnad
HSM	Signature of the Harvard Semitic Museum
HUCA	*Hebrew Union College Annual*
Iraq	(journal of the British School of Archaeology in Iraq)
JAOS	*Journal of the American Oriental Society*
JCS	*Journal of Cuneiform Studies*
JESHO	*Journal of the Social and Economic History of the Orient*
JNES	*Journal of Near Eastern Studies*
JRAS	*Journal of the Royal Asiatic Society*
Klengel, Beitraege	*Beitraege zur sozialen Struktur des alten Vorderasien*, ed. H. Klengel
KUB	*Keilschrifturkunden aus Boghazköi*
La banque	*Les origines antiques de la banque de dépôt*, R. Bogaert
Labat, *Manuel*	*Manuel d'épigraphie akkadienne*, R. Labat
LFBD	*Letters of the first Babylonian dynasty*, T. Fish
LTBA	*Die lexikalischen Tafelserie der Babylonier und Assyrer in dem Berliner Museum*, W. von Soden
MAH	Signature of the Musée d'art et d'histoire of Geneva
MAOG	*Mitteilungen der Altorientalischen Gesellschaft*
Merchant	*The Old Babylonian Merchant*, W. F. Leemans
MLC	Signature of the J. P. Morgan Library Collection, Yale University
MSL	*Materialien zum sumerischen Lexikon*
MVAG	*Mitteilungen der vorderasiatisch-aegyptischen Gesellschaft*
NBC	Signature of the James B. Nies Babylonian Collection, Yale University
OA	Old Assyria(n)
OB	Old Babylonia(n)
PBS	*Publications of the Babylonian Section, University Museum, University of Pennsylvania*
Personenmiete	*Altbabylonische Personenmiete und Erntearbeitervertraege*, J. Lautner
RA	*Revue d'assyriologie et d'archéologie orientale*

RIDA	*Revue Internationale des droits de l'Antiquité*
RlA	*Reallexikon der Assyriologie*
Roellig, Bier	*Das Bier im alten Mesopotamien,* W. Roellig
RSO	*Rivista degli studi orientali*
SD	*Studia et documenta ad iura Orientis Antiqui pertinentia*
S-d	Samsu-ditana
SFS	*Une saison de fouilles à Sippar,* V. Scheil
SGL	*Sumerische Goetterlieder,* vol. I, A. Falkenstein; vol. II, J. J. van Dijk
S-i	Samsu-iluna
SLB	*Studia ad tabulas cuneiformes collectas a F. M. Th. de Liagre Boehl pertinentia*
ŠL	*Šumerisches Lexikon,* A. Deimel
STT	*The Sultantepe Tablets* vol. II, O. Gurney and P. Hulin
Studies Oppenheim	*Studies Presented to A. L. Oppenheim*
SVJAD	*Starovavilonskie juridičeskie i administrativnie dokumenti v sobranijach SSSR,* A. Riftin
Taxation	*Taxation and Land Revenues in the Old Babylonian Period,* M. deJ. Ellis
Tablettes	*Tablettes économiques et administratives d'époque babylonienne ancienne,* M. Birot
TCL	*Musée du Louvre, Textes cunéiformes*
TCS	*Texts from Cuneiform Sources*
TJG	*Tablettes juridiques de la Ire dynastie de Babylone, conservées au Musée d'art et d'histoire de Genève,* E. Szlechter
TJM	*Tablettes juridiques et administratives de la IIIe dynastie d'Ur et de la Ire dynastie de Babylone, conservées au Musée de l'université de Manchester . . .,* E. Szlechter
TIM	*Texts in the Iraq Museum*
TLB	*Tabulae cuneiformes a F. M. Th. de Liagre Boehl collectae*
UAZP	*Urkunden des altbabylonischen Zivil- und Prozessrechts,* M. Schorr
UCP	*University of California Publications in Semitic Philology*
UET	*Ur Excavation Texts*
VAB	*Vorderasisatische Bibliothek*
VDI	*Vestnik drevnej istorii*
VS	*Vorderasiatische Schriftdenkmaeler der Koeniglichen Museen zu Berlin*
W	Waterman, *Business Documents of the Hammurabi Period* = *AJSL* 29, 145ff, 288ff. and *AJSL* 30, 48ff. *AJSL* copies used in this study
Warenpreise	*Warenpreise in Babylonien,* B. Meissner
Wirtschaftsleben	*Zum altbabylonischen Wirtschaftsleben,* W. Schwenzner
YOS	*Yale Oriental Series*
ZANF	*Zeitschrift fuer Assyriologie und vorderasiatische Archaeologie, Neue Folge*
ZDMG	*Zeitschrift der Deutschen Morgenlaendischen Gesellschaft*
ZZB	*Die "Zweite Zwischenzeit" Babyloniens,* D. O. Edzard

PREFACE

As the scope of this monograph is not clearly indicated by its rather sweeping title, a clarification of the aims of this study and of the intent of the title are appropriate at the outset. In the first place, the use of the term "economic role" does not imply the goal of isolating the particular dynamics of production, consumption and exchange in Babylonia. The intention is, rather, to deal with certain aspects of Babylonian social structure that may be approached from the study of documents explicitly drawn up as records of financial transactions. It would be ambitious, indeed, to try to delimit a set of phenomena as having an "economic" role to the exclusion of those phenemena also possessing "social" or "political" purpose. No attempt will be made, therefore, to maintain that economic considerations can be or ought to be separated from the larger fabric of relationships that comprise the structure of Babylonian society.

Although the majority of the economic records examined here emanate from various bureaus of the royal administration, it is clear that the contents of the texts were not restricted to intramural bureaucratic affairs. The political systems (i.e., states) in ancient civilizations, like their counterparts in more recent times, were not independent entities monolithically able to direct all spheres of legal action and economic production and distribution throughout the social order. Rather, the state interacted with relatively autonomous local units, each with its particular pattern of socio-economic integration. The state stood above all of these local units, however, having the power to make decisions concerning the public welfare and prosperity of the society as a whole. Thus, the documents of state bureaucracies report on governmental relations with these locally organized social units as well as record internal administrative undertakings. In discussing the "economic role of the crown," we mean not only to delineate the hierarchical structure of certain administrative bureaus concerned with fiscal affairs, but also to describe the function of the bureaucracy in conveying centralized political decisions to, and monitoring the responses to those decisions from, these institutionalized elements in society with which the administration had to deal.

The time-range implied by the term "Old Babylonian" is itself in need of elaboration. Most of the attention in this monograph is devoted to the northern part of Babylonia and to the time of the last kings of the "First Dynasty of Babylon." The events of this particular "late Old Babylonian" time and place, however, are closely related to the historical process of the conquest and administration of the south by king Hammurapi of Babylon and are even partly conditioned by the circumstances through which Babylon gradually became pre-eminent among the competing cities in the north after the collapse of the "Third Dynasty of Ur" (ca. 2000 B.C.). While the presentation of quantities of original text editions that date predominantly to the latter part of the Old Babylonian period has precluded more detailed discussion of the earlier part, my intention is ultimately to expand this study backward in time (through an examination of texts from Kish that date throughout the entire period) and to make more explicit the few remarks concerning this earlier period, passed over so fleetingly now.

Assyriological publications dealing with editions and expositions of textual data have conspicuously limited their interpretive comments to neat summaries of the contents of the texts. Larger explanatory statements for which no direct textual citation might be adduced have been consciously avoided. One obvious consequence of this hyper-cautious approach to scholarship has been the production of works that are accessible only to specialists, sometimes only to those who are expert in the minutiae of a certain period. While criticism of compressed and particular Assyriological studies of texts and terms as being too trivial has not been wanting among Assyriologists themselves, the richness and variety of Mesopotamian data have largely remained unknown to, or been cast in a form unusable by, historians and social scientists who might be interested in certain theoretical problems to which Mesopotamian data can make a real contribution.

One route out of this paradoxical situation would be to employ more explicitly an interpretive methodology that departs from the traditional goals of philological classification and seriation of textual data. An orientation that seeks to use textual materials to answer carefully chosen kinds of questions has certain immediate advantages over one that uses texts as a means from which questions are to be generated. At the same time that it impels the analyst to deal directly with fundamental historical and cultural processes, it also serves to bring the importance of Mesopotamian data to the attention of these not solely committed to a ramble among the customs and curios of one particular early civilization. The disadvantage in this approach lies mainly in the analyst's susceptibility to the charge that he may not be able to substantiate every interpretive statement with appropriate textual chapter and verse. Nevertheless, the goals of interpretation seem worth this risk.

While any study utilizing Mesopotamian texts must obviously contain many detailed philological discussions, I have tried to keep in mind that few circumstances in (late) Old Babylonian society are likely to have been phenomena unique to that time and place. The inferences and explanations drawn from the texts gathered here are not restricted to the description and evaluation of the contents of this particular corpus of materials, but rather are ordered in an attempt to deal with the process of historical change in Mesopotamia. It is hoped that this study might thereby be considered not only pertinent for students of the Old Babylonian period, but also suggestive for Assyriologists who are concerned with the study of other times in Mesopotamian history. A still more ambitious aim is that this monograph might serve as a case-study in the operation of (ancient) bureaucratic systems, and in the process of socio-political change within a complex society, and thus be of interest to social scientists and historians concerned with these topics.

To any of those latter groups of readers who may pick up this study the following warning must be made: most of the data in the monograph is presented according to Assyriological convention and will be completely intelligible only to those having competence in Mesopotamian languages and their scholarship. I am exceedingly grateful, therefore to

Prof. Giorgio Buccellati, the editor of this series, for suggesting that I undertake a separate publication amplifying the interpretive sections herein and omitting the more technical linguistic discussions so that this work may be made more easily accessible to non-Assyriologists. This synopsis will appear in his series *Sources and Monographs in the Ancient Near East.*

The present study began as a dissertation written under the supervision of the late Prof. J. J. Finkelstein and was submitted to Yale University in the spring of 1973. I learned from Prof. Finkelstein, not only in the classroom, but also in personal and friendly conversation, that texts were not to be translated analytically and antiseptically, but as the vivid documentation of once vital and complex social systems. It seems only cold appreciation now, but I have him to thank here for placing his pre-publication *YOS* 13 materials at my disposal and for discussing many points in their interpretation.

I have further to thank Prof. D. O. Edzard, with whom I studied for two semesters in his Assyriological Seminar in Munich, and who first suggested to me the general idea of studying Old Babylonian business and administrative documents, although he could not foresee the direction of this study. I want to acknowledge Prof. W. W. Hallo's permission to cite a few unpublished examples from the *YOS* 12 volume, and to thank Dr. Mark Cohen for calling them to my attention. In addition, I am indebted to Profs. †Oppenheim and Reiner for permission to consult the lexical files of the *CAD* and the article *mu'errum* from the "Wurstmaschine" edition of volume M. I also wish to thank Dr. Maria deJ. Ellis for kindly placing her dissertation manuscript at my disposal and discussing with me many of the issues raised therein. Finally, I am grateful to Dr. Maureen Gallery who consented to read through the entire manuscript and has suggested a number of very useful re-evaluations and to Mr. M. Desrochers and Mrs. M. L. Penchoen for their skill and care in editing the volume. The final product, of course, is my sole responsibility.

I have avoided assigning absolute dates to the regnal years mentioned throughout this study. The problem of competing chronologies may be summarized as follows:

Sumu-abum	1894-1881	1830-1817	(14 years)
Sumula'el	1880-1845	1816-1781	(36 years)
Sabium	1844-1831	1780-1767	(14 years)
Apil-Sin	1830-1813	1766-1749	(18 years)
Sin-muballiṭ	1812-1793	1748-1729	(20 years)
Hammurapi	1792-1750	1728-1686	(43 years)
Samsu-iluna	1749-1712	1685-1648	(38 years)
Abi-ešuḫ	1711-1684	1647-1620	(28 years)
Ammi-ditana	1683-1647	1619-1583	(37 years)
Ammi-ṣaduqa	1646-1626	1582-1562	(21 years)
Samsu-ditana	1625-1595	1561-1531	(31 years)

CHAPTER 1

Introduction: Administrative Documents and the Study of the Palace in the Old Babylonian Period

The discipline of Assyriology is one of the younger academic sciences. It was only in 1857, little more than a century ago, that Rawlinson, Hincks, Oppert and Talbot gathered in London each to try his hand independently at translating a common text so as to demonstrate to a skeptical academic community the basic accomplishment of the decipherment of the cuneiform script. By about the first decade of the twentieth century, texts could be established readily and the data gleaned from them used fairly reliably to reconstruct the course of Mesopotamian history and the cultures spanning almost three millennia.

Throughout the development of the discipline, undoubtedly owing to the vast amount of documentation suddenly brought to light covering such a long span of time, Assyriologists have seen their foremost duty to be the publishing and editing of texts. Problems of interpretation, consequently, have often been circumscribed as commentaries to specific texts or groups of texts. In order to expand the level of discussion beyond these texts, the modern analyst usually tries to focus on key terms in the texts and then to draw other texts that mention the same terms into the examination. In this way the amount of data available for close inspection is increased, while a basic restriction on the field of interpretation to lexically related materials is preserved. These basic philological principles will be observed in this study but with one important difference: instead of choosing only those terms that are found in a particular set of texts, thereby generating interpretations inductively, we shall first select a problem and then examine texts in the attempt to deal with that problem. Hypotheses, involving particular terminological discussions and building upon one another, will be systematically stated. Existing data will then be inspected in order to show how they tend to confirm or fail to confirm each hypothetical statement.

The Palace as a Category of Study

In any study of the Babylonian palace it would be obviously difficult to limit research only to those documents that mention the *ekallum*, the Babylonian word for palace. Such a conservative approach would result in a collection of descriptive oddments which, with few exceptions, would serve only to characterize the palace as an expression of royal power, or to provide a vehicle for tracing the careers of its royal inhabitants. If we want to examine in any breadth the economic affairs of the bureaucratic administration of the palace, we must be prepared to assume the existence of records that do not mention the palace explicitly but nonetheless document its economic activity.[1]

To isolate the palace as a category of study within Babylonian society, we must begin by considering the traditional criteria for determining what texts refer to the palace. The first documents to be inspected are, of course, the ones which can be most securely linked with the palace, namely those documents mentioning the *ekallum* and describing activities labelled by F. R. Kraus "Die Geschaefte des 'Palastes' "[2] ("the business affairs of the crown"). It is our contention that the "palace" does not refer to one building[3] in one city and does not necessarily refer to a royal residence. *ekallum* implies, rather, the crown's administrative institutions chiefly in relation to its economic interests. Therefore to try to pinpoint the specific edifice to which *ekallum* in administrative documents may refer will lie outside the goals set here; it may not refer to any. In these texts, then, *ekallum* ('Palast') may most usefully be translated, "of, or pertaining to, the crown's administration," or simply, "crown."

Beginning with these explicitly denoted crown "business documents," we can immediately catalogue a set of resources managed by the crown and can specify the particular techniques through which these resources were distributed to various clients. Because these crown business documents are few in number, however, we want to review in this chapter the traditional criteria for considering which texts are pertinent to the study of the crown's economic enterprises. Since these standards will be seen as inadequate, in Chapter 2 we shall concentrate on developing new criteria in order to broaden the amount of material appropriate to this field of inquiry. Then, in successive chapters, we shall focus on several key terms selected so as to provide tests for a series of hypotheses designed to explore the nature of several offices in the hierarchy of the financial bureaus of the crown and to determine the ranges of these official activities.

By enlarging the number of texts recording the ways in which available resources in Old Babylonian society are manipulated toward certain ends by the political system, we shall be able to assess more accurately the economic impact of the crown's administrative policies. In addition, by concentrating on that section of the bureaucratic structure of the crown charged with the management of fiscal resources, and by observing how these activities change through time, we can add new and more detailed perspectives to our current historical picture of the Old Babylonian period. Providing a control on the usual sources for the reconstruction of the sequence of events in Mesopotamia, this study of "non-historical" documents will rely only minimally on native historical conceptions, which while obviously valuable, are more often than not tendentious and self-serving.

In the final chapter, in the course of presenting a model to explain why particular sets of financial activities were undertaken, we shall also consider the factors affecting the availability of resources to the crown, and the effects of political decisions made by the crown on the economic stability of the Old Babylonian society as a whole.

The Palace as Economic Entity

The economic role of the palace has come under scrutiny mainly in terms of the authority of the king or dynasty in power, and consequently has been appraised according to the strength of the military and political authority wielded by the throne. A vigorous monarch (or dynasty) has been interpreted as exercising a pervasive influence in the economic life of the society - specifically by limiting the quantity of land privately held, by obliging payments in agricultural taxes and other dues and by requiring corvée labor. It has been asserted, for example, that the royal house of the Third Dynasty of Ur dominated society, possessed almost all the land, and sat atop an all-encompassing bureaucratic pyramid that all but suffocated the individual economic enterprise of its subjects.[4] While this picture of the Ur III socio-economic organization as monopolized by the palace is being gradually amended to include some role for the private (communal) sector,[5] it should be noted that this more balanced view of the economy has emerged not so much through direct textual attestation of the role of the private sector as through circumstantial indications of privately disposed land and commodities from administrative documents and literary compositions.[6] The overwhelming preponderance of Ur III documents left by the royal bureaucracy effectively screens our proper appreciation of the community's participation in the economy; and the enormously energetic, though certainly not ubiquitous, authority of the royal administration still dominates our evaluation of the socio-economic structure in the Ur III period.

The Old Babylonian period[7] is usually contrasted in socio-economic terms with that of Ur III. Especially striking is the smaller quantity of patently administrative documents[8] whose enormous numbers in the Ur III period attested to a complex and pervasive royal bureaucratic organization. This change in documentation in the OB period is commonly supposed to reflect a change in social structure in which the private economy predominated at the expense of the power of the palace.[9] The growth of the private sphere, in turn, is generally attributed to the influx of new elements of population.[10] Thus, from the Ur III period to the Old Babylonian, the palace has not only been reduced in military and political power, but has also been supplanted as the paramount economic force in its society.

The large number of Old Babylonian private documents has drawn analysts' attention to the relationships among private individuals in much the same way that the Ur III administrative documents drew almost all attention to the palace in studies of that period. Consequently, there have been few investigations on the nature of the Old Babylonian palace or of the palace's economic activities. The aim of this study is to redress this imbalance - to examine certain features of the palace's role in the economic affairs of the Old Babylonian period.

However, in contrast to the difficulty of reformulating the picture of the economy of Ur III, when private documents are not abundant, the task of studying the economic role of the Old Babylonian palace is considerably facilitated by the existence of many administrative documents attesting to its economic activities. A major problem has been the inability of many scholars to recognize the administrative nature of certain texts that, when studied in microscopic isolation, were thought to be private documents. Indeed, it will become clear that there were well-organized bureaucracies of officials in the service of the OB palace, and that these officials presided over redistributive systems of commodities and were in charge of the management of large tracts of arable land. In short, revision of the picture of the OB period as an age of private enterprise par excellence is overdue.

Old Babylonian Administrative Documents

In 1923 Ungnad and Koschaker were already fighting an uphill battle to complete translations of all the published "legal and administrative documents of the first Babylonian and its contemporary dynasties,"[11] approximately 2000 in number. Since that time the number of published texts has increased at least three-fold, but no similar "corpus" of translations has appeared attempting to put some order to them. The earlier categorizations of these "non-literary"[12] texts were along juridical lines, often egregiously anachronistic. Kohler, for example, followed the organizational scheme of the *Deutsches Buergerliches Gesetzbuch*! [13] -- and experts of "cuneiform law" have dominated the analysis of these documents to this day.[14] Though this means of analysis has often yielded fruitful results, it has at the same time imposed a certain way of looking at texts and has tended to establish the techniques of formal legal methodology as the criteria for determining textual significance.[15]

A turning point in the analysis of OB "legal documents," often cited but seldom fully appreciated, was marked by Landsberger's study of the archive of Ubarum in *JCS* 9, p.121ff. There, in a few brief words, Landsberger pointed out a new principle without which contracts could not be properly interpreted – the necessity of ascertaining the "chain of authority"[16] within whose jurisdiction the stipulations of the document were to be executed. It follows, then, that no contract can be analyzed solely on the basis of abstract legal formulations. The implications of this principle of analysis involve no less than an attempt to come to grips with the nature of the socio-economic system of organization in the Old Babylonian period.

There were various administrative structures at this time and the category "administrative" has a broader reference than simply to the state. Accordingly, the interpreter must examine not only the terms of a document, but also the status and character of its participants. This means inspecting all the titular identifications found in the body of the document, and in addition, examining the witnesses and their possible interests in the conditions of the transaction.

That Landsberger's opinions resulted from the study of an archive was, of course, no accident, for it is only through the study of a group of internally connected texts that these kinds of administrative networks can be effectively researched. A genuine archive from a single provenience and published in one place[17] occasioned Landsberger's attention. As will be demonstrated however, other meaningful groups of texts may be assembled according to internal criteria to form "artificial archives."

The accumulation of texts into "artificial archives" based on prosopographic research into the world of Old Babylonian officialdom forms the philological underpinning on which this study of the palace's socio-economic structure and function is founded. It remains, of course, to show the relationship between these officials and the palace.

The only detailed study of a wide range of social and economic conditions in the OB period, one which, moreover, takes special cognizance of the administrative affairs of the palace, is F. R. Kraus's *Ein Edikt des Koenigs Ammi-ṣaduqa von Babylon.*[18] In his explication of the *mīšarum*-edict Kraus collected an enormous amount of information in order to document the practices which the edict mentions or to which it alludes. The source materials that Kraus utilized were primarily the "legal and administrative contracts," for it is in these documents that one finds the fullest exposition of official titles and technical terms. Here it is perhaps worthwhile reflecting a moment on Leemans' comment that "all three categories (letters, contracts and administrative documents) are of equal value for our knowledge of the economic and social history of ancient Mesopotamia and all three categories complement each other."[19]

One certainly cannot dispute the value of using all possible source materials to complement each other in the reconstruction of past events. Nevertheless, in the course of preparing this particular economic history the detailed study of letters was found to be much less fruitful than the examination of contracts and administrative documents. In spite of the more personal and vital quality of letters, it is often impossible to ascertain the referent of their communication (that is, the position of their authors in Landsberger's "chains of authority"). Even in the instance of royal correspondence, without specific knowledge of the participants or of the events preceding the matter at hand, the administrative details are often only tantalizing, and more often, just opaque. The elements generally missing in letters, patronyms and titular (official) identifications, are precisely the most important factors in establishing and grouping like administrative activities, and without these groupings research cannot proceed much beyond the stage of linguistic analysis. Singly, of course, the documents also lack explicitness. It is only in their concatenation according to internal criteria that prosopographic investigations may be undertaken. From these investigations the activities of many officials can be shown to define the nature of the office itself, and ultimately, the outlines of structures in the social order and in legal application may be drawn.

In an intentional departure from previous nomenclature, I use the word "document" to refer to what others have termed "contracts and administrative documents,"[20] "*Rechts- und Verwaltungsurkurden,*"[21] "Juridical texts and contracts,"[22] *Rechts- und Wirtschaftsurkunden,*"[23] and other variations on a theme first expressed by Koschaker in *HG* VI, p. 155-6. Koschaker used the criterion of the presence or absence of witnesses in a text to classify that text as a private contract or as an administrative record. It was exactly the problematic witnessed contract recording an administrative affair of the palace, however, that forced him to lump documents of this sort in a "Mischtypus," rare exceptions to the formal distinction between private and administrative documents. Koschaker's standard naturally limited the number of documents that he classified and analyzed as administrative.

Unfortunately, this standard has persisted to this day,[24] in spite of Landsberger's demonstrations of its inapplicability (in his Ubarum archive remarks).[25] There he showed that *only* by a careful examination of the witnesses in a document is one able (in many cases) to apprehend the presence of an administrative authority. The absence of witnesses in a document, therefore, merely denotes its character as an inventory, a bookkeeping record or a directive. A contract, on the other hand, implies simply an agreement with, or acceptance of, a condition; it may be either administrative or private and is witnessed in either case. For these reasons we must analyze documents by criteria other than the presence or absence of witnesses in order to ascertain whether they are private or administrative. "Administrative documents", therefore, must ultimately include a far greater range of materials than Koschaker, under the severe limitations of his formal distinction, had in mind in 1923 when he wrote, "Die Verwaltungsurkunden sind so gut wie nicht erforscht"[26] ("administrative documents might as well not have been researched at all"). Unfortunately, except for Koschaker's own study of what he termed the Larsa state fish monopoly[27] and Kraus's *Edikt,* the same might be said today.[28]

NOTES

[1]This argument follows Kraus's line of reasoning in *Ein Edikt des Koenigs Ammi-ṣaduqa von Babylon* (Leiden, 1958), p. 98, but intends to broaden the field of inquiry at the point where Kraus withdraws.

[2]*Edikt*, Chs. 6-7, pp. 75-112.

[3]Cf. *Edikt*, p. 82, however, where Kraus sometimes takes "palace" to mean "local palace."

[4]Cf. Falkenstein, *Die altorientalischen Reiche I*, Fischer Weltgeschichte (Frankfurt, 1964), pp. 146-47; Diakonoff, in Klengel, ed., *Beitraege zur sozialen Struktur des alten Vorderasien,* "On the Structure of Old Babylonian Society" (Berlin, 1971), p. 20; Gelb, in *Studi in Onore di Edoardo Volterra,* vol. VI (1969), "On the Alleged Temple and State Economies in Ancient Mesopotamia," p. 137 ff. Gelb tries to trace the history of the "Staatsozialismus" theories in Assyriology, p. 146 ff. He knows of no reference in Western literature that questions the fact that the state owned all the land in Ur III times.

[5]Mainly by Diakonoff, e.g., in Klengel, *Beitraege,* p. 18, and in *Ancient Mesopotamia* (Moscow, 1969), "The Rise of the Despotic State in Ancient Mesopotamia," p. 173 ff., esp. p. 194-197, contending that there was some private land in the Ur III period. At the same time, though, he stresses the "complete domination" of the state in other matters. The traditional Assyriological notion is to see some activity of the private sector in ditilla's and "contracts" (cf. Gadd, *CAH* vol. II, Part 1, Ch. 5–fascicle 35 , 1965, p. 28-9), but to assume the state owned all the land. Gelb, in *Studi in Onore di Edoardo Volterra*, vol. VI, p. 146 ff. has presented the first article showing the definite written records of private ownership of land in Ur III. His article undoubtedly signals a fresh look at the economy of Ur III that does not automatically assume the absolute control of the state in all economic matters.

[6]Diakonoff, in Klengel, *Beitraege*, p. 18-19 for a good example of such a reading of a literary work.

[7]The term Old Babylonia (n) is used here for that period between the end of Ur III and the end of the reign of Samsu-ditana.

[8]Edzard, *Die Altorientalischen Reiche I*, p. 193:

> In der altbabylonischen Zeit sind Urkunden der staatlichen Verwaltung viel seltener als sonstige nichtliterarische Zeugnisse: Privatvertraege, Gerichtsurkunden, Abrechnungstafeln und kleine Notizen ueber die Verwaltung privater Wirtschaftsbetriebe und vor allem Briefe–durchweg in akkadischer Sprache–, teils aus der Korrespondenz des 'Palastes', teils von Privatperson an Privatperson gerichtet.

[9]Edzard, *loc. cit.*:

> Dieser Unterschied in der Quellenlage beruht nicht etwa auf dem Zufall der Funde. Er ist bezeichnend fuer den Wandel der sozialen Struktur Babyloniens.

[10]Edzard, *Die 'zweite Zwischenzeit' Babyloniens* (1957), p. 8-9; Kraus, *Cahiers d'histoire mondiale I* (1955), p. 524; Pettinato, *Oriens Antiquus* VII (1968), p. 40.

[11]Ungnad and Koschaker, *Hammurabi's Gesetz* (hereafter *HG*, 1923) vol. VI, p. v.

[12]Edzard, *Die altorientalischen Reiche, vol. I, op. cit.*, p. 193, "sonstige nichtliterarische Zeugnisse".

[13]*HG* VI p. vii. Schorr, in *UAZP*, also divided documents according to formal legal classifications; Lindl, *Das Priester- und Beamtentum der altbabylonischen Kontrakte* (1913), simply gives a chronological arrangement of texts with lists of "priests and officials" (as far as he determines them) appended.

[14]See, for example, the bibliography, *Droits cunéiformes*, Cardascia and Klíma (1966), where almost all discussions of institutions and specific non-literary texts are fitted into the rubric "law." Specific studies on the OB economy (including neither Schwenzner, *Wirtschaftsleben*, nor Meissner, *Warenpreise*) are accorded six numbers (621-627) and "institutions administratives" four (565-68)—the latter being a sub-category of "Études de droit public." Walther, *Gerichtswesen*, is listed under the public law category as well, sub-heading "institutions judiciares." Landsberger's article, "Remarks on the Archive of the Soldier Ubarum" is found under "études de droit privée," sub-category "biens," sub-heading, "sur la tenure de service." Actually this principle of legal taxonomy is not entirely inappropriate; for most *studies* of the OB economy and administrative structures are themselves only afterthoughts to arguments concerned with juridical classification and explication. (Lautner's book, *Personenmiete*, valuable as it is, is an example). Administrative structures, especially, have not been deemed a proper subject for consideration on their own terms.

[15]Landsberger first questioned certain of the premises of cuneiform law in his article in *Festschrift Koschaker* (1939), pp. 219-234, "Die babylonischen Termini fuer Gesetz und Recht," and it is still to his arguments that all further discussions of the Babylonian legal process must turn. Cf. Finkelstein, *JAOS* 90 (1970), p. 255-6.

[16]*JCS* 9, p. 122, for this division into four chains of authority. The important thing for this study is the principle of division, not Landsberger's exact model. Cf. pp 126-8 for instances of the importance of recognizing the operative authority in the analysis of specific contracts.

[17]*JCS* 9, p. 121 with notes 1-2 .

[18]*SD* 5, Leiden, 1958, (abbreviated throughout as Kraus, *Edikt*).

[19]Leemans, *JESHO* 11, (1968) "Old Babylonian Letters and Economic History, A Review Article with a Digression on Foreign Trade," p. 171.

[20]Leemans, *JESHO* 11, p. 171.

[21]*HG* 6, p. v (1923).

[22]van Dijk, *TIM* 5 (1968), preface, where they are distinguished from administrative texts.

[23]Edzard, *Altbabylonische Rechts- und Wirtschaftsurkunden aus Tell ed-Dēr im Iraq Museum*, 1970 (hereafter, Edzard, *ed-Dēr*).

[24]Cf. Lautner, *Personenmiete*, (1936), p. 155:

> Nach dem fuer oeffentliche Verwaltungsakte bekannte Kriterium der Zeugenlosigkeit . . .

and Edzard, *ed-Dēr*, (1970), p. 17 with note 21:

> Gegenueber den Rechtsurkunden im engeren Sinne (d.h. den von einer Zeugenliste begleiteten Vertraegen und den Gerichtsurkunden) . . .

[25]Landsberger's study in *JCS* 9 parallels in some ways ancient Mesopotamian Wissenschaft: he proved his theories by working with them rather than by stating them apodictically as general rules.

[26]*HG* 6, p. 156.

[27]In *ZA* 47, (1942), p. 135-180, "Zur staatlichen Wirtschaftsverwaltung in altbabylonischer Zeit, insbesondere nach Urkunden aus Larsa." This is the only attempt of which I am aware that tries to document an administrative redistributive system in Mesopotamia, a process often spoken of by Assyriologists. Cf. Leemans' comments on this article in *The Old Babylonian Merchant,* 1950, p. 51ff; and cf. its influence on Kraus, *Edict*, p. 104.

[28]In this brief roster must also be included the doctoral dissertation of M. deJ. Ellis, *Taxation and Land Revenues in the Old Babylonian Period* (Yale, 1969; hereafter, Ellis, *Taxation*) which is being revised for publication. F. R. Kraus's *Staatliche Viehhaltung im altbabylonischen Lande Larsa* (Amsterdam, 1966), while having to do with "administrative documents," is more concerned with elucidating the technical terminology of several related texts concerning state-owned herds of animals (primarily sheep), than with an exposition of the economic importance of the animals to the state. Kraus supposes that the herds were very likely tended by semi-official, private individuals who contracted for this responsibility with the state (p. 50).

CHAPTER 2

Utul-Ištar and "The Business Affairs of the Crown"

The documents Kraus treated in the seventh chapter in the *Edikt* (1958), "Die Geschaefte des 'Palastes' nach den Urkunden,"[1] had previously been collected and briefly discussed by Walther (1917),[2] Koschaker (1923[3] and 1942[4]) and Leemans (1950).[5] Kohler and Ungnad in 1909[6] first categorized these texts, only thirteen of which had been published up to that date, as loans, but divided them according to the presence of an "Inhaberklausel."[7] The six documents without that clause were placed under the subcategory "Darlehen von Palast und Tempel" ("loans from palace and temple"), although the other seven texts that include the clause are also palace loans. One document, *BE* 6/2 120, was omitted in Kraus's collection.[8] Altogether there are now nineteen texts in this " 'Palast'geschaefte" group,[9] all from Sippar and Dilbat, and all dating from Ammi-ditana 26 through Ammi-ṣaduqa 15, a 27-year span.[10] Although their major features have been well well studied in the *Edikt*, It will be useful to review and restate some of the important points in this chapter as well.[11]

Since the " 'Palast'geschaefte" documents unambiguously refer to the crown (*ekallum*), they will form the first step toward the larger investigation of the crown's economic affairs. Kraus noted that there were likely to be other texts referring to the affairs of the crown that did not contain the word *ekallum*, but that were nonetheless transacted by crown officials. However, he specifically refrained from expanding his analysis of crown affairs beyond those texts containing the word "palace" because he considered such a project would involve too many unsupported assumptions,[12] and because going beyond these *ekallum*-texts would have entailed an investigation far beyond his intention of explicating the Edict.

Statement of Hypotheses

If the economic activities of the crown are performed by officials in texts not mentioning the "palace," and if, as noted in Chapter 1, administrative texts may be witnessed, procedures must be undertaken to identify those official documents that pertain to administrative, economic matters. These procedures may begin from a careful examination of the careers of important and well-attested officials in a group of texts mentioning the "palace." The activities of these individuals recorded in such "official" texts may then be compared with their activities in texts identifying them by their titles, but lacking an explicit reference to the palace. This comparison may be stated in the form of an hypothesis: If texts lack an explicit reference to the crown but mention a certain titled official who is known to be associated with the palace in other contexts, then these texts (may) record other administrative duties of that official. Comparison of these two groups of texts will thus provide the test of whether a (well-attested) individual bearing an official title undertakes responsibilities for the crown in texts not explicitly mentioning the palace. If this initial hypothesis is confirmed, two corollary hypotheses may be stated: (1) If this titled individual serves in the crown's administration, then the title held by this particular crown official designates a fairly specific locus of activities performed in service to the crown, and (2) If this official title denotes a rank held in the service of the crown, then texts involving other officials bearing this same title also document crown administrative activities.

It is suspected that many documents, when analyzed as individual artifacts, were routinely considered to reflect private business transactions because of the absence of any specific reference to the palace or simply because of the presence of a list of witnesses. In the light of a gradual accumulation of the possibly official roles of the participants in these documents, however, re-evaluations of the purpose of these transactions may be undertaken. Thus, the notion of the paucity of crown administrative documents in the Old Babylonian period was based primarily on *a priori* assumptions that excluded any analysis of the official sphere in most Old Babylonian texts. An investigation of the economic role of the crown was never undertaken, consequently, as there never seemed to be sufficient material to warrant such a study. From the accretion of information through prosopographic analysis as a means of testing whether titled officials explicitly connected with the palace in some texts also act in service to the crown in texts where they are titled but without any reference to the palace, this putative insufficiency of material to study the economic affairs of the crown may be remedied.

The Bureau of Wool Accounts

Resources and Profit

The 19 documents referring to the "business affairs of the crown" belong to what may be provisionally termed the "crown bureau of wool accounts." This bureau received wool from sources that cannot be directly documented, but probably from crown herds, and then made "loans" to acquire silver, which in turn could be used to purchase barley, which itself could also be loaned.[13]

The first process in the transaction of the wool loan was to specify a silver equivalency:

> (Amount of) wool belonging to the crown,[14]
> at the equivalent price (ratio) of 1 talent wool =
> 10 shekels silver . . .[15]

Kraus called this transaction "a sale of wool on credit," as in each case silver was required as the means of repayment. The exact mechanism of its repayment could also be variously designated,[16] and then this (repaid) silver could be loaned,

> (amount) silver
> šà šám sig *ša* é-gal ("from the wool accounts of the crown")

with silver to be repaid.[17] Barley was also loaned.[18] According to Kraus, the relationship among the three products is to be perceived in the document *BE* 6/1 85:

14 gín kù-babbar
a-na šám *še-e*
šà šám é-gal

(Amount) silver,
from the crown's (wool) accounts
to buy barley.

This form of barley transaction, in which the repayment within 10 days had to be weighed out in Sippar, was not a true loan (according to the canons of "cuneiform law") but a "purchase in advance" (German: "Praenumerationskauf").[19] There were, however, a number of normal barley loans that were made with the barley acquired from these "purchases." It is certain that these crown accounts were from the bureau of wool affairs even when síg (= wool) is not written, for the administrative personnel of these texts can be shown to be the same as in the wool and silver transactions.

The document *BE* 6/2 120, inadvertently omitted from Kraus's chapter, shows again the relationship among wool, silver and barley:

8 še gur ^{giš}bán-^{d}utu
šám 14 gín kù-babbar
šà šám síg *ša* é-gal

(Amount of) barley according to the *sūtu*-measure of Šamaš,
equivalent price in silver,[20]
from the wool accounts of the crown . . .

The tablet is broken, but we can assume that barley was to be repaid. Using Kraus's explanation, then, the barley that was loaned was acquired as payment for a loan of silver; and this silver was originally acquired from a wool loan.

There are some problems with this interpretation, however, which directly relate to economic theories of the medium of exchange in the Old Babylonian period. Edzard last brought up the issue in his excursus on the contract type, "Silberdarlehen, Rueckzahlung von Gerste," that is, documents in which silver is loaned, but barley is specified as the means of repayment.[21] He discussed the previous interpretations of "Lieferungskauf" ("purchase made on delivery") and "verhuellter Fruchtwucher" ("disguised appreciation"), but did not include documents from the bureau of wool accounts in those discussions. After much review of the past literature on the subject, Edzard came to the conclusion that a silver loan with barley repayment is a "normales Darlehen."[22] This conclusion was directed mainly against the opinions of Szlechter,[23] who thought that barley, whose value was reckoned in silver, was the subject of the loan as well as the medium of repayment, and of Pritsch,[24] who also thought that silver was only an equivalent price. Nevertheless, we can see that in the crown documents silver was indeed used as a standard by which the value of commodities was determined:

CT 8 21a

1 gú-un síg *ša* é-gal
šám 10 gín kù-babbar
ki PN
PN$_2$ šu ba-an-ti

(Amount of) wool belonging to the crown,
equivalent price in silver,
from PN (an official), PN$_2$ borrowed.

As we fortunately possess the receipt for the repayment of this loan, we see that the conditions of the loan are recapitulated before the statement of its repayment is written:

W 30

5 gín[25] kù-babbar na$_4$-^{d}utu
šà šám 1 gú-un síg$^{hi\text{-}a}$
ša é-gal
ša ki PN
PN$_2$ *im-ḫu-ru*[26]
mu-DU PN$_2$
nam-ḫar-ti PN

(Amount) silver, by the standard of Šamaš,
according to the equivalent price of 1 talent of wool
belonging to the crown,
which, from PN (an official),
PN$_2$ (three people) had received;
the repayment[27] of PN$_2$
was duly received by PN.

Kraus considered the entire transaction simply as a sale on credit, but as he noted, there is a certain ambiguity in the term šám (= *šīmum*), which he rendered both "Kaufpreis" ("saleprice") and "Kaufgegenstand"[28] ("material for sale"). In the context of *CT* 8 11c, we would prefer the translation "equivalent price," which connotes in these transactions the value of an item whether the item is sold, bought or kept:

CT 8 11c

1 gú-un síg *nam-ḫar-ti* é-gal
ganba 6 ma-na *a-na* 1 gín kù-babbar
šám 10 gín kù-babbar

1 talent of wool received by the crown,
at the market price of 6 minas (wool): 1 shekel silver—
the equivalent price is (thus) 10 shekels silver . . .

The translation "equivalent price" also seemed most appropriate for the text *BE* 6/2 120 (above p.14) in which barley was calculated according to its equivalent price in silver which came from the proceeds of the bureau of wool accounts.

Equivalencies and Markets

The question of equivalencies, markets, and, necessarily, the term šám has been most recently discussed by K. R. Veenhof in his study on Old Assyrian trade.[29] In the Old Assyrian texts šám is not used in contexts similar to those of the texts of this Old Babylonian crown bureau, and Veenhof's insistence on "the verbal, abstract notion 'purchase' "[30] is of no concern here. More relevant are his comments on the theories of Polanyi concerning the absence of markets and the medium of exchange in Mesopotamia.[31] Polanyi's ideas on these subjects, as expressed in three important essays,[32] are summarized by Veenhof as follows: Basically, Polanyi denies the existence of a market, or even a marketplace in Mesopotamia, and sees silver used not as an "indirect means of exchange," but rather as "money of account."[33] Various products, according to Polanyi's view, were exchanged in a system of barter and redistribution of accumulated goods, while silver was mostly used as the standard in a system of equivalencies for these redistributions. After discussing these problems in light of the Old Assyrian trading texts, however, Veenhof contends:

> . . . in OA trade silver served a purely commercial purpose and functioned as money in all the meanings of the word . . . We further have to conclude that markets did exist . . .[34]

Veenhof thus finds Polanyi's theories refuted by the evidence from Old Assyrian documents and letters. Since Polanyi used Old Assyria as one of his main examples, Veenhof's criticisms are justifiable for that period. For the Old Babylonian period, however, Polanyi's theories need to be re-examined in a different context. The documents of the crown bureau of wool accounts show, for example, that commodities were in fact evaluated on a silver standard. Although Veenhof did not dismiss completely the uses of silver as "administrative devices and <a> 'banking' < medium>"[35] in the Old Assyrian period, those texts that he analyzed, which are only part of the records of a long-distance trading network of merchants centered in Assur, hardly reflect all the uses of silver within Old Assyrian society. Though plentiful and fascinating, Old Assyrian documents shed light only on certain facets of a much larger socio-economic system.

For the Old Babylonian period the sample of documentation is much different. Concerning the use of silver in economic exchanges, Oppenheim wrote in 1964:

> During the Old Babylonian period, payments for real estate, slaves, goods and services seem to have been only rarely made in silver, although prices as a rule are quoted according to that standard. Specific allusions in texts support this assumption, and since no concern at all is expressed in Old Babylonian legal documents as to the quality and fineness of the silver used in payments, the silver probably did not change hands.[36]

The economy of Babylonia was based largely on the production of large-scale cereal agriculture and was pervaded by the existence of extensive manorial estates; stored wealth was converted into power through systems of redistribution. A complex network of equivalencies was developed consequently to deal with the various mechanisms of redistribution, and many records of payments for goods and services were transacted as allocations within manorial estates. Palaces, temples and holders of large tracts of private property remunerated their dependents with payments of various products grown on their lands. These payments would be specified as often as not, in terms of silver, but in fact they were distributed in the form of rations and silver seldom changed hands. We shall show in our discussion of the pay records of the crown "bureau of agricultural affairs" that occasionally texts directly mention payment of an amount of grain or another commodity, while other payments to the same class of workers record silver. The logical, albeit circumstantial, inference is that these agricultural laborers held contracts by which payments were calculated on a silver standard for bookkeeping purposes, but that they were paid in various products.

With respect to the arguments of Veenhof and Polanyi, it may be stated that there did exist mechanisms of equivalencies in Babylonia and that many exchanges were structured on a silver standard. It is unnecessary, however, to deny categorically the existence of the direct exchange of silver. We have already observed that in some texts, not only was an amount of wool to be loaned measured on a silver standard, but that silver was in fact repaid. The situation, in short, is more complicated than either Veenhof, with his biased sample of commercial trading records, or Polanyi, with his facile assumptions of the state-directed nature of Mesopotamian economy, have considered.

If silver functioned often as a standard of payment by which the value of goods and services were calculated, this bookkeeping technique was not characteristic of all exchanges in Babylonian society. It was precisely the great estates that made use of redistributional mechanisms as they were basically self-sufficient organizations insofar as subsistence needs were concerned. These great manorial estates, however, did not encompass the entire economic fabric of society. Commercial enterprises, long-distance trading and fluctuating prices of commodities demonstrate the existence of a flourishing market economy in Babylonia as well as in Assyria. This market system interacted extensively with the redistributive systems of the manorial organizations. For its part, the crown attempted to influence market exchange and the utilization of equivalent valuations in silver by restricting access to certain important objects of exchange.

Through its herds of animals, craftsmen (shepherds, fullers, weavers, and so on), and storage facilities, the crown was able not only to process wool on its own estates, but also to offer wool for sale through its bureau of wool accounts. This bureau acted as a credit institution, one of the variables (and one of the more important ones) affecting the course of the Babylonian markets. The bureau was able to convert wool into silver by means of a "loan" to be repaid in silver. Silver could be then negotiated into grain, as we see in *BE* 6/1 86:

> 10 še gur ^{giš}bán-^{d}utu
> *e-zu-ub ka-ni-ki-šu ša* 3 gín kù-babbar
> šà šám é-gal

(Amt. of) grain by the *sūtu*-standard of Šamaš,
apart from his (earlier) transaction of (an amt.) silver
from the crown's (wool) accounts

This grain was loaned to a man by the personnel of the bureau of wool accounts. That kind of "earlier transaction" was documented in *BE* 6/1 85 (above p.14) where "an amt. of silver from the crown's (wool) accounts" was loaned "to acquire grain." The crown's purpose in converting wool into silver and then into grain becomes obvious, for the rate of interest on silver is 20% and on grain 33 1/3%.[37] Why the crown needed to acquire grain in this manner is never stated, but this question will be treated as part of the explanatory model presented in the concluding chapter.

Personnel

We have spoken thus far of the operations of the "crown bureau of wool accounts" but have not discussed the personnel of the bureau (or bureaus). Seventeen of the nineteen documents are from Sippar; fifteen of these mention Utul-Ištar as the person responsible for the disbursement and receipt of commodities and two of them record subordinates of Utul-Ištar as supervising the transactions. In the remaining two documents which are from Dilbat, neither Utul-Ištar nor his subordinates are mentioned.

THE TERM *níg-šu*

The phrase denoting Utul-Ištar's jurisdiction in fourteen of the fifteen cases in which he appears is níg-šu, in the fifteenth the phrase *ša pīḫat.* That the latter term does not explain níg-šu, which in Akkadian is *ša qāti,* was proved by Landsberger in 1915.[38] In *CT* 6 35c, *ša pīḫat Utul-Ištar* refers to "the representative of Utul-Ištar,"[39] whereas níg-šu refers to the commodities, or better, the whole transaction that was thus "under the jurisdiction of Utul-Ištar." Lautner contended that the phrase níg-šu was not necessarily employed in the administrative sphere,[40] but the very nature of the expression "under the jurisdiction of," implies a system of hierarchical responsibilities such as would be found in the complex bureaucratic organization of the crown. In the letters published in the *AbB* series where níg-šu alternates freely with its Akkadian equivalent *ša qāti,* sometimes in the same letter,[41] various translations have been suggested: "unter Leitung des,"[42] "zuhanden des,"[43] dem PN unterstehen,"[44] "dem PN unterstellen,"[45] "im Besitze des."[46] Only the last, "in possession of," seems inappropriate and has led to misinterpretation. The letter involved concerns a complaint of an improperly irrigated field a-šà gú-un níg-šu ^{d}nanna-tum. The field is clearly a rented field (Pachtfeld) administered by one Nannatum, and on which he must pay the *biltum*-tax;[47] we suspect from Hammurapi's order not to impose a penalty[48] on Nannatum (on account of the irrigation difficulties) that the field belonged ultimately to the crown.

Edzard translated níg-šu literally, "zu Haenden von," in texts that he considered to be administrative documents because of the presence of the g̃ir-official.[49] Walther, commenting on the crown wool documents in 1917, translated more to the point, "Abteilung (woertlich: das von der Hand) des."[50]

Although Utul-Ištar appeared as the official responsible for the general operations of the bureau, he directed a number of subordinates who actually carried out the daily transactions. A subordinate was in charge of the commodity to be loaned (from Utul-Ištar's jurisdiction), then disbursed it to the borrowing party. This was most commonly expressed

níg-šu *utul-ištar*
ki PN (subordinate official)
PN_2 (borrower) šu ba-an-ti.

Occasionally this is fleshed out by the addition of the statement that the subordinate official received the commodity from the bureau of Utul-Ištar:

(Amt.) commodity
níg-šu *utul-ištar*
ša PN (subordinate official)
imḫuru
ki PN (subordinate official)
PN_2 (borrower) šu ba-an-ti

This phraseology appears in the repayment receipt *CT* 33 31[51] wherein the original terms of the loan are recapitulated before the statement of its repayment to the subordinate official. The entire text is as follows:

CT 33 31

(amt.) silver
šà šám síg *ša* é-gal
níg-šu *ú-túl-ištar* dub-sar
ša ᵈutu-šu-mu-un-dab di-ku_5
im-ḫu-ru-ma
i-na qá-ti ᵈutu-šu-mu-un-dab di-ku_5
PN (borrower)
im-ḫu-ru
mu-DU PN (borrower)
nam-ḫa-ar-ti ᵈutu-šu-mu-un-dab

ina qāti is used here for the more usual ki (= *itti*) of other documents, but this was just a scribal variation—there is no change in meaning. Utu-šumundab appears also in two grain loan documents without any mention of the authority of Utul-Ištar, but in the other five documents in which Utu-šumundab is present, he functions as the subordinate of Utul-Ištar.

In two other grain loans, *VS* 7 72 and 78, both of which attest a bureau of wool accounts in Dilbat, there is no mention of a director responsible (níg-šu) for the transaction, which is thus carried out by the disbursing (subordinate) officials. These officials have the rank *abi ṣābim* and *dayānum*, titles held by Utul-Ištar and Utu-šumundab respectively.

The position of the subordinate official in this crown bureau appears to have been hereditary, and the official himself possessed high status. Utu-šumundab appears with the rank di-ku$_5$ in five texts (A-d 29–A-ṣ 2), and with the rank ugula dam-gàr$^{(\text{meš})}$ in two texts of later date (A-ṣ5). His father, Ilšu-ibni, was also an ugula dam-gàr, and in the earliest of the bureau's documents,[52] was himself the subordinate official under Utul-Ištar's jurisdiction. The son not only succeeded to his father's position in the crown's service, but also assumed his rank. In the context of the crown's service, then, we must assume that ugula dam-gàr$^{(\text{meš})}$–*wakil tamkārī*–was a higher rank than di-ku$_5$–*dayānum.*[53]

Six documents attest the participation of a single family in the affairs of the crown bureau. Iddin-Ea, a *dayānum,* appears in three texts, and Sîn-išme'anni, *tamkārum,* in one. The other two members of this family who also serve as subordinate officials to Utul-Ištar, are not titled in the documents. The family may be reconstructed:

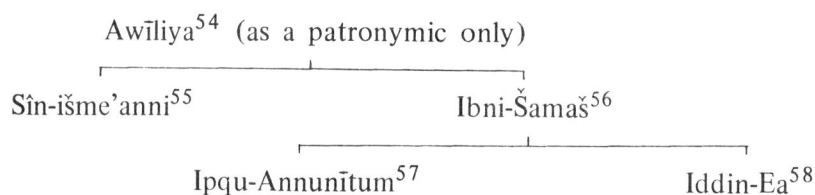

Awīliya[54] (as a patronymic only)

Sîn-išme'anni[55] Ibni-Šamaš[56]

Ipqu-Annunītum[57] Iddin-Ea[58]

As noted in connection with the documents that represent receipts for payments to the palace, the subordinate was also responsible for the collection of the loan. The original loan documents provided for this repayment through various intermediaries. These were the "bearer of his tablet" (*nāši kanīkišu*) or the "collector" of the crown (*mušaddinum*). The "collector" was not a distinct office, but a function performed on occasion by a member of the appropriate crown bureau.[59] In *AbB* 2 30 a *tamkārum* serves as a *mušaddinum,* and in *AbB* 2 89 the writer acts "as a *mušaddinum.*"[60] The crown could also demand payment of the obligation, according to the phrase *ūm ekallum kaspam irriš.*[61]

Just as a subordinate official in this bureau, Utu-šumundab,[62] "advanced" in rank from *dayānum* to *wakil tamkārī,* the chief of the bureau, Utul-Ištar also changed in status, going from dubsar (*ṭupšarrum*) to *abi* erén$^{(\text{meš})}$ = abi ṣābim. The translation "scribe"[63] for the title dub-sar is inadequate since the range of administrative duties does not include specifically scribal functions, although we may assume Utul-Ištar was trained in the scribal arts. It would, moreover, seem inappropriate for a "judge" or a "mayor"[64] to be under the jurisdiction of a "scribe." Utul-Ištar was, rather, the chief of the crown bureau of wool accounts, under whose jurisdiction a complex set of activities and a well-organized bureaucratic system was administered.

We shall now want to examine other documents in which Utul-Ištar appears with his titles *ṭupšarrum* and *abi ṣābim,* but without explicit reference to the *ekallum,* in order to compare his activities depicted in those documents with his duties that were explicitly in the service to the crown. Kraus considered that the " 'Palast'geschaefte" texts showed only a small part of the crown's economic affairs in the Old Babylonian period.[65] If we can show that texts not mentioning the *ekallum* were nonetheless crown administrative documents, we would thereby be able to explore the nature of the business "affairs of the crown" much more fully.

Texts Mentioning Utul-Ištar by Title

The fifteen " 'Palast'geschaefte" documents mentioning Utul-Ištar span a 27-year period—from Ammi-ditana 26 to Ammi-ṣaduqa 15. Until A-ṣ 6 he was identified as *ṭupšarrum,* from A-ṣ 10-15 as *abi ṣābim.* From Table 1, listing all the texts mentioning Utul-Ištar by title, it can be seen that this advancement in rank took place in A-ṣ 8, although the advancement itself did not seem to occasion a change in his responsibility in the crown's bureau of wool accounts. We shall try to determine from the additional texts, therefore, whether there might have been *any* change in authority that accompanied this change of title.

Table I: Texts Mentioning Utul-Ištar by Title

Year	Place of Publication
ṭupšarrum	
A-d 22	*CT* 48 66
A-d 26	*CT* 8 36a
A-d 29	*CT* 6 37c
	W 19
A-d 31	*CT* 33 31
A-d 32	*BE* 6/1 85
	YOS 13 281
A-d 33	*PBS* 8/2 214
A-d 36	*BE* 6/1, 87
	AS 16, 211-216
A-d 37	*BE* 6/1 86
A-ṣ 1	*YOS* 13 317
	VS 7 69
	CT 48 119
	CT 8 11c
	VS 7 145
	VS 7 139 (?)

Year		Place of Publication
	ṭupšarrum (cont.)	
A-ṣ 2		*ed-Dēr* 45
		CT 6 35c
A-ṣ 4		*BE* 6/2 120
A-ṣ 6		*PBS* 8/2 241
A-ṣ 7		*ed-Dēr* 30
	abi ṣābim	
A-ṣ 8		*YOS* 13 62
		67
		69
		70
		73
		362
		478
A-ṣ 10		*BAP* 4
A-ṣ 13		*CT* 8 21a
		BAP 74
A-ṣ 14		*TJG* p.38
A-ṣ 15		*CT* 8 10a
		CT 8 30b
		W 30
Date lost		*TLB* 1 226

The Early Career of Utul-Ištar

Slave Buyer

In *BAP* 74 Utul-Ištar, *abi ṣābim,* is mentioned as the father of Marduk-mušallim in a land-rental agreement. On the basis of this information the documents *BE* 6/1 103 (A-ṣ 1) and the letter *CT* 6 39b, which are concerned with the activities of *Marduk-mušallim* dumu *Utul-Ištar,* can be considered relevant to Utul-Ištar's biography. Since the name of Utul-Ištar's father is unknown, however, one cannot establish whether he might have inherited his position or even whether his father held any official position. The name Utul-Ištar[66] is quite common in the Old Babylonian period—there are eight different individuals by this name in the *YOS* 13 index alone—and since a writing, "Utul-Ištar, title, son of PN," is very unusual (either the title or the patronym was written, but seldom both), it is difficult to ascertain who was the father of the well known crown official.

We do not know, of course, Utul-Ištar's age when he is first documented with the rank of *ṭupšarrum* in A-d 22, but fifteen years later, his son was old enough to be involved in litigation (in A-ṣ 1, *BE* 6/1 103). The earliest text (A-d 22) mentioning Utul-Ištar with a title shows him commissioning the purchase of two Subarian slaves from "Mesopotamia."[67]

CT 48 66

[x ma-na] 4 gín kù-babbar na_4-lugal[68]
[ ][69] 2 sag-ìr su-bir_4^{ki} *nam-ru*
[*bi-ri-it*] i_7
ki [*ú-túl*]-*ištar* dub-sar
^{I}*i-ku-un-*pi_4-^{d}*sîn*
dumu *ip-qu-ša*
šu ba-an-ti
a-na iti-1-kam
2 sag-ìr *nam-ru*
bi-ri-it i_7
a-na ú-túl-ištar dub-sar
ú-ub-ba-lam-ma
ka-ni-ik-šu i-ḫi-ip-pí

---

igi *a-wi-la-tum*
dumu SI.A.TU-é-mah
igi ^{d}nanna-ma-an-sum dub-sar

---

iti du_6-kù u_4-10-kam
mu *am-mi-di-ta-na* lugal-e
en šà aš-gub-a x-[-x-x]
i_7 *am-mi-di-ta-na* mi-[ ]

Translation:

(Amt.) of) silver according to the royal standard, [in order to purchase] two first-class Subarian slaves from "Mesopotamia,"[70] Ikūn-pî-Sîn, son of Ipquša, has received from Utul-Ištar, the "scribe." In one month he will bring to Utul-Ištar, the "scribe," the two first-class Mesopotamian slaves; and his contract he will break.

The text *VS* 7 53 concerns the purchase of a female "Mesopotamian" slave from two joint-owners, one of whom is a certain Utul-Ištar, son of Sîn-iddinam.[71] The purchaser is a well known inhabitant of Dilbat, Uṣriya, son of Warassa.[72] Since *VS* 7 53 is from Dilbat, since the Utul-Ištar mentioned is untitled, and since the activities of the bureau of wool accounts directed by Utul-Ištar are all performed in Sippar (though there was a similar bureau in Dilbat), it could be argued that the Utul-Ištar in *VS* 7 53 was not the crown official of the same name. The date of *VS* 7 53, moreover, is two years earlier than Utul-Ištar's first titled attestation.

It may be seen from Table I, however, that documents from Dilbat (published in *VS* 7) do indeed mention an Utul-Ištar with the title dub-sar. It will also be observed that Utul-Ištar maintained an active interest in the slave trade, which he pursued in the official service to the crown.

The recently published *ed-Dēr* text no. 45 points to this connection between Utul-Ištar's slave interests and his crown functions. It belongs to the " 'Palast'geschaefte" genre—the silver paid for the two slaves is designated šà šám é-gal. We may add this text, then, to the list of transactions of the bureau of wool accounts. The date, A-ṣ 2, shows that this text falls within the temporal range of Utul-Ištar's activities as head of that bureau. His overall responsibility in this bureaucratic transaction is also indicated by the use of the term níg-šu in the text. That síg (wool) was omitted from the phrase šà šám é-gal is not critical since it was also omitted in some of the other documents we have reviewed that were transacted by the personnel of the bureau of wool accounts.

Edzard grouped *ed-Dēr* 45 with five other texts (nos. 46-50) since the terms mu-DU and *namḫarti* indicate they could all be classified as administrative documents, although in *ed-Dēr* 45 both words must be supplied in breaks. Edzard read the title of the "subordinate official" in line 6:

ša ⸢...-x⸣-^{d}é-a šà-[tam]

which should actually read,

ša ⌈*i-din*-⌉^{d}é-a di$^{!}$-[ku$_{5}$].

Iddin-Ea occurs in three other " 'Palast'geschaefte" documents of the bureau of wool accounts and is the most prominent member of the family of officials sketched above (p. 20). In his excursus to *ed-Dēr* text 1, Edzard had argued that šu ba-an-ti (= *leqûm* not *maḫārum*) implied the obligation of repayment on the part of the borrower. Here, however, he assumes that the person in line 6 was the borrower (*ša* PN *imḫuru*), while line 8 was the statement of his repayment ([mu-DU P]N). The text, *ed-Dēr* 45, which is an elaboration of the normal repayment receipt of the crown (*e.g.*, as seen in *W* 30, *CT* 33 31) probably reads as follows:

2 sag-géme [x]
gú(?)⸢-i$_{7}$⸣-ma-ra-da^{ki}
šám 7 5/6 gín kù-babbar
šà šám é-gal
níg-šu *ú-túl-ištar* dub-sar

ša ⌜*i-din-*⌝^{d}*é-a* di-$^{!}$[ku$_5$]
[*im*]-*ḫu-ru*
[ki *i-din*]-^{d}*é-a*
[PN šu ba-an-ti]
[mu-DU PN]
[nam-ḫar-ti]
r.1' ⌜i-din⌝-[^{d}é-a](?)

This document[73] is, therefore, an administrative record, showing Utul-Ištar purchasing slaves with crown funds.

BAP 4, dating to A-ṣ 10, also indicating the long-standing concern of Utul-Ištar with the slave-trade,[74] now titled *abi ṣābim,* should be considered along with *ed-Dēr* 45 and *CT* 48 66:

> (An Amt. of) sesame-oil measured according to the *sūtu*-standard of Šamaš, its price being (an amt. of) silver, Warad-Marduk, son of Ibni-Marduk, received from (the bureau of) Utul-Ištar, *abi ṣābim,* at the behest of (the subordinate official) Lu-Iškurra, son of Ili-usāti, in order to buy first-class Gutian slaves. In one month he will bring the first-class Gutian slaves. If he does not bring (them) by one month, Lu-Iškurra, son of Ili-usāti, will pay (the amt. of) silver to the bearer of his contract.

Lu-Iškurra is a subordinate of Utul-Ištar's[75] with the designated responsibility to purchase slaves and, although he himself contracts with a "slaver" who will actually do the purchasing, he is responsible for their prompt delivery to Utul-Ištar.[76] We do not know the purpose for which Utul-Ištar employed the slaves, but, on the basis of the administrative text *ed-Dēr* 45, we may be justified in viewing these slave purchases as evidence of the broad range of his functions as a crown official.

In addition to *VS* 7 53 other documents from Dilbat mention Utul-Ištar though these do not seem to refer to his official duties with the crown. With the title "scribe," he leases a field from someone (*VS* 7 69) and in turn he lets a field to someone else (*VS* 7 145). In *VS* 7 139 Utul-Ištar, "scribe," witnessed a field-rental agreement. One laconic document from Dilbat, *VS* 7 86, which shows a certain Utul-Ištar in a position of some authority, does not accord him any official title:

1 máš-gal
a-na ta-ku-ul-ti ⌜nin⌝ ^{d}*ŝin-im-gur-an-ni*
dumu-é-dub-ba-a *ša ú-túl-ištar*
mu-DU
^{I}*ri-ša-tum* sipa
nam-ḫa-ar-ti
^{Imunus}*an-na-bu* dumu-munus lugal
gìr *a-bi-i-lí* rá-gab (A-ṣ 10)

This text shows that an obligation was owed the sister of Sîn-imguranni, a dumu-é-dub-ba-a official who, in an unspecified way, was in the service of Utul-Ištar. We have suggested that the obligation was due the *sister* of Sîn-imguranni on the basis of the possibility that she might be the *nadītum,* sister of a Sîn-imguranni, in *CT* 6 6.[77] It can be shown that officials with the "scribal ranks" dub-sar and dumu-é-dub-ba-a are frequently mentioned in the body of the text or as witnesses in documents concerning high crown officials. Landsberger thought that these two scribal ranks were synonymous,[78] but there is some indication that certain individuals held only one of these positions at a time; thus the implication is that there was some meaningful distinction between dumu-é-dub-ba-a and dub-sar.

In addition to these Dilbat documents, two texts, *TLB* I 226 (date lost) and *CT* 8 10 a (A-ṣ 15), show Utul-Ištar, *abi ṣābim,* renting property. There is no indication that any of these rentals were part of Utul-Ištar's official functions.

Tax Collector

THE TERM *mušaddinum*

In the " 'Palast'geschaefte" documents the repayment of a crown loan was sometimes accomplished "when the *mušaddinum* of the crown calls for the silver," the *mušaddinum* being a person assigned the duties of collection for a specific occasion.[79] In those documents Utul-Ištar directed the collection, but he also could function as a *mušaddinum* himself. In *ed-Dēr* no. 30, "silver, the *isiḫtum* of Warad-Gipar was given over to Utul-Ištar, 'the scribe' for collection," *ša ana Utul-Ištar* dub-sar *ana šuddunim nadnu.* According to Edzard, the *isiḫtum* "ist zweifellos eine Zuweisung von amtswegen"[80] that was to be collected by Utul-Ištar from the guarantor of Warad-Gipar. Two similar texts from *YOS* 13 also show Utul-Ištar in the role of a *mušaddinum:*

YOS 13 317

10 gín kù-babbar
šà kù-babbar *še-e* lú-kúrun-na^{meš} ŠA LA AH?[ ]
ne-me-et-ti ^{d}*sîn-i-din-nam* si[pa u_8-udu$^{hi.a}$ é-gal
wa-ši-ib ì-lip^{ki}
ša mu *am-mi-ṣa-du-qá* lugal-e
^{d}en-líl-le nam-en-na-ni-šè bí-íb-[gu-ul-la]
ša a-na ú-túl-ištar dub-sar
a-na šu-ud-du-nim na-ad-nu
mu-DU ^{d}*sîn*[*-i-din-nam*]
nam-ḫar-ti ša-al-l[*u-rum*]
ù ìl-šu-ba-ni
seal: *ša-al-lu-rum*
dub-sar
ìr-^{d}*na-bi-um*
iti du_6-kù u_4-20-kam
mu *am-mi-ṣa-du-qá* lugal-e

^{d}en-líl-le nam-en-na-ni-šè
bí-íb-gu-ul-la (A-ṣ 1)

YOS 13 281

10 gín kù-babbar
šà 12 gín kù-babbar *še-e* lú-kúrun-na
ne-me-et-ti
^{Id}*sîn-i-din-nam* sipa u$_8$-udu^{hi-a} é-[gal]
wa-ši-ib ì-lip^{ki}
ša mu *am-mi-di-ta-na* [lugal-e]
bàd *iš-ku-u*[*n*]
ša ú-túl-ištar d[ub-sar]
[*a-na šu-ud-du-nim na-ad-nu*]
mu-[DU ^{d}*sîn-i-din-nam*]
nam-ḫa-a[*r-ti*]
^{I}*ša-al-lu-rum ù ì*[*l-šu-ba-ni*]

---

iti ab-è u$_4$-4-kam
mu *am-mi-di-*[*ta-na* lugal-e]
bàd *iš-ku-*[*un*]
gú i$_7$-[ ]
bí-in-dù-àm (A-d 32)

Translation of *YOS* 13 281:

> 10 shekels silver from the 12 shekels silver of the grain (accounts) of the brewers[81]—the *nēmettum*—obligation of Sîn-iddinam, the shepherd of the crown flocks, dweller of Ilip[82]—which in year A-d 32 was given over for collection to Utul-Ištar, the "scribe." (It was) brought in by Sîn-iddinam (and) received by Šallurum and Ilšu-bani.

An obligation of grain of certain brewers, stated in its silver equivalency, was brought in by Sîn-iddinam (relationship to the principals unspecified) and received by the subordinates of Utul-Ištar who was himself responsible for its collection.

Kraus discusses the *mušaddinum* and the phrase *ana šuddunum nadānum* (which indicates the function of a *mušaddinum*) in terms of the number of participants involved in the collection process.[82a] In the above two *YOS* 13 texts, 5 parties are enumerated: the brewers; their representative (?), Sîn-iddinam; Utul-Ištar, who was responsible for the collection; Šallurum and Ilšu-bani who received it;[83] and, implicitly, the crown which designated Utul-Ištar as the *mušaddinum* in the first place. The number of participants in collection documents does not so much define the type of collection, however, as it indicates the stage in the collection process. In the case of the two *YOS* 13 documents, which are acknowledgments of payment, the maximum number of parties are involved since the agents of the collector and the agents of the obligated parties must be enumerated as well as the principals.[84]

THE *nēmettum*–PAYMENT

The obligation to be collected by Utul-Ištar in the two *YOS* 13 texts–the *nēmettum*–occurs as well in the text published by Goetze in *AS* 16, pp. 211-16. That text also mentions lú-kúrun-na (=*sabū* "brewers") and, as the collector in charge of the *nēmettum*-payment, Utul-Ištar, *ṭupšarrum.*[85] Indeed, the text belongs formally to the " 'Palast'-geschaefte" genre, for é-gal is twice mentioned, and the entire matter of payment is summarized, line 41, *pīḫatam ekallam ippalū,* "the obligation is payable to the crown." The text begins,

> *aš-šum* lú-kúrun-n[a^{meš}] *ù* muhaldim^{meš} *wa-*[*ši-bu*][86]
> *ša* mu A-d 36
> *ša a-na ú-túl-ištar* dub-sar
> *a-na šu-ud-du-nim na-ad-nu*
> *gu-um-mu-ri šu-uš-ṭù-ri-im-ma*
> kù-babbar *ne-me-et-ti-šu-nu a-na* é-gal *ba-ba-lim*

Goetze's translation:

> Concerning getting the tavern keepers and cookshop operators liv[ing in Ilip], during the year A-d 36, who to Utul-Ištar, the scribe, have been assigned for collecting (the taxes), completely inscribed (in the register), (concerning) bringing the silver of their impost to the palace . . .

The collection of the *nēmettum*-payment by the crown, the subject of the two *YOS* 13 texts, is the main concern of this interesting and difficult text along with the registration of "tavern keepers and cookshop operators." The remainder of Goetze's text deals with other rules and obligations owed the crown and an oath by various *rabi'ānū* of their compliance with these rules.

Goetze had previously translated *nēmettum* as "impost," commenting on a large economic document in which *nēmettum* is contrasted in the ledger with mu-DU:

> It follows that for them [Iltani and her herdsmen] *nēmettum* was a revenue, an 'impost' that someone else had to deliver to them.[86a]

The *AHw* translates *nēmettum,* "a) Auflage," following Goetze, and "b) Beschwerdegrund"[87] following a recent article by Renger.[88] In Renger's investigation of the "Praedikatsergaenzungen" (various nouns used with certain verbs) of *răšûm* and *šuršûm* in the OB period,[89] he considered that the usual translation of *nēmettum,* "Auflage," would not do for the occurrences of that word in the phrase *nēmettam rašûm/šuršûm,* and offered the translation "Schwierigkeiten."[90] In this translation he was preceded by P. Kraus, 1932, "Beeintraechtigung" (injury, detraction);[91] Ungnad, 1914, "Vorwurf" (reproach);[92] Leemans, 1960, "charge";[93] F. R. Kraus, 1964, "Vorwurf,"[94] "Ruege"[95] (censure), "Regress"[96] (recourse), *inter alia.* In Renger's meaning, "difficulty," he sees an extension of the "concrete" definition "impost"–that is, it was "difficult" for the liable party to pay his taxes.[97] Kraus, who referred to *nēmettum* in passing within his section on the *mušaddinum* in the

Edikt, concluded that "arrears . . . were given over to the *mušaddinum* for collection."[98] The interpretation as "arrears" (as will be seen below) suits the context of the *nēmettum*-payment far better than Renger's labored explanation, "difficulty" (and the previous interpretations from which it was extrapolated):

> Es sei in diesem Zusammenhang an den deutschen Ausdruck 'die Zeche fur etwas bezahlen muessen' erinnert [to suffer the consequences; pay the piper].[99]

Renger concludes his study with the argument that phrases using the verb *šuršûm* with various objects are technical terms, "creations of the royal chancellory in Babylon."[100] One may wonder, however, whether "difficulty" is an appropriate technical term to be used by the crown's administrative bureaucracy.

In documents, the translation "impost" for *nēmettum* is considered appropriate by all, (e.g., *JNES* 27, p. 138, "eine Leistungspflicht, die aber nicht mit 'Lehns'plicht (*ilkum*) identisch ist"). Thus only in letters is a translation "difficulty" deemed more accurate. In the letters cited by Renger, however, it may be noticed, that, with a single exception, *nēmettum* appears in a "negative" context. The numbering below refers to Renger's article:

/8.1/ *nēmettam la irašši*
/8.2/ *nēmettam la iraššû*
/8.3/ *nēmettam la iraššû*
/8.4/ *nēmettam la iraššû*
/8.5/ *nēme[ttam] la tuš[ar]šaššunūti*
/8.6/ see below
/8.7/ *nēmettam ina muhhiya la irašši*
/8.8/ *aššum ina muhhiya nēmettam la rašê*
/8.9/ *nēmettam elika la irašši*
/8.10/ *nēmettam la irašši*[101]
/8.11/ *nēmettam la ir[ašši]*
/8.12/ *nēmettam la irašši*
/9.1/ *nēmettam ul tišu*

The letter /8.6/ (*TCL* 7 18 = *AbB* 4 18), quoted only in part by Renger, contains the only positive context of *nēmettam rašûm*. We present the letter in its entirety as its context clearly exemplifies why *nēmettum* almost invariably appears in a negative formulation:

Hammurapi writes Šamaš-hāzir: "Nannatum said to me the following:

i-na a-šà gú-un-*ya*
a-šà-*um ma-du-um-ma ú-ul im-ku-ur*
ki-a-am iq-bi-a-am
a-na a-šà gú-un níg-šu ^{d}nanna-tum
a-li-ik-ma

a-šà-*am ša a-na* ^{d}nanna-tum
a-na gú-un *na-ad-nu-ma*
a-na me-e e-lu-ma la im-ku-ru
a-mu-ur-ma
i-na a-šà-*im ša a-aḫ* i_7[ ]
ša re-eš é-gal *ú-k*[*a-al-lu*]
a-ša-*am ma-ak-r*[*a-am* Renger: *pu-uh* a-šà][102]
ša la im-[*ku-ru*]
a-na ^{d}nanna-tum [*i-di-in*]
a-na še gú-un-*šu ne-me-et-tam l*[*a i-r*]*a-aš-ši*
a-šà-*am ma-ak-ra-am a-na* ^{d}nanna-tum
ú-ul ta-na-ad-di-in
ne-me![103]*-et-tam i-ra-aš-ši-ma*
ḫe-ṭì-it gú-un-*šu*
i-na mu-uḫ-ḫi-ka
iš-ša-ak-ka-an

'From my *biltu*-field,[104] a large section was not able to be irrigated;' thus he (Nannatum) said to me. 'Go to the *biltu*-field under the jurisdiction of Nannatum,[105] the field which was given over to Nannatum under a *biltu*-agreement and examine the high-lying water which prevented irrigation. From the field on the bank of the [x-]canal, which are crown reserve lands,[106] give to Nannatum an irrigable field [as a substitute for the field] which was unable to be irrigated. Concerning his *biltu*-tax in barley, he shall incur no *nēmettum*-payment. But if you do not give an irrigable field to Nannatum, and he does incur a *nēmettum*-payment, the deficit of his *biltu*-tax will be imposed on you!'[107]

Nannatum cultivates land under a *biltu*-rental agreement under which he must pay a percentage of his crop to the crown. Part of his land will not yield a harvest, however, because high-standing water prevented proper irrigation. Hammurapi, therefore, orders Šamaš-ḫāzir to supply another piece of land from the crown's holdings. Because of the condition of the former land, no *nēmettum*-payment would be levied for the late payment of his *biltum*-obligation. But if Šamaš-ḫāzir does not promptly supply the exchange-land to Nannatum, and the relevant crown bureau does levy a *nēmettum*-payment, then Šamaš-ḫāzir will be liable for that payment.

The force of the negative usages of *nēmettum* in letters thus refers to contexts where an administrative authority threatens that if a situation is not corrected, someone will incur a *nēmettum*-payment that will be added to an original obligation. We suggest, therefore, that *nēmettum* be translated, "penalty, surcharge," and that there is no need to adopt one translation for documents and another for letters. This translation of *nēmettum* is also what one would expect from a *maprast*-formation of *emēdum,* "something imposed, an imposed payment, penalty, surcharge, impost." In the lexical citation *MSL* 6 127, note a, we find *nēmettum* used as follows:

$^{giš\text{-}gi\text{-}ri}$giš-šu-lú/dingir = *ne-me-et-tum ša a-*[*wi-lim*]/*i-lim,*

According to Landsberger, *nēmettum* means "pillory, stock," a wooden penalizing device, as it were. In the later historical development of the word, the *maprast-* of *emēdum* apparently got confused between "something imposed" and "something to lean on"; consequently one finds in later periods also the meanings, "Stuhllehne, Ruhelager."[108]

The function of the *mušaddinum,* a specially appointed collector, fits in very well with the collection of this penalty/surcharge as we saw above. In the two *YOS* 13 texts a *nēmettum*-payment was collected under the authority of Utul-Ištar acting as *mušaddinum,* and in *AS* 16 p. 211ff, Utul-Ištar administered the collection of obligations and registered certain categories of people. The dates were A-d 32, A-d 36, A-ṣ 1, during which years Utul-Ištar's title was "scribe." In A-ṣ 7, the year before he assumed the title *abi ṣābim,* he collected an *isiḫtum*-payment, which was also an assigned obligation.[109] Thus, in addition to his responsibilities in the "bureau of wool accounts," Utul-Ištar's duties included that of tax collector.

The Bureau of Agricultural Affairs

The Cultivation of Crown Lands

Another group of texts illustrates an additional facet of Utul-Istar's service, the administration of arable lands belonging to the crown. There were several ways in the OB period by which the crown used its land resources to derive (agricultural) revenues. One way was to lease land to certain beneficiaries who were not directly dependent on the crown (community members) in return for a rental fee. The crown also made beneficiaries of various high officials and priests whose rental dues also had to be paid to the crown storehouses, but these officials could in turn lease out the lands to third parties. The yield of these fields would then be apportioned in three ways: to the farmer who leased the land, to the direct beneficiary, and to the crown. The crown also gave land as subsistence (*šukūsum*) fields to minor dependents, soldiers, palace supernumeraries, and others owing service to the palace, but they still owed a rental payment to the crown. The rental dues of these minor dependents of the crown, the *nāši biltim* of the *mīšarum*-edicts and "law codes," were occasionally remitted by the king. The custom of periodic tax remission, however, never extended to high officials, beneficiaries of large tracts of land who could sub-let parcels for profit.[110]

The final means by which the crown derived benefits from its lands was to cultivate them directly with its own dependents and staff. In the letter *TCL* 7 18 cited above, it was clear that the crown controlled unassigned tracts of land. The following texts from the year Ammi-ṣaduqa 8 show that the cultivation of such crown lands was conducted by an agricultural bureau under the jurisdiction of Utul-Ištar.

TEXTS AND TRANSLATIONS

YOS 13 62

2 gín kù-babbar
e-zu-ub pí-i ka-ni-ki-šu pa-ni-i
a-na saḫar$^{\text{ḫi-a}}$ šà a-šà
ša pí-ḫa-at bu-la-ṭa-tum e-pí-ši
a-na á *ku-ub-bu-rum* dumu-ni
šu-ti-a
^{Id}iškur-*ra-bi* IŠ ^{d}za-ba$_4$-ba$_4$
ki *ú-túl-ištar a-bi* erén

---

igi ^{d}*é-a-bu-šu* [dumu x-x]*-ištar*
igi *ìl-šu-*[x-x]

---

iti ne-ne-gar u$_4$-[12-kam]
mu *am-mi-ṣa-du-qá* lugal-[e]
giš-KU-gar-guškin-g[a]-a
ki bàd-gub-a-aš ì-túm-ma
kišib ^{d}iškur-*ra-bi* (A-ṣ 8)

(the equivalent of) 2 shekels silver,
apart from his former transaction—
for doing earth works
in the field(s) under the responsibility of Bulaṭatum,
as the wages of his son, Kubburum—
received by
Adad-rabi, *kizûm* of Zababa.[111]
From (the bureau of) Utul-Ištar, *abi ṣābim.*

YOS 13 67

½ gín kù-babbar
e-zu-ub ka-ni-ki-šu pa-ni-i
a-na APIN-*tim*
i-na a-šà *ú-túl-ištar a-bi* erén
ša pí-ḫa-at bu-la-ṭa-tum

e-pí-ši-im
šu-ti-a
^{I}*A-na-pa-ni-ištar-na-di*

---

igi *ib-ni-*^{d}*marduk* dumu *gi-mil-*^{d}*marduk*
igi *bi-la-kum* dumu *mu-ha-ad-du-ú*

---

iti gan-gan-è u$_{4}$-22-kam
mu *am-mi-ṣa-du-qá* lugal-e
giš-KU-gar-guškin-ga-a
ki-bàd-gub-a-aš ì-túm-ma (A-ṣ 8)

(the equivalent of) ½ shekel silver—
apart from his former transaction
for cultivating
in the field(s) of Utul-Ištar, *abi ṣābim,*
under the responsibility of Bulaṭatum—
received by
Ana-pānī-Ištar-nadi.

YOS 13 69

1 gín kù-babbar
2 (PI) 3 bán še
e-zu-ub ka-ni-ki-šu pa-ni-i
a-na saḫar^{hi-a} šà a-šà *ša pí-ḫa-at*
^{I}*bu-la-ṭa-tum e-pí-ši-im*
šu-ti-a
^{I}*i-din-*^{d}*sîn su-ḫu-um*^{ki}
ki *ú-túl-ištar a-bi* erén

---

igi *ib-ni-*^{d}*marduk* dumu *gi-mil-*^{d}*marduk*
igi *ig-mil-ištar* dumu *be-la-nu*
igi *bi-la-kum* dumu *mu-ḫa-ad-du-ú*

---

iti apin-du$_8$-a u$_4$-5-kam
mu *am-mi-ṣa-du-qá* lugal-e
giš-KU-gar guškin-ga-a
ki bàd-gub-a-aš ì-túm-ma (A-ṣ 8)

(the equivalent of) 1 shekel silver—
(that is) 150 liters of barley,[112]
apart from his former transaction,
for doing earth works in the field(s)
under the responsibility of Bulaṭatum—
received by Iddin-Sin of Suḫum;
from (the bureau of) Utul-Ištar, *abi ṣābim.*

YOS 13 70

2 gín kù-babbar
e-zu-ub pí-i ka-ni-ki-šu pa-ni-i
a-na APIN-*tim i-na* a-šà *pí-ḫa-ti*
ša bu-la-ṭa-tum e-pí-ši
šu-ti-a [x-x-]tum engar
dumu *ib-ni-*^{d}*še-rum*
ki *ú-túl-ištar a-bi* erén

---

igi *ri-iš*-é-dub ugula mar[-tu]
igi *a-wi-il-*^{d}*sîn* dumu *e-ṭi-rum*

---

iti ne-ne-gar u$_4$-12-kam
mu *am-mi-ṣa-du-qá* lugal-e
giš-KU-gar guškin-ga-a
ki bàd-gub-a-aš ì-túm-ma (A-ṣ 8)

Seals: *ri-iš*-é-[dub]
ugula-[mar-tu]
dumu *i-na-pa-[li-šu]*
ìr-*am-mi-[ṣa-du-qá]*
a-wi-il-[^{d}*sîn]*
dumu *e-ṭi-[rum]*

(the equivalent of) 2 shekels silver—
apart from his former transaction,
for cultivating in the fields under the responsibility
of Bulaṭatum
received by PN, the *errēšum*-farmer,
son of Ibni-Šērum;
from (the bureau of) Utul-Ištar, *abi ṣābim.*

YOS 13 73

10 ma-na *qí-is-ti-*^{d}*marduk*
6$^{(?)}$ ma-na ìr-^{d}utu
[*ša*] ^{I}*i-lu-ni*
[*ilqû*(?)] 4 ma-na urudu
[*a-na*] ^{urudu}šu-kin
[*ša*]*-pa-ki-im-ma*
še-e ša a-šà *pí-ḫa-ti-šu-nu*
ka-ma-si-[*im*]
ki *ú-túl-ištar a-bi* erén

---

gìr dumu-20-kam en[sí]
—indistinct seal—
iti še-gur$_{10}$-ku$_{5}$ u$_{4}$-20-[kam]
mu [*am-mi-ṣa-du-qá* lugal-e]
giš-KU-gar guškin-ga (A-ṣ 8)

10 minas—Qīšti-Marduk,
6 minas—Warad-Šamaš,
which Iluni [received (?)];
4 minas copper
for casting copper sickles
(used) to gather grain in the fields
for which they were responsible;
from (the bureau of) Utul-Ištar, *abi ṣābim.*
Overseeing official: Mār-ešrâ, *iššakkum.*

YOS 13 362

1 gín kù-babbar
e-zu-ub ka-ni-ki-šu pa-ni-i
a-na ša-qú-tim

i-na a-šà *ú-túl-ištar a-bi* erén
ša pí-ḫa-at bu-la-ṭa-tum e-pí-ši
šu-ti-a
ìl-šu-ib-ni
dumu *ib-ni-*^{d}*marduk*

---

igi *ib-ni-*^{d}*marduk* dumu *gi-mil-*^{d}*marduk*
igi *bi-la-kum* dumu *mu-ḫa-ad-du-ú*
iti gan-gan-è u$_4$-29-kam
mu *am-mi-ṣa-du-qá* lugal-e
giš-KU-gar guškin-ga-a
ki-bàd-gub-a-aš ì-túm-ma (A-ṣ 8)

(the equivalent of) 1 shekel silver—
apart from his former transaction,
for performing irrigation activities
in the field(s) of Utul-Ištar, *abi ṣābim,*
under the responsibility of Bulaṭatum—
received by
Ilšu-ibni, son of Ibni-Marduk.

YOS 13 478

[g]ín kù-babbar
[*e-zu-ub k*]*a-ni-ki-šu pa-ni-i*
[*a-n*]*a* APIN-*tim*
i-na a-šà *ú-túl-ištar a-bi* erén
ša pí-ḫa-at bu-la-ṭa-tum agrig
e-pí-ši-im
šu-ti-a
^{I}*ba-aš-ilu* dumu *nu-na-ak-ka*

---

igi *ib-ni-*^{d}*marduk* dumu *gi-mil-*^{d}*marduk*
igi ^{d}za-ba$_4$-ba$_4$-lú-ti
igi *ta-ri-ba-tum* dumu *i-din-*^{d}*na-na-a*

---

iti gan-gan-è u$_4$-25-kam
[mu *am-*]*mi-ṣa-du-qá* lugul-e
giš-KU-gar-guškin-ga-a (A-ṣ 8)

Seal: *ib-ni-*^{d} [*marduk*]
[dumu *gi-mil-*^{d}*marduk*]
ìr-^{d} [ ]
ù ^{d}[ ]

(the equivalent of) x shekels silver–
apart from his former transaction,
for cultivating in the field(s) of Utul-Ištar, *abi ṣābim,*
under the responsibility of Bulaṭatum, *abarakkum*–
received by
Baši-ilu son of Nunakka.

DISCUSSION

In these seven documents presented above, Utul-Ištar is referred to as *abi ṣābim.* He assumed that rank only in the year A-ṣ 8, as the text *ed-Dēr* 30, dated to A-ṣ 7, still identifies him as a *ṭupšarrum.* Texts before A-ṣ 8 showing Utul-Ištar's management of lands and agricultural materials are thus far not attested, and we assume that this lack implies that his new rank brought with it a new set of responsibilities. While *YOS* 13 73 can best be explained in connection with another group of documents, the six remaining texts all refer to the same locus of activities. Bulaṭatum, titled agrig (=*abarakkum*) in no. 478:5, occurs in all six. Ibni-Marduk, son of Gimil-Marduk, witnesses four documents and Bilakum, son of Muḫaddu, witnesses three of those four. These texts are clearly part of a large series of transactions, as each document states *ezub (pî) kanīkišu pānî,* "apart from his former document." These examples are, therefore, only a small representation of countless other administrative dealings that were overseen by Utul-Ištar as head of a bureau concerned with the management of crown lands.

YOS 13 69 differs from the other documents in that it lists in apposition to the amount of silver, an amount of grain, which was received by a person for certain work. In the other texts only silver is recorded as being paid out as wages for the workers on these lands. The rate of the silver/grain exchange in *YOS* 13 69 is exactly one-half of the specified ratio of the "laws of Eshnunna," which is 1 šeqel silver = 300 *qa* grain.[113] According to another paragraph (no. 11) in the Eshnunna laws, this amount of grain would be the wages of a hired laborer for an entire month, but as the prices during the reign of Ammi-ṣaduqa were much inflated even over the idealizations of the Eshnunna laws, this standard cannot be assumed for this text.[114] The even payments in these texts (2 shekels, ½, 1, 2 and 1 shekel) indicate that a regular work-period was being remunerated, but the length of each period cannot be determined.

The work itself was designated in texts *YOS* 13 62 and 69 as *ana* saḫar^{hi-a} *epēšim*; in texts 67, 70, 478 as *ana* APIN-*tim epēšim;* and in text 362 as *ana šaqūtim epēšim.* These terms present some difficulties.

ana APIN-*tim* is probably to be read *ana ikkarūtim,* "for cultivation." *ana saḫar*$^{hi\text{-}a}$ *epēšim* is literally *ana eperī epēšim,* "to do earthworks."[115] Walters considered that the phrase *eperam epēšum,* "to perform earth (operations)," was specifically employed in connection with irrigation affairs.[116] This interpretation seems confirmed by its association with the phrase *ana šaqūtim epēšim,* which, although not heretofore attested in the OB period, nevertheless has to do with irrigation.[117]

These activities were performed in fields under the supervision of Utul-Ištar, *abi ṣābim.* In texts *YOS* 13 67, 362 and 478 the fields are described as *eqel Utul-Ištar*; and in texts 62, 69, 70 and 73 the payments for the workers are disbursed by him (*itti Utul-Ištar*). The "fields belonging to Utul-Ištar" is merely a formulaic convention denoting his authority over the work done on those fields; and the disbursement of grain payments implies, as well, that the entire transaction was accomplished under his jurisdiction. *itti Utul-Ištar* can thus be compared to the phrase níg-šu *Utul-Ištar* found in the " 'Palast'geschaefte" documents. The payments, in all likelihood, were not handed over by the chief himself, but by subordinates, which may account for the repeated occurrence of certain witnesses—Utul-Ištar's agents (?)—in these texts.

Utul-Ištar's official representative in the field, responsible for the daily irrigation and cultivation of the land, was Bulaṭatum, the *abarakkum,* "steward." The phrase denoting his responsibility, *eqlum ša pīḫat Bulaṭatum,* refers to the location—"the field (of Utul-Ištar) under the responsibility of Bulaṭatum"—where the work was done. Landsberger noted that the relationship implied in the phrase *eqlum pīḫat PN* was that of a subordinate official working on crown land.[118] Additional responsibilities of Bulaṭatum will be examined in texts to be discussed below.

The above documents are receipts of grain payments that were part of large-scale paylists of a crown bureau of land management. The tablets are quite small (4 cm x 3 cm), rapidly written in an extremely cursive style, and the wedges barely impressed in the clay. They give the impression, externally and internally, of being bookkeeping records, but individually analyzed and in the absence of knowledge of the participants, it is doubtful that their relationship to the crown would have been perceived.

The Accounting of Agricultural Implements

The specific nature of Bulaṭatum's responsibilities on crown lands can be documented in several other texts published in *YOS* 13. *YOS* 13 73, already transliterated and translated (above p. 35) will be considered together with these five texts, as it can be most easily placed in the context described by them. At the same time it provides a link between these texts and the ones describing the activities of Utul-Ištar.

TEXTS AND TRANSLATIONS

YOS 13 49

30 ma-na urudu
a-na a-ša *pí-ḫa-ti-šu*
e[-*ṣi*]-*di-im*
š[u-ti-]a
[PN]
ki *bu-la-ṭa-tum* dumu-é-dub-ba-a

---

seal: [ ]
[ ]
ìr-^{d}*marduk*

iti še-gur$_{10}$-ku$_5$ u$_4$-23-kam
mu *am-mi-ṣa-du-gá* lugal-e
^{d}lama-didli-a
é-babbar-ra-šè in-ne-en-ku$_4$-ra (A-ṣ 7)

30 minas copper—
for harvesting
in the field(s) under his responsibility—
received by
[PN];
from (the bureau of) Bulaṭatum, dumu-é-dub-ba-a.

YOS 13 71

10 ma-na urudu
KA dub-a-ni nu-me-a
a-na ^{urudu}šu-kin
ša a-šà *pí-ḫa-ti-šu e-pí-ši-im*
šu-ti-a
^{I}ìr-^{d}*mi-šar*
ensí
ki *bu-la-ṭa-tum* agrig

(indistinct seals)
iti bara-zà-gar u_4-3-kam
mu *am-mi-ṣa-du-qá* lugal-e
alam-nam-nir-gál-a-ni
zub-bi guškin-ga-ke_4
é-babbar-ra-sè in-ne-en-ku_4-[ra] (A-ṣ 9)

10 minas copper
—there was no prior transaction of his—[119]
for doing "sickle-work"
in the field(s) under his responsibility,
received by
Warad-mīšar
iššakkum;
from (the bureau of) Bulaṭatum, *abarakkum.*

YOS 13 72

72 ^{urudu}šu-kin
ki-lal 20 ma-na urudu
kin-til-la
a-na še-e ša a-šà kiš^{ki}
ka-ma-si-im
šu-ti-a
^{Id}*sîn-na-di-in-šu-mi*
^{I} dumu ^{d}*sîn-i-qí-ša-a*[*m*]
ù u-bar-^{d}*sîn* [x]
ki *bu-la-ṭa-tum* agrig

(indistinct seals)
iti bára-zà-gar u_4-18-kam
mu *am-mi-ṣa-du-qá* lugal-e
alam-nam-nir-gál-a-ni
é-babbar-ra-šè in-na-an-ku_4-[ra] (A-ṣ 9)

72 sickles—
weight 20 minas of copper,
finished work,
for reaping grain
in the field(s) of Kish—
received by
Sîn-nādin-šumi,
son of Sîn-iqīšam,
and Ubar-Sîn [x];
from (the bureau of) Bulaṭatum, *abarakkum.*

YOS 13 75

iš-tu iti-apin-du$_8$-a
u$_4$-7-kam
2 *bán* káš-ta-àm
a-na ma-aš-ti-it ^{munus}*se-eḫ-*[*ra*]*-tum* (erasures)
i-na é é-sag-íl-*mu-ša-lim* lú-kúrun-na
^{I}*bu-la-ṭa-tum* dumu-é-dub-ba-a
iṣ-bat

---

iti apin-du$_8$-a u$_4$-7-kam
mu *am-mi-ṣa-du-qá* lugal-e
šu-nir-ra u$_4$-dim (A-ṣ 6)

From the 8th month,
7th day,
2 seahs beer each,
for the beer rations of the young girls,
from the estate of Esagil-mušallim, the brewer,
Bulaṭatum, dumu-é-dub-ba-a,
took in possession.

YOS 13 235

10 ^{urudu}ḫa-bu-da
a-na a-šà ^{uru}ma-lah$_4$^{ki}
pí-ḫa-at gi-mil-lum dumu-é-dub-ba-a
ka-sa-mi
šu-ti-a
^{I}*gi-mil-lum* dumu-é-dub-ba-a
dumu *a-ta-na-aḫ-ištar*
ki *bu-la-ṭa-tum* agrig

---

gìr ^{d}*sîn-ma-gir*
seals: ì-*lí-i-din-*[*nam*]
dumu-^{d}*sîn-iš-*[me-an-ni]
ìr-^{d}nin-[ ]
iti šu-numun-a u$_4$-24-kam
mu *am-mi-ṣa-du-qá* lugal-e
alam-nam-nir-gál-la-ni
é-babbar-ra-šè (A-ṣ 9)

10 copper hoes –
for weeding
in the field(s) of the city Malaḫ,
under the responsibility of Gimillum, dumu-é-dub-ba-a –
received by
Gimillum, dumu-é-dub-ba-a, son of Ātanaḫ-Ištar,
from (the bureau of) Bulaṭatum, *abarakkum;*
controller: Sîn-magir.

DISCUSSION

The texts presented here refer to Bulaṭatum's responsibilities for distributing and maintaining various agricultural implements that were used by his work-force. These implements were also the subject of *YOS* 13 73 (above p. 35), a document that does not mention Bulaṭatum but does show that the maintenance of these implements was supervised by the bureau of agricultural affairs under the authority of Utul-Ištar. In this document several quantities of copper were received, one amount being specified as intended for casting into sickles that would then be used in the "fields of their responsibilities."[120] As seen in these additional texts, Bulaṭatum, the *abarakkum*-steward in the bureau, was the official most actively responsible for the maintenance of the copper tools.

He distributed to the workers of his precinct copper sickles and hoes, and then collected the worn implements and delivered them to be recast into new tools. Certain subordinates of his–in *YOS* 13 71 an *iššakkum*, in *YOS* 13 235 a dumu-é-dub-ba-a–were required to keep meticulous records of the weight of the worn tools that had been previously distributed. Quite a number of these tools were involved in the land work–in *YOS* 13 72, 20 minas of copper yielded 72 sickles, and weights of 30 minas in *YOS* 13 49 and 10 minas in *YOS* 13 71 are also recorded.

In *YOS* 13 75 another facet of Bulaṭatum's responsibilities is revealed, namely, that of securing beer rations from a brewer. The nature of the service performed by the "young girls," who in return received these rations, is unspecified; however, the collection of the beer from brewers recalls Utul-Ištar's own *mušaddinum*-activities in the collection of *nēmettum*-payments from brewers (in *YOS* 13 281 and 317, and in *AS* 16 p. 211ff).[121]

The title of Bulaṭatum in *YOS* 13 75 is dumu-é-dub-ba-a, a title he held also in *YOS* 13 49. As these two documents are dated in A-ṣ 6 and 7 respectively, we can see that he assumed the title *abarakkum* in A-ṣ 8 (*YOS* 13 478) and continued to hold it in A-ṣ 9 (*YOS* 13 71, 72, 235). Also, in A-ṣ 8 Utul-Ištar has the title *abi ṣābim,* a change in rank that most likely implies an advancement from the more generalized title "scribe." That *abarakkum* was a higher rank than dumu-é-dub-ba-a in this bureau is indicated in *YOS* 13 235 where Gimillum, a dumu-é-dub-ba-a, appears as a subordinate of Bulaṭatum, the *abarakkum.*

The title dumu-é-dub-ba-a has been confused occasionally with GÁ-dub-ba (= $\check{s}a_x$-dub-ba), the *šandabakkum,* one of the highest posts of the administrative hierarchy.[122] GÁ-dub-ba is never written with the extra -a, while in economic documents dumu-é-dub-ba-a invariably includes -a. In letters, however, dumu-é-dub-ba is occasionally written.

dumu-é-dub-ba-a has been translated "military scribe"[123] and "archivist."[124] These translations do not apply very well to Bulaṭatum's functions, and their difficulty underscores that in translating the "scribal" title of Utul-Ištar. Landsberger considered dub-sar and dumu-é-dub-ba-a as synonyms,[125] but considered that the latter title "was restricted to scribes of the royal administration, especially military scribes . . . and not carried by an ordinary village scribe."[126] Although we have not made a full collection of these titles, we do know that dub-sar was also a rather high rank within the bureaucracy of the crown. The difference between these two "scribal" titles, therefore (if there is any difference), does not necessarily reflect a consistent difference in function. One might provisionally posit that certain well-born youths were sent to scribal academies where they were trained to assume administrative posts. Any assumption of advancement from "scribal ranks" to higher posts, however, will not account for the facts that Utul-Ištar continued in his tasks in the bureau of wool accounts after his change in title to *abi ṣābim,* and that Bulaṭatum managed lands in the bureau of agricultural accounts when he held the titles of both dumu-é-dub-ba-a and *abarakkum.*

Conclusion

This chapter began with the hypothesis that texts concerning "the business of affairs of the crown" could be identified as such although an explicit textual reference to the crown was absent from them. The test of this hypothesis involved comparing the duties of an important, well-attested and explicitly denoted crown official with his activities in texts not mentioning the crown. We chose Utul-Ištar, the chief of the crown bureau of wool accounts, who presided over transactions of wool to acquire grain which could then be loaned on a short-term for a greater amount of profit. Under his jurisdiction, various officials of high rank, the *dayānum,* the *tamkārum* and the *wakil tamkārī,* whose titles were traditional in their families, received and dispensed the various commodities negotiated by this bureau.

From the tablets recording functions that Utul-Ištar was performing in the crown's service, we proceeded to the examination of texts that were less explicit in terms of the nature of his responsibilities. We observed that in his early career Utul-Ištar was engaged in collecting delinquent imposts of brewers and was in charge of the registration of crown dependents and the obligations that they owed the crown. Also in his early career, Utul-Ištar initiated what became a strong interest in the foreign slave trade. The purposes for which these slaves were acquired are never mentioned, and their limited number reflects the relative unimportance of slave labor during this period. One of the texts concerning his acquisition of slaves, however, did involve funds from the bureau of wool accounts.

While in the service of the bureau of wool accounts, Utul-Ištar held two different titles, *ṭupšarrum* and *abi ṣābim,* the latter of which he assumed in the year A-ṣ 8. In that same year, if the sample of extant texts can be trusted, he also assumed the leadership of what we have termed the bureau of agricultural affairs. As chief of this bureau, he had charge of the cultivation and maintenance of crown lands and the distribution of ration payments to the people who worked on them. Under his authorization, precincts were delineated and managed by agricultural specialists who were his subordinates. We can follow the activities of one of these management specialists, Bulaṭatum, as he fulfilled his duties of supplying valuable copper reaping instruments (cast by the crown's workshops?) to the harvesters of his precinct. He meticulously collected and recorded by weight the pieces of worn tools which would be melted down and recast into new implements. Bulaṭatum was also responsible for the distribution of beer rations to the workers in his precinct.

The many subordinate officials in this bureau of agricultural affairs–*abarakkum, iššakkum,* dumu-é-dub-ba-a–were under the jurisdiction of Utul-Ištar, the *abi ṣābim*-official, who, it should be noted, was at the same time still functioning in his position as chief of the bureau of wool accounts. By following the career, therefore, of an individual who must have been one of the most influential figures of his time, we have also observed the external workings of an elaborate bureaucratic system. This bureaucracy consisted of a well-defined hierarchy of titled officials who were administering a complex redistributive system. We have also seen that part of the bureaucracy functioned as a credit institution, dealing with people outside the redistributive system of the crown by negotiating some of the products of that system.

Throughout this chapter we have kept in mind Kraus's admonition against using a prosopographic method to aid in ascertaining "the business affairs of the crown." We believe it may be fairly said, however, in concluding this chapter, that the demonstration of the extent of crown affairs that has been presented here–including the functions of the bureau of wool accounts, the bureau of agricultural affairs and the collection of delinquent imposts–was made possible *only* through the study of texts mentioning Utul-Ištar and his subordinates. Let us now turn to our second hypothesis and an examination of the texts involving officials who held the same rank as did Utul-Ištar.

NOTES

[1]Kraus, *Edikt,* pp. 98-111.

[2]Walther. *Gerichtswesen,* p. 43 ff.

[3]Koschaker, *HG* 6 p. 18, note to *W.* 30 (1459).

[4]Koschaker, *ZA* 47, (1942), p. 141 note 15.

[5]Leemans, *The Old Babylonian Merchant, SD* 3, p. 102 f. The above four references are all noted by Kraus, *Edikt,* p. 98.

[6]Kohler, Ungnad, *HG* 3, pp. 56-59.

[7]*HG* 3, p. 58-59. Cf. the latest discussion of the "Inhaberklausel," *ana nāši kanīkišu* which states that the payment of a loan will be made "to the bearer of his [the debtor's] contract"), in Edzard, *ed-Dēr,* p. 69 ff (and below Ch. 4 p. 110f.). The table pp. 70-72 includes the seven documents in HG 3 systemetized according to the distinctions of "cuneiform law": "Empfang von Silber (diverse Zwecke)." "Empfang von Gerste (diverse Zwecke)," "Lieferungskauf," and "Kreditkauf." While it is not "wrong"

to classify documents according to their disparate phraseologies, the classification becomes only an exercise if it detracts from the larger significance of what the documents are about. Questions of juridical terminology must not be allowed to define the nature of the activity represented in texts or to interfere with categorization into significant groups according to that activity.

[8] *HG* 3 918, cf. Leemans, *Merchant,* p. 103, n. 258.

[9] Grant, *Smith College* no. 262, Kraus no. 19, must be omitted pending collation of the tablet.

[10] *CT* 48 119, as noted in that volume, is a "duplicate" of *CT* 8 llc. The year date is A-ṣ "17+c" which Kraus proposed to read A-ṣ 2, *Edikt,* pp. 106-111, following (at least chronologically) Walther, *Gerichtswesen,* p. 264, Nachtrag to p. 24. Finkelstein in *JCS* 15 pp. 92-3 (1961) in his review of the *Edikt* proved "17+c" is really year one, and that date will be adopted here. Also in the *CT* 48 volume is number 72 which belongs to the same type as analyzed by Kraus, *Edikt,* pp. 102-104. The *KU* 3 (=*HG*) citation, *Edikt* p. 102, for *CT* 8, 2b was misprinted 313; correct to 113.

[11] Kraus' discussion was very schematic as his purpose was to present the bare evidence of the crown's business activities, not to discuss all their ramifications.

[12] *Edikt,* p. 98.

[13] *Edikt,* p. 105; for the management of crown herds, see Kraus, *Staatliche Viehhaltung,* Amsterdam, 1966.

[14] The various choices of phrase for this statement are summed up in the *Edikt,* p. 99ff:

síg *ša* é-gal
síg na_4 *namḫarti* é-gal
síg na_4 *namḫarti* šà šám síg *ša* é-gal
síg *namḫarti* é-gal

[15] The phrases denoting the conversion of wool to silver are:

kù-bi (amt.) silver
kīma kargulli é-gal
šám (amt.) silver.

W 30 is not an exception to this equivalency ratio, see below, p. 15ff. and n. 25.

[16] The agents of collection were the *mušaddinum* or the *nāši kanīkim*; or the palace could just call for the silver. See discussion below.

[17] *Edikt,* p. 101.

[18] *Edikt,* pp. 100-101.

[19] *Edikt,* p. 101 n. 4; Kraus decided not to become embroiled in a discussion of the term. He had already spent some time on it in *JCS* 3 (1951) p. 52 with note 9.

[20] According to the "law code" of Eshnunna, 1 kor of barley is worth 1 shekel silver. This inflated price in barley, 1 kor: 1¾ shekels, is usual in the later OB period. See Schwenzner, *Zum altbabylonischen Wirtschaftsleben, MVAG* 19, 1915, Table I, p. 51, but note the circularity of the argument since this very text is cited as an example there.

[21] Edzard, *ed-Dēr,* excursus to text 2, pp. 30-34.

[22] *ed-Dēr* p. 34.

[23] *JCS* 7, p. 89, No. 12.

[24] *Bonner Biblische Beitraege* 1 (1950), p. 183.

[25] The amount repaid is ½ the original sum borrowed (cf. *CT* 8 21a). Therefore, this example is really not an exception to the usual ratio of silver to barley, 1 gú-un: 10 gín.

[26] In *ed-Dēr* excursus to text 1, p. 29, Edzard tries to differentiate between šu . . . ti = 1. *leqûm*, 2. *maḫārum*. *leqûm* is used to imply "Empfangshaftung," that something received must be repaid,

while *maḫārum* can be used for simple "receive." His most convincing argument is drawn from the wool accounts text *CT* 8 21b where an official receives (*maḫārum*) barley from a storehouse, and then other individuals "borrowed" (*leqûm*) it from him. The text *CT* 33 31, also from the records of the bureau of wool accounts, does not, however, adhere to Edzard's rule. In line 5, PN "borrows" (*maḫārum*) silver from an official. Edzard may be right in his analysis, but in ancient times the scribes sometimes became confused with the distinction; *W* 30 also departs from Edzard's rule.

[27]Cf. note 84 of this chapter.

[28]*Edikt,* p. 75.

[29]K. R. Veenof, *Aspects of Old Assyrian Trade and Its Terminology* (1972), *SD* 10, pp. 345-400.

[30]Veenhof, *ibid.,* p. 359; p. 365.

[31]Veenhof, *ibid.,* pp. 345-357.

[32]Veenhof, *ibid.,* p. 348: "Marketless Trading in the Time of Hammurabi" in *Trade and Market in the Early Empires,* Glencoe, 1957; and two essays in *Primitive, Archaic and Modern Economies,* ed. Dalton, New York, 1968, (another edition Boston, 1971) chs. 8 and 10. On p. 258 (Boston) Polanyi takes into cognizance the rather unflattering review of Heichelheim in *JESHO* 3 (1960), pp. 108-110.

[33]Polanyi, *ibid.,* pp. 188-189 (Boston); cf. below p. 21 and the review of Veenhof by the author, *JNES* 35 (1976), pp. 62-65.

[34]Veenhof, *Aspects,* p. 399.

[35]Veenhof, *Aspects,* p. 399.

[36]Oppenheim, *Ancient Mesopotamia,* Chicago, 1964, p. 87.

[37]Leemans, The Rate of Interest in Old Babylonian Times, *RIDA* 5, (1950), pp. 7-34; cf. also, "Laws of Ešnunna" paragraph 20 as restored by Landsberger in *David Fs.* (1968), p. 74, where someone who had loaned grain was forbidden "to change the grain to silver" and had to pay back interest according to the higher rate on grain.

[38]*ZDMG* 69 (1915), p. 497ff.

[39]Landsberger, *ZDMG* 69, p. 496, "jemandem (von amtswegen) unterstellt."

[40]Lautner, *Personenmiete,* p. 155.

[41]*AbB* 4 23: 16-18.

aš-šum i-na me-e ensí
ša qá-at zi-im-ru-akšak^{ki}
ensí^{meš} níg-šu u_4-bala-na-nam-hé

[42]*AbB* 4 23: 17-18.

[43]*AbB* 1 37: 9 reverse.

[44]*AbB* 2 8: 11.

[45]*AbB* 2 9: 8.

[46]*AbB* 4 18: 10.

[47]For a discussion on *biltu*-fields and land tenure, see M. deJ. Ellis, Yale University, Ph.D. dissertation, 1969, *Taxation and Land Revenues in the Old Babylonian Period,* Ch. 2.

[48]For a discussion of *nēmettum* and a translation of this letter, *TCL* 7, 18 (=*AbB* 4 18), see below, p. 29f.

[49]*ed-Dēr* p. 195; see also Lautner, *Personenmiete,* p. 202 with note 588.

[50]Walther, *Gerichtswesen,* pp. 23-24. On the question of whether níg-šu is merely an ideographic writing for *šá qāti* the evidence is the following: *MSL* 5 p. 60, še-níg-šu = *še-im qá-ti.* In *Das Akkadische Syllabar, An. Or.* 42, von Soden and Roellig, 1967, no. 323, (NINDA), appears in "OB nur zur

Wiedergabe des Pronomens *ša* (z.B. *LIH* 9, 8; 35, 6)." Both references are to níg-su. In syllabic writings of *ša qāti* the spelling is always *ša,* however (Labat, *Manuel* no. 353). This is sometimes confusing as in the older literature (e.g., Landsberger *ZDMG* 69, Walther, *Gerichtswesen,* Delitsch *BA* IV 486, Thureau-Dangin *RA* 8 146, n. 2) NINDA was transliterated *ša* and Labat 353 was *šá.* It is certain that *ša qāti* is, in the best sense of the term, a translation of níg-šu; but it is unlikely that níg-šu is the ideographic writing of *ša qāti.*

51 *W* 30 has a slightly different format; see note 26 above.

52 A-d 26, *CT* 8 36a.

53 Leemans' study of the *tamkārum* and *wakil tamkārī* in 1950, *The OB Merchant,* is still the broadest-based study on these titles. On p. 102-3 he discusses briefly the wool accounts texts and especially the role of Utu-šumundab in them. A more complete study of the Sippar material will be published by R. Harris, including an examination of these officials as integrated within the socio-economic order. In the meantime Oppenheim's article, based on the files of the Sippar project, "A New Look at the Structure of Mesopotamian Society" (*JESHO* 10, 1967 pp. 1-16) argues that the ugula dam-gàr^{meš} was a city-mayor (p. 6) and he speaks further of the "autonomy" of the free citizens in the Mesopotamian city. However, from the evidence from the bureau of wool accounts, it seems that some *wakil tamkārī* were acting as crown agents. Utu-šumundab is also attested in other documents performing crown-related functions (Kraus, *Edikt*, p. 102ff and note 6 above).

54 *BE* 6/1 85 father of Sîn-išmeʾanni.

55 *BE* 6/1 85.

56 *PBS* 8/2 214 as father in texts noted in ns. 53, 54.

57 *PBS* 8/2 241.

58 *BE* 6/1 86, *BE* 6/1 87; *BE* 6/2 120.

59 *Edikt,* pp. 50-54; Ellis, *Taxation,* p. 14.

60 *ša ana mušaddinim tašpuranni,* "(was den Obersaenger betrifft,) zu dem du mich als Eintreiber geschickt hast, . . ."

61 cf. *Edikt,* pp. 99-100 for the phrases:

ūm ekallum kaspam irriš
ūm mušaddini ekallim ana kaspim išassû
ūm mušaddinu ekallim išassû
ūm ti-ru ekallim iššassû
ūm ši-si ekallim iššassû

62 Walther, *Gerichtswesen,* pp. 43-45 collected for his time (1917) the complete file on Utu-šumundab.

63 There is no monograph-length study on scribes and the scribal arts. Landsberger at one time was engaged in writing one (statement of his intention in *JCS* 9 125, n. 22), but we must be content with his summaries in the abstracts of the 23rd Congress of Orientalists, Cambridge, 1954, "Babylonian Scribal Craft and Its Terminology," pp. 123-126 and his contribution in *City Invincible,* ed, Kraeling and Adams, 1960, Chicago, pp. 94-123. Goetze in *AS* 16, p. 211 no. 3 expressed his own dissatisfaction with the translation "scribe" for the title of Utul-Ištar (for that document see below p. 38ff). In that same *AS* 16 volume Oppenheim reviewed some aspects of scribal activities, "A Note on the Scribes in Mesopotamia," pp. 153-256. From letters to the royal court at Mari, Amarna, and Nineveh he showed that scribes functioned as secretaries-advisors to the king. He seems content with the term scribe, "in the service of the great households (temple and palace)," but says little about the quality of that service. For bibliographies on scribes see pp. 211-212 of *City Invincible* and *Oppenheim, Ancient Mesopotamia,* p. 377 n. 17. For certain important additions see Biggs, "Semitic Names in the Fara Period," *OrNS* 36 (1967) pp. 60-61 esp. who points out that the scribes

of Abū Ṣalābikh mostly bore Semitic names; Schneider, "Der dub-sar als Verwaltungsbeamte" *OrNS* 15 pp. 64-88 who gathers references for the Ur III period; and Ḫallo, "The House of Ur-Meme," *JNES* 31 (1972) 37ff., who discusses the history of a scribal family (see esp. note 7, p. 38). In *City Invincible* p. 99, Landsberger contended that in the Ur III period the scribe could be a high administrator for the crown, but after that period he was mainly a "secretary" and in the OB period was often a "street scribe." The texts referring to Utul-Ištar, however, show that a *ṭupšarrum* could also be a high administrative post in the OB period as well.

[64] Oppenheim, *JESHO* 10 (1967), p. 7.

[65] *Edikt,* p. 105. "Ueberbleibsel," "zufaellige Spezimina."

[66] The name according to Stamm, *Namengebung,* p. 275 with note 2, means "Schutz der Ištar." (See also Stamm, *Namengebung,* p. 273).

[67] Subarian slaves were highly prized in Babylonia. With Veenhof, *SD* 10, note 168, I maintain the translation "good, first-class" rather than "light-colored" for *namrum;* cf. Finkelstein, *JCS* 9 p. 6 n. 52 for further literature.

[68] na$_4$-lugal is probably to be compared with na$_4$ *namḫarti* é-gal of the " 'Palast'geschaefte" texts.

[69] [*ana* šám] suggested restoration.

[70] Finkelstein, *JNES* 21, p. 73ff. (1962), "Mesopotamia."

[71] *VS* 7 53:

1 sag-géme zu-ul-gi mu-ni-[im]
uru śi-na-aḫ^{ki} *ma-at bi-ri-*[*tim*]^{ki}
sag-géme ìr-^{d}*marduk* dumu ^{d}*marduk-na-ṣi-ir*
ù ú-túl-ištar dumu ^{d}*sîn-i-din-nam*
ki ìr-^{d}*marduk* dumu ^{d}*marduk-na-ṣi-ir*
ù ú-túl-ištar dumu ^{d}*sîn-i-din-nam*
be-le-e-ša
^{I}*uṣ-ri-ya* dumu ìr-*sa*
in-ši-in-šám
šám-til-la-bi-šè
5/6 ma-na 7 gín kù-babbar
in-na-an-lá
ù 1 gín kù-babbar diri-ga [*iš-ku-un*]
u$_4$-3-kam *te-ib-i-tum*
iti-1-kam *be-en-nu-um*
a-na ba-aq-ri-ša
ki-ma ṣi-im-da-at lugal
iz-za-a-az-zu
igi ^{d}*sîn-mu-ša-lim* di-ku$_5$
igi *ib-ni-*^{d}*marduk* ugula-šu-peš (HA)-UD.DA
igi é-gal-maḫ-kal-la-íb-ti dumu ^{d}*da-mu*-ENGAR (=*šamuḫ*)*
igi ^{d}*sîn-mu-ša-lim* kù-dím dumu ^{d}marduk-*mu-ša-lim*
igi ìr-^{d}a-ta-ba-a^{ki} *a-ḫi-ya* dumu ìr-^{d}utu
iti apin-du$_8$-a u$_4$-27-kam
mu *am-mi-di-ta-na* lugal-e
ki-dur-šà-du$_{10}$-ga-ke$_4$

This text is mentioned by Finkelstein, *JCS* 9 (1955), p. 7 ns. 66-67.
* cf. van Dijk, *Heidelberger Studien,* p. 241 with note 41.

[72]Cf. Ch. 4, p. 102ff.

[73]Cf. *ed-Dēr*, p. 88. Although there is not enough indication in the copy in *TIM* 6 to tell how much space is available for reconstruction, the full formulas for an administrative receipt are given here.

[74]For the sake of comparison I provide again the transliteration of *BAP* 4; cf. also Leemans, *Foreign Trade*, p. 94.

3 (PI) 2 (*sūt*) 4 2/3 sìla ì-giš ^{giš}bán-^{d}utu
kù-bi 1/3 ma-na 2/3 gín kù-babbar
a-na šám sag-ìr^{meš} gu-ti-i ^{ki}
nam-ru-tim
ki *ú-túl-istar a-bi* erén
a-na qá-bé-e lú-^{d}iškur-ra
dumu *ì-lí-ú-sa-ti*
ìr-^{d}*marduk* dumu *ib-ni-*^{d}*marduk*
šu ba-an-ti
a-na iti-l-kam sag-ìr^{meš} gu-ti-[i^{ki}]
nam-ru-tim
ú-ub-ba-lam a-na iti-l-kam
ú-ul ú-ub-ba-lam-ma
1/3 ma-na 2/3 gín kù-babbar
lú-^{d}iškur-ra dumu *ì-lí-ú-sa-ti*
a-na na-aš ka-ni-ki-šu
ì-lá-e

---

igi *ìl-šu-ib-ni* dumu ^{d}*sîn-e-ri-ba-am*
igi *i-lu-ni* dumu *ip-qu-ša*
igi *be-el-šu-nu* dumu *ìl-šu-ba-ni*
igi *ip-qá-tum* dumu *ta-ri-bu-um*

---

iti ne-ne-gar u_4-6-kam
mu *am-mi-ṣa-du-qá* lugal-e
sipa nam-sè-ga ^{d}utu-^{d}*marduk*-bi-da-ke_4

[75]For a discussion of the phrase *ana qabê* PN, see Cf. 4, p. 110ff.

[76]San Nicolò, *Beitraege zur Rechtsgeschichte im Bereiche der keilschriftlichen Rechtsquellen*, Oslo, 1931, p. 226 considered that Lu-Iškurra was a slave seller who received a commission from Utul-Ištar and then named his agent who would actually deliver the slaves.

[77]Cf. Harris, *JCS* 16 p. 1 (1962); in *HG* 3 119, the translation is "zur Speisung der Frau," taking the sign we have interpreted NIN as DAM.

[78]Landsberger, *23rd Congress of Orientalists*, p. 124.

[79]Cf. notes 59-61 above.

[80]*ed-Dēr* p. 67, 4., "einzelnes zu Nr. 30."

[81]lú-kúrun-na = *sabû* is translated in *AHw* as "Bierbrauer, Schankwirt," in Roellig, *Das Bier*, p. 87 note 188 as "Schankwirt." The translation "brewer" is provisionally adopted here (except in direct quotation of other opinions).

[82]For Ilip see Reiner, *JCS* 15, p. 124. The spellings i-li-ip, ì-lip, and KI.BAL.MAŠ.DÀ[ki] all occur among the *YOS* 13 texts, cf. index, "Names of Places and Peoples."

[82a]*Edikt,* p. 47ff.

[83]Both names are attested among the bureau of wool accounts texts, but the names are common. Šallurum is a fairly well-known dub-sar and dumu-é-dub-ba-a in the latter part of the OB period.

[84]Edzard comments in *ed-Dēr* 45, p. 88, that the expressions mu-DU PN, *namḫarti* PN identify late OB administrative documents and suggests that further analysis of the type is only possible within the bounds of a larger discussion of the "Geschaefte des 'Palastes' " genre. We can see that the type of document he speaks of, however, is simply an official receipt. These phrases are usually preceded by remarks to the effect that PN had already been "loaned" a commodity and, now was fulfilling his obligation of repayment. mu-DU (*ed-Dēr* p. 87 for a discussion of the Akkadian equivalent *šūrubtum* or *šūbultum*) PN always refers to the obligated party. This kind of document should not be set aside typologically from the documents of loans (and disbursements) that preceded it.

[85]Goetze, *AS* 16, p. 211, n. 4 very reluctantly translated his title, "scribe."

[86]We may probably suggest on the basis of the *sabū* and Utul-Ištar's *nēmettum*-collection responsibilities in *YOS* 13 281, 317 the reconstruction ⌈i-lip[ki]⌉.

[86a]*JCS* 2 (1948) p. 83.

[87]*AHw* p. 777a.

[88]*JNES* 27, (1968), pp. 136-140, "*ṭēmam pānam šuršûm* und verwandte Ausdruecke."

[89]The first part of Renger's article concerning the phrase *ṭēmam pānam šuršûm* has been reviewed by Kraus in *RA* 64 (1970), "Akkadische Woerter und Ausdruecke II," p. 55ff.

[90]*JNES* 27, 138.

[91]This is Renger's only citation to previous literature–*MVAG* 36/1, 197.

[92]Ungnad, *Babylonische Briefe, VAB* 6. 233:29, hereafter *BB.*

[93]*Foreign Trade,* p. 105:29-30.

[94]*AbB* 1 17:29.

[95]*AbB* 1 131:29.

[96]*AbB* 4 18:19.

[97]Renger, *JNES* 27, 138.

> Der konkrete Sinn, der sich hinter "Schwierigkeiten" verbirgt, darf dabei nicht aus dem Auge gelassen werden. D. h., "Schwierigkeiten bekommen" heisst "(mit einer Auflage) belastet werden, fuer etwas bezahlen, einstehen muessen, fuer etwas haftbar sein."

[98]*Edikt,* p. 51.

[99]*JNES* 27, p. 138.

[100]*JNES* 27, p. 140. I agree with this conclusion.

[101]/8.10/ misreferenced by Renger as *CT* 43 131:28-29, apparently referring to Kraus' translation, *AbB* 1 131:18-19. The text is *CT* 44 55.

[102]This restoration was originally suggested by Thureau-Dangin. (Reference in Kraus, *AbB* 4 18:16 note a).

[103]DI in text. Cf. *AbB* 4 18 note to line 22, "So, K[opie] statt zu erwartenden ne-me-."

[104]Cf. Ellis, *Taxation, Ch. 2.*

[105]Cf. above Ch. 2, p. 18 and note 48.

[106]For this interpretation of *eqlum ša rēš ekallim ukallû* cf. Diakonoff, *Ancient Mesopotamia,* p. 197.

[107]Cf. Kraus, *RA* 64, (1970) p. 53ff., "Akkadische Woerter und Ausdruecke I, *ḫiṭītum* = Schadenersatz. "(s)o wird dir der Schadenersatz fuer den Ausfall seiner Pachtausgabe auferlegt werden."

[108]*AHw, nēmettum,* p. 777; cf. also Landsberger, *Date Palm,* n. 80 for further references.

[109]*ed-Dēr* 30 cited above p. 26 and n. 80. *isiḫtum (isḫatu, esiḫtu, isiktu, esiktu),* under *CAD* I: "1. assignment, assigned working material, share 2. certificate of assignment."

[110]Ellis, *Taxation,* p. 161-164; cf. Edict of Ammi-ṣaduqa, paragraph 15 (in Finkelstain's numbering, *RA* 63 (1969), p. 45ff); on the periodicity of *mīšarum*-edicts, see Finkelstein, Ammiṣaduqa's Edict and the Babylonian "Law Codes," *JCS* 15 (1961), pp. 91-104.

[111]*AHw* translates *kizû,* "Diener"; *CAD*: "1. herdsman(?), 2. groom, personal attendant"; *AbB* 4 110: 6–IŠ *ša* ᵈiškur, "Wagenfahrer des Adad"; *AbB* 2 26: 4–ᵈ*sîn-ma-gir* IŠ, der *kizû*-Beamte Sîn-māgir"; cf. Sjoeberg, *JCS* 21 (1967), p. 277, SAḪAR=kus_x=*kizû*; also Owen, *JCS* 24 (1972), p. 133.

[112]For translations of weights and measures, see Kraus, *AbB* 4, p. xi.

[113]Goetze, *The Laws of Eshnunna,* 1956, pp. 24-30.

[114]On inflation in the time of Ammi-ṣaduqa, see Schwenzner, *Wirtschaftsleben,* 1915, p. 52, and on wages in the OB period, Meissner, *Warenpreise,* 1936, both in drastic need of up-dating.

[115]Oppenheim, *Eames,* E 23, p. 52.

[116]Walters, *Water for Larsa,* p. 38. Cf. also texts 31, 32, 83, 88 and p. 147.

[117]*šaqû*="bewaessern" (to irrigate); cf. *MSL* 1 Tf. 4 i 51; *ŠL* 378:22; *ŠL* 579:324b; Oppenheim, *Eames,* F i, p. 57; the usual form of the word, "irrigation," is *šiqītum.*

[118]*MSL* 1 130.

[119]ka dub-a-ni nu-me-a = **pî kanīkišu ul ibašši.* This is an artificial Sumerian formation, constructed to look like a *terminus technicus,* the opposite of *ezub pî kanīkišu pānî,* "apart from his prior document (transaction)." See Ch. 3, p. 65ff.

[120]The translation "sickle" for ᵘʳᵘᵈᵘšu-kin was already suggested by Finkelstein, *JAOS* 90 (1970), p. 248 with notes 24, 25 although, to my knowledge, this writing for sickle, which is normally written ᵘʳᵘᵈᵘkin or ᵘʳᵘᵈᵘše-kin, is not otherwise attested; cf. Salonen, *Agricultura Mesopotamica* (1968), p. 164ff, Landsberger, *ZDMG* 69 (1915), pp. 522-23. Akkadian for ᵘʳᵘᵈᵘkin, ᵘʳᵘᵈᵘše-kin is *niggallum.* The citation in *MSL* 6, p. 146, ᵍⁱšu-kin = *qá-a-tu ša ni-gal-lim,* "handle of a sickle," is a patent "Volks-etymologie," although šu-kin, "handle," has found its way into some discussions (Oppenheim, *Eames,* p. 145 n. 2); cf. Soden, *LTBA* II 17:46; Ebeling, *MAOG* 10/2, p. 81. In HAR-ra = *ḫubullu,* šu-kin appears as part of ᵍⁱšapin-šu-kin (=*ḫarbum*) a type of plow (Salonen, *Agricultura,* p. 60ff); ᵍⁱšin-nu-šu-kin (=*naḫbašum*), another type of plow (Salonen, *Agricultura,* p. 180ff; apin-šu-kin (=*mayārum*), a third type of plow (Salonen, *Agricultura,* p. 65). Landsberger suggested that the normal word-sign for *ḫarbum,* ᵍⁱšapin-túk-kin (this variant Salonen considered to betray the substrate language word *thukin! –*Agricultura,* p. 60), was a scribal error for ᵍⁱšapin-šu-kin (*MSL* I, p. 161), a position Oppenheim ascribed to Landsberger's misplaced confidence in late syllabaries. *AHw* and *CAD* now take apin-túk-kin = *ḫarbum,* apin-šu-kin = *mayārum.* Salonen sees šu-kin as meaning, "mit der Hand (Haecksel) machen," (*Agricultura,* p. 180), but this etymology is not recognized in the Akkadian translations of the words for implements whose Sumerian counterparts contain šu-kin. šu-kin in Deimel, *ŠL* 354:392, = šūrum, a kind of reed, cf. *CAD* K, 241a, but is not relevant to the primary significance of šu-kin in the descriptions of agricultural tools.

In *YOS* 13 72 and 73 the sickle is used to "gather" (*kamāsum*), i.e., reap, grain. In *YOS* 13 235 ᵘʳᵘᵈᵘḫa-bu-da (=*ḫapūtum*), "light hoes," are mentioned, recalling Salonen's comment that hoes (ḫa-bu-da) and sickles (še-kin), along with axes (ḫa-zi-in), are the most common metal objects in Ur III texts (*Agricultura,* p. 144). Salonen noted that the text *HUCA* 29, p. 88 n. 15, records the numbers and

weights of the hoes with the remark kin-dub-ba, "hammered work." Hallo compared this phrase, which he translated "broken work," with the more frequently found kin-til-la, "finished work," which also turns up in *YOS* 13 72. (Hallo, *HUCA* 29 (1958), Contributions to Neo-Sumerian, p. 92. For "hammered work," see Limet, *Le travail,* p. 131). In *YOS* 13 72 the number of sickles is recorded with their weight, and the remark, kin-til-la, designates the finished process. (Salonen, *Agricultura,* p. 165, calculates sickles weigh between 65-150 grams. In *YOS* 13 72 a sickle weighed on the average 140 grams). Copper sickles became quickly worn during the course of the harvesting season and had to be collected and reworked into new products. kin-til-la thus denotes these finished products. Careful records had to be kept recording the weight of the broken sickles which were returned for recasting. These *YOS* texts are partial records of these procedures.
Although the writing ^{urudu}šu-kin does not occur in Mesopotamia, Prof. Harry Hoffner has kindly pointed out the existence of the springtime Hittite festival, EZEN.(URUDU.)ŠU.KIN.(DU), *KUB* 12 2 iv 4-7, when the occasion called for the "releasing" (Hittite: tarna-) of this implement. Hoffner further notes that this spring festival eliminates any identification with the various words for plow which contain the element šu-kin since plows were used to break up soil in the autumn. The tool "released," Prof. Hoffner agrees, was the sickle.

121 For a similar text see Leemans, Texts Sissa, *JCS* 20 (1966), no. 8, p. 35, translation p. 47.

122 Cf. Landsberger, *JCS* 9 (1955), p. 125 n. 22, for earlier literature and the reading $\check{s}a_x$-dub-ba; also Goetze, *Sumer* 14 (1958), p. 3ff; note *MSL* 12, 97:133, é-dub-ba-a = *šá-an-da-bak-ku,* a late confusion of the situation.

123 *AbB* 2 27:9, "Militaerschreiber."

124 Walther, *Gerichtswesen,* p. 159, "Archivar"; cf. also, *AbB* 3 55:7 "Staatschreiber."

125 Landsberger, *23rd Congress of Orientalists,* p. 124.

126 Landsberger, *JCS* 9, p. 125 n. 22.

CHAPTER 3

The *abi ṣābim*

Research Hypothesis

In the previous chapter we have seen that Utul-Ištar assumed the rank of *abi ṣābim* in the year Ammi-ṣaduqa 8 and could be attested as having held the title through A-ṣ 15. During that period he continued his service to the crown as chief of the bureau of wool accounts, a function he had performed before A-ṣ 8, with the title *ṭupšarrum.* Also during his tenure as *abi ṣābim,* he was in charge of the management of crown lands, which he supervised through his field administrators. Utul-Ištar's bureau not only paid the field laborers with rations of food and drink, but also supplied them with the tools with which the labor was performed.

We noted above that the title *ṭupšarrum,* "scribe," and the connotations of that title, did not adequately characterize the range of activities in which Utul-Ištar was engaged. While his later title, *abi ṣābim,* might be hoped to afford a clearer indication of the nature of his service to the crown, this title has been only sparsely attested up to now in the cuneiform letters and documents of the Old Babylonian period and has not been the subject of a detailed study. The recent publication of new texts,[1] however, enables us to initiate the study of this important office and the associated social and economic structures in which the individuals who bore that title acted. One purpose of this chapter, then, will be to characterize the range of activities of the *abi ṣābim* and to compare these to the functions that we have previously observed Utul-Ištar to have been performing. Since Utul-Ištar was a high crown official—though his earlier rank of "scribe" gave no indication of that status—we may hypothesize at this time that *abi ṣābim* was an explicit rank within the crown's bureaucracy. In the course of analyzing the rank *abi ṣābim,* we shall thus test the hypothesis that this rank was used only to categorize officials of rather high status who were engaged in specific kinds of activities in service to the crown.

Previous Literature

The most complete discussion of the *abi ṣābim* to date is the paragraph Walther devoted to the "Leutevater."[2] Walther commented on the basis of the texts known to him (in 1917), and not intending any thorough-going analysis on the subject,[3] that the *abi ṣābim* was an official whose duties were many-sided.[4] He specifically identified Utul-Ištar as a palace official but denied previous opinions that the rank was a military designation[5] or involved police functions.[6] Walther noted that the *abi ṣābim*-officials were addressed with unusual respect since *awīlum* was sometimes added to their title, (i.e., *awīlum abi ṣābim*, "the honorable *abi ṣābim*,") and that other officials seemed to have been under his jurisdiction.

The translation "Leutevater" (or " 'Leute'vater") appeared in the first text editions in which the title was found[7] and has persisted to this day. Some variety has crept into the definition, however, according to the different interpretations of the word *ṣābum* by various scholars. Goetze (1965)[8] wrote " 'father' of the (work)men"; R. Harris (1964),[9] "father of the troops"; and Szlechter (1958),[10] "chef (litt. père) des mercenaires." Von Soden has sanctified this tradition of literal translation in the *AHw* under *abu* 6(d), " 'Leutevater,' ein Beamter."

There have also been divergent methods of transcribing the title in Akkadian since the second word is always written as a Sumerogram, erén. Only Ungnad[11] ever rendered erén = *ummānum*, but several commentators, especially in some of the older treatments, have transliterated erén = *ṣābī*, that is, as a grammatical plural (in the genitive). Thus: Lautner, *abi ṣābī*;[12] Lindl, *abi ṣâbî*;[13] Szlechter, *abi ṣâbê*.[14] The *CAD*, vol. Ṣ (1962), lists a possible plural *ṣābū*, but adds that the basic sense of the word is a collective, hence a grammatical singular, "a group of people." Occasionally the Akkadian-speaking scribes wrote erén^{meš}, but this must be considered an overpunctilious form of writing–how the Akkadian scribes thought Sumerian should correctly reflect an Akkadian collective: plural idea, plural indicator. In either case, erén or erén^{meš}, the Akkadian should be *ṣābum*, genitive *ṣābim*. This is the opinion of both dictionaries and will be followed here.

The *CAD*, vol. A/1, pp. 51-2, eschews all of the above etymologically-based translations of *abi ṣābim* and simply writes, "(an official in charge of personnel)." The lexical citations summarized there are all late compilations and do not reflect first-hand knowledge of the title, which appears only in OB texts. No attestation of *abi ṣābim*, however, appears in OB lú = *ša* or any of its related series.[15] The title was certainly no venerable appellation and, if our sample is trustworthy, was not even in use during the entire OB period.[16]

The *CAD* noted in its discussion of *abi ṣābim* (vol. A/1, p. 52) that a certain Ili-iqīšam appears in several texts with the title gal-unken-na erén-ká-é-gal, but also in one text as *abi ṣābim*. The editors speculated from this fact that these two titles may have been equivalent. They noted that gal-unken-na, which in lexical lists is the Akkadian *mu'errum*, is never syllabically written out in the OB period, and furthermore, that the two titles are occasionally prefixed by the same honorific, *awīlum*. We shall see in the course of this and the next chapter, however, that this kind of evidence for equating two titles is very tenuous indeed. More to the point, *mu'errum* is, in fact, syllabically spelled in the OB period. Nevertheless, these two ranks do have some relationship, inasmuch as they both reflect high status in the crown's service. The *mu'errum*, a more venerable rank and much better attested in the OB period, is the subject of the following chapter. Here we shall follow the careers of the individuals who held the title *abi ṣābim* in order to gain a fuller understanding of the meaning of this title.

Table II: Texts Mentioning Individuals with the Title *abi ṣābim*

Text Edition	Name of *abi ṣābim*	Date of Text
BAP 4	Utul-Ištar	A-ṣ 10
BAP 74	Utul-Ištar	A-ṣ 13
CT 4 17a	Ili-iqīšam	A-ṣ 9
CT 4 19a (*AbB* 2 90)		letter
CT 4 39d (*AbB* 2 104)		letter
CT 6 29	Marduk-lamassašu, Sîn-mušallim	A-d 1
CT 8 3b	Marduk-muballiṭ	A-ṣ 3
CT 8 10a	Utul-Ištar	A-ṣ 15
CT 8 19b	Ili-iqīšam	A-ṣ 11
CT 8 21a	Utul-Ištar	A-ṣ 13
CT 8 21c	Ili-iqīšam	A-ṣ 10
CT 8 30b	Utul-Ištar	A-ṣ 13
CT 8 36a	Utul-Ištar	A-ṣ 15
CT 33 27	Marduk-lamassašu	A-d 4
CT 45 48	Gimil-Marduk, Marduk-lamassašu, Marduk-mušallim	A-d 14
CT 45 54	Marduk-lamassašu	A-d [ ]
CT 45 61	Nanna-mansum	A-ṣ 17+b
PBS 7 108	Marduk-muballiṭ	letter
PBS 8/2 238	Unnamed	A-ṣ 15
TCL 1 158	Marduk-lamassašu	A-d [ ]
TCL 1 164	Unnamed	A-ṣ 9
TJG p. 38	Utul-Ištar	A-ṣ 14
TJM p. 93	Marduk-muballiṭ	A-d 37
TLB 1 226	Utul-Ištar	date lost
VS 7 72	Marduk-muballiṭ	A-ṣ 3
VS 7 86	Utul-Ištar	A-ṣ 10
VS 7 195	Unnamed	letter
VS 16 202	Unnamed	letter
W 30	Utul-Ištar	A-ṣ 15
W 33	Marduk-muballiṭ	(date lost)
YOS 13 5	Marduk-lamassašu	(date lost)
YOS 13 33	[ ]-mušallim	A-d 33

YOS 13 62	Utul-Ištar	A-ṣ 8
YOS 13 66	Nabium-mālik	S-d 14
YOS 13 67	Utul-Ištar	A-ṣ 8
YOS 13 69	Utul-Ištar	A-ṣ 8
YOS 13 70	Utul-Ištar	A-ṣ 8
YOS 13 73	Utul-Ištar	A-ṣ 8
YOS 13 142	Unnamed	(no date)
YOS 13 262	Marduk-muballiṭ	S-d 2 (patronym)
YOS 13 289	Marduk-muballiṭ	A-d 34
YOS 13 309	Marduk-muballiṭ	A-d (lost)
YOS 13 337	Nabium-mālik	S-d 13
YOS 13 362	Utul-Ištar	A-ṣ 8
YOS 13 428	Ibni-Šamaš	S-d 14
YOS 13 444	Nabium-mālik	S-d 14
YOS 13 478	Utul-Ištar	A-ṣ 8

Table III: Names of *abi ṣābim*-officials

Name	Text	Date
Gimil-Marduk	*CT* 45 48	A-d 14
Ibni-Šamaš	*YOS* 13 428	S-d 3
Ili-iqīšam	*CT* 4 17a	A-ṣ 9
	CT 8 21c	A-ṣ 10
	CT 8 19b	A-ṣ 11
Marduk-lamassašu	*CT* 6 29	A-d 1
	CT 33 27	A-d 4
	CT 45 48	A-d 14
	CT 45 54	A-d [ ]
	TCL 1 158	A-d [ ]
	YOS 13 5	(date lost)
Marduk-muballiṭ	*YOS* 13 289	A-d 37
	YOS 13 309	A-d [ ]
	TJM p. 93	A-d 37
	CT 8 3b	A-s 3

Marduk-muballiṭ	*VS* 7 72	A-ṣ 3
	PBS 7 108	letter
	W 33	(date lost)
	YOS 13 262	S-d 2 (patronym)
Marduk-mušallim	*CT* 45 48	A-d 14
[ ]-mušallim	*YOS* 13 33	A-d 33
Nabium-mālik	*YOS* 13 66	S-d 14
	YOS 13 444	S-d 14
	YOS 13 337	S-d 13
Nanna-mansum	*CT* 45 61	A-ṣ 17+b
Sîn-mušallim	*CT* 6 29	A-d 1
Utul-Ištar (See Table I, Chapter 1)		

Texts Mentioning Marduk-lamassašu

The *abi ṣābim* as policeman?

Marduk-lamassašu, the earliest and one of the better attested figures who held the title *abi ṣābim,* was active during the early years of Ammi-ditana. The text *CT* 6 29, dated to A-d 1, has been treated in *HG* 3 740 and edited by Schorr.[17] Since this well-known and important text has formed the cornerstone in the theory that the *abi ṣābim* exercised a police function, and because parts of the text are still not fully understood, it is presented here in full.

CT 6 29

^{I}ìr-^{d}bu-ne-ne
ša pir-ḫi-ì-lí-šu be-el-šu
a-na áš-nun-na *a-na* 1½ ma-na kù-babbar
id-di-nu-šu
mu-5-kam *i-na li-ib-bi* áš-nun-na^{ki}
be-lu-tam il-li-ik-ma
a-na ká-dingir-ra^{ki} *it-ta-bi-tam*
^{Id}*sîn-mu-ša-lim ù* ^{d}*marduk-la-ma-sà-šu a-bi* erén^{meš}
^{I}ìr-^{d}bu-ne-ne *iṣ-<ba>-su-ú-ma*
ki-a-am iq-bu-šum
um-ma šu-nu-ma
el-le-ta ap-pu-ut-ta-ka
gu-ul-lu-ba-at ta-al-la-ak i-na aga-uš^{meš}
^{I}ìr-^{d}bu-ne-ne *šu-ú*
ki-a-am i-pu-ul

um-<ma>*šu-ú-ma*
i-na aga-us^{meš}*ú-ul a-al-la-ak*
il-ka ša é *a-bi-ya*
a-al-la-ak
^{I}*li-pí-it*-^{d}iškur ^{d}iškur-*lu-ze-rum*
ù ib-ni-^{d}utu *aḫ-ḫu-šu*
mu ^{d}*marduk ù am-mi-di-ta-na* lugal-e
in-pà-dè-e-meš
a-na ìr-^{d}bu-ne-ne *a-ḫi-šu-nu*
a-na ri-šu-tim la ra-ga-mi
^{i}ìr-^{d}bu-ne-ne *a-di ba-al-ṭù*
it-ti aḫ-ḫi-šu
i-lik é *a-bi-šu-nu*
i-il-la-ak

---

igi *a-wi-il*-^{d}iškur ugula mar-tu
igi AN-*pi*$_{4}$-*ša* dumu ^{d}*sîn-i-din-nam*

---

iti šu-numun-a u$_{4}$-25-kam
mu *am-mi-di-ta-na* lugal-e
ad-gi$_{4}$-a gu-la ^{d}utu ^{d}marduk-bi-da

Warad-Bunene, whom Pirḫi-ilišu, his master, had sold to Ešnunna for one and one-half minas silver—after he had served 5 years in Ešnunna, had fled to Babylon. Sîn-mušallim and Marduk-lamassašu, the *abi ṣābim*-officials, seized Warad-Bunene and said to him the following: "You are cleansed,[18] your slave-mark is shaved off. You will serve with the *rēdû*-forces." Warad-Bunene replied as follows: "I will not go among the *rēdû*-forces. I will perform the *ilku*-service of my father's estate." Lipit-Ištar, Adad-lu-zerum and Ibni-Šamaš, his brothers, swore by Marduk and King Ammi-ditana. Against Warad-Bunene there is no slave-claim. Warad-Bunene, as long as he lives, will perform with his brothers the *ilku*-service of the estate of their father.

This document raises several questions in regard to the status of the slave in ancient Mesopotamia and in regard to the problem of the *ilkum*-service. Paragraph 280 of the Code of Hammurapi may be relevant here if the situation is that Warad-Bunene received his freedom as a slave who had been sold in a foreign country and had returned home—the condition of freedom mentioned in that paragraph (see below). According to the "Code," slaves could be freed in four ways: according to paragraph 117, the wife and children of a debtor would be freed after three years of service to his creditor; according to paragraph 171, a slave woman who bore a free man children would be set free after his death; according to paragraph 175, the children of a marriage between a free woman and a slave would be automatically free; and finally, according to paragraph 280, a native Babylonian slave sold in a foreign country would be freed on return to Babylon. Slaves were acquired by purchase, attained as plunder from military campaigns, taken as debtors in service, or were house-born. The status of Warad-Bunene is, of course, not known, but he must have been of considerable value, as his inordinately high sale-price of 1½ minas indicates. Although the circumstances of Warad-Bunene's refusal to join the *rēdû*-troops is not mentioned in this text, some understanding of this refusal may be gained with the aid of another manumission document.

In *BIN* 2 76,[19] a manumission document from the south, a certain Ilabrat-tayyār, slave of Apil-ilišu, was freed and his forehead cleansed. He was granted the legal privilege to "perform the *ilkum*-service and the corvée-work as the sons of Apil-ilišu":

ilkam u ḫarrānam kīma mārī apil-ilišu illak

In spite of Koschaker's statement that in the south no formal adoption took place in manumission documents,[20] Ilabrat-tayyār was clearly an adopted son who, in return for fulfilling his responsibilities of supporting his adopted father, received part of the inheritance and was to be regarded as a full family member. Similarly, the case of Warad-Bunene is an instance of an adopted slave returning to claim his share in his adopted family's estate. An outline of the general circumstances of the case can be reconstructed as follows: While still the slave of his adopted father, he was sold to another party in Ešnunna. After five years, during which time Pirḫi-ilišu had died, thus automatically freeing him,[18] he managed to escape to Babylon, where his freedom would have been effected as is seen in *CH* 280 and where his brothers were forced to admit his legal status and accept him as a co-member of their father's houshold. Concomitantly, he was obliged to perform the *ilkum*-services incumbent on that family.

It is easy to see why Schorr was drawn to the notion that the two *abi ṣabīm*-officials in this document were performing police functions. Sîn-mušallim and Marduk-lamassašu detain Warad-Bunene and subsequently declare that he is a free citizen of Babylon. This declaration may be seen as part of the normal state of affairs when a Babylonian slave has returned from serving in a foreign place or has otherwise been freed by his master. It seems that such a slave became a "free" citizen, but if he was not specifically included in a family organization[21] by his manumittor, he became a dependant of the state with the obligation to serve with the *rēdû*-forces, soldiers of the crown.

Warad-Bunene refused to join the *rēdû*-forces, contending that he was a member of the family of Pirḫi-ilišu, his adopted father. He was able to prove this, and instead of being conscripted into the *rēdû*-forces had to assume the normal *ilkum*-duties, probably consisting of a fixed period of service, of his adopted family.[22] The first witness in the document was an ugula mar-tu, whose presence evidenced the interest of the military in the disposition of Warad-Bunene's case. The military was not represented by the *abi ṣābim*-officials, nor did these officials act as (civil) police, detaining individuals before they came to court.

To fully understand the interplay of social forces in this text we must clearly differentiate among the several lines of authority present in the case. The military under whom the returned slave would have to serve is represented by the first witness. The military, however, does not have independent authority in the matter, but may conscript Warad-Bunene only if it is determined that he is not recognized as a son in the family of Pirḫi-ilišu. If his status as a family member is in fact established, then Warad-Bunene owes only service for a specified period, i.e., *ilkum*-service. The conflict revolves around whether Warad-Bunene is a free citizen but not a community member, or whether he was freed (under an adoption agreement) and taken into the community with the same rights and obligations as other community members.

The function of the *abi ṣābim*-officials in the case was to serve as a liaison with the community, and, as crown officials, once the community's decision on the status of the adopted slave was resolved, to oversee the compliance with the *ilkum*-service (on the nature of which the document does not dwell, but perhaps having to do with agricultural labor). The central, if not the only direct issue of this document, is to ratify or reject the military's claims on the returned slave. The "legal" position of Warad-Bunene in the community was not decided in this case and was not, in fact, a matter for the crown to decide. The community's decision, already made, was that Warad-Bunene could assume the full rights of his adopted brothers. The case then fell under the authority of the *abi ṣābim*-officials, who had only to implement the community's decision by rejecting the military's claims.

The basic duties of the *abi ṣābim* as a crown official led him in some instances to be the agent interposed between the community with its traditional structures and powers, and those obligations that community members owed the state. This function enabled him to mediate certain issues between the community and other crown-related authorities who made claims on the services of individuals. The primary responsibilities of the *abi ṣābim* (as will be documented below) lay in the realm of agricultural management, where he was in charge of crown lands and agricultural activities and was particularly responsible for the storehouses in which the crown accumulated grain. Using this grain as stored wealth, the crown was able to monitor the exchange of goods and services within the larger OB economic structure. From this basic authority over the management of agricultural products, which entailed the mobilization of material resources from the community, as well as from the estates of the crown, the power of the *abi ṣābim* naturally expanded into the regulation of certain other relationships between community and crown. Before generalizing more on this subject, however, let us turn to other texts that exemplify the basic responsibilities of specific *abi ṣābim*-officials.

The *abi ṣābim* in the Bureau of Agricultural Affairs

In *CT* 33 27, dating to A-d 4, Marduk-lamassašu appears as the father of a *nadītum* of Šamaš named Narubtum. The text itself is a contract to buy oil, and is cited by Harris[23] as an example of the high status of fathers of *nadītum*-women, Marduk-lamassašu being classified by Harris as a military official, "father of the troops."

Three *abi ṣābim*-officials, Marduk-lamassašu, Marduk-mušallim and Gimil-Marduk, are named in a text dated to A-d 14 (*CT* 45 48), thus showing that several *abi ṣābim*-officials held that title at the same time. Their duties were to distribute grain and flour to infantry living in Sippar-Amnānum,[24] each being responsible for overseeing a precinct.[25] The grain and flour were kept in storehouses in Sippar-Yaḫrurum, from which the distributions were duly registered.[26]

The administrative authority of the *abi ṣābim*-official over expenditures of grain may also be seen in the fragmentary text *CT* 45 54, a companion document to *CT* 45 48. In this text ration allotments are disbursed to Kassite charioteers in the administrative precinct of Marduk-lamassašu.[27] The expenditures were again designated (*iššakkan*) from the storehouses in Sippar-Yaḫrurum.

Marduk-lamassašu further appears in *TCL* 1 158, dating to the reign of Ammi-ditana.[28] This text is presented here in its entirety for its informative content on the nature of the *abi ṣābim*'s official range of duties.[29]

1 še gur ^{giš}bán-[^{d}*marduk*]
a-na šuku 5 erén! ḫun-gá [x-x-x]
a-na pa$_5$-e *ša-di-a-tim ša* i$_7$ *še-⌜ri-im-tum*?⌝
hi-ri-e-im ù gú-un a-šà é-gal ^{giš}apin^{hi-a}
ša ma-har ib-ni-^{d}*sîn za-ba-⌜lim⌝*
a-na qá-bi-e da-du-ša ya-sì-il
^{I}*ib-ni-é-a ù ra-ab-bi-e-ra-aḫ*
ki ^{d}*marduk-la-ma-sà-šu a-bi* erén
^{I}*ya-wi-*^{d}*da-gan*
níg-su *ya-sì-il*
^{I}*zi-im-ra-tum*
níg-šu *ib-ni-é-a*
^{Id}utu-*na-ṣi-ir* níg-šu *da-du-ša*
^{I}*za-ki-rum*
^{I}*ra-ab-bi-e-ra-aḫ*
2 níg-šu *ra-ab-bi-e-ra-aḫ*
šu ba-an-ti
ú-sa-ad-da-ru-ma
i-il-la-ku-ma
ú-ul i-il-la-ku-ma
ṣi-im-da-at šar-ri-im
igi *ipqu-*AN*-tum*
igi *a-wi-il-*^{d}iškur
igi *na-bi-*[ ]
igi [ ]
iti ab-[è u$_4$-x-kam]
mu *am-mi-di-*[*ta-na* lugal-e]
mu gi[bil]

Seals: *ya-sì-il*
ib-ni-é-a
ra-ab-bi-e-ra-aḫ
*ipqu-*AN*-tum*
a-wi-il-^{d}iškur

> 1 kor of grain according to the seah-measure of Marduk, for the provisioning of 5 hirelings [ ], for digging ditches in GN and providing the field tax of the palace and for plows which are presently before Ibni-Sîn. At the behest of Daduša, Yasi-il, Ibni-Ea and Rabbi-eraḫ from the bureau of Marduk-lamassašu, the *abi ṣābim*: Yawi-Dagan under the jurisdiction of Yasi-il; Zimratum under the jurisdiction of Ibni-Ea; Šamaš-nāṣir under the jurisdiction of Daduša; Zakīrum and Rabbi-Eraḫ, 2 men under the the jurisdiction of Rabbi-Eraḫ, received the grain. They entered (this) in the accounts. They will perform the work. If they do not perform, then it is according to the *ṣimdat šarrim.*

The subject of the documents is the recording of the payment of 1 kor of grain as rations for the subsistence (or support) of 5 hirelings who were engaged in digging irrigation ditches. Each of these workers is duly entered in the books as being under the jurisdiction of a work-captain, one work-captain also being recorded as receiving rations and being accounted for in his own work-gang.[30] The phrase indicating the subordinate relationship of the workers in lines 10, 12, 13, 16 is níg-šu, the familiar term that denoted the overall responsibility of Utul-Ištar in the bureau of wool accounts texts. Marduk-lamassašu appears thus in a function similar to that of Utul-Ištar in the agricultural administration documents; it is from Marduk-lamassašu's bureau that the ration payments to the workers are made.

Lautner noted the official significance of the text in the following words:

> Es handelt sich offensichtlich um oeffentliche Arbeiten, zumal die Leistung erbringende Person als *abi ṣābī* bezeichnet ist.[31]

In spite of this statement, however, Lautner was still worried about the presence of witnesses in the contract and the private nature of the šubanti-clause as possible hindrances to perceiving the "official" nature of the contract.

The accounting procedures of the crown in this digging/dredging operation complement the agricultural administration and wool accounts texts of Utul-Ištar. The administrative archives had to record not only the payments received by the workers, but also the intermediaries at whose behest (*ana qabê*) the payments were made. The technical terms in the document, *ana qabê,* níg-šu, *šukūsum,* when taken together, as well as the explicit reference to the "palace" (*bilat eqel ekallim*), leave no doubt that this document was an official bookkeeping account of the crown. The *ṣimdat šarrim* was thought by Lautner not to refer to any measure of force, as some previous commentators had proposed,[32] but rather to a fine the worker had to pay as compensation if he did not comply with the terms of his contract.[33]

In summation, the role of Marduk-lamassašu, an *abi ṣābim*-official in the time of Ammiditana, can be compared to that of the *abi ṣābim* Utul-Ištar, who was in charge of the administration of crown lands under Ammi-ṣaduqa. In at least one document Utul-Ištar was associated with the management of irrigation facilities and with the distribution of ration payments for workers who were doing earth-removal operations under the jurisdiction of his subordinate.[34] In addition to *TCL* I 158, the two *CT* 45 documents mention

Marduk-lamassašu making payments of grain, indicating his specific authority over disbursements from the storehouse. This may be accounted for by the fact that the crown was managing certain agricultural activities on its own lands and hiring workers to take care of those lands. From its stores of grain, the crown then funded other operations—for example, those of the military. These payments were directed by Marduk-Lamassašu, presiding over the storehouse, and were implemented by his subordinates in the field.

A final text mentioning Marduk-lamassašu with the title *abi ṣābim* is the slave sale *YOS* 13 5. In this document, whose date is lost, Marduk-lamassašu buys a house-born slave of Babylon from two brothers. The warranty concluding this document, regarding the health of the slave is normal for this type of contract.

Many other documents mention people named Marduk-lamassašu who may be identical with the *abi ṣābim*-official, but this identification can seldom be argued since title and patronymic are lacking. In texts that pertain to crown enterprises in the latter part of the OB period the individuals recorded are almost always titled. Many texts, such as the *YOS* 13 5 slave sale, appear to be strictly private business affairs mentioning people with titles. Toward the very end of the period, especially during the reign of Samsu-ditana, the appearance of titled individuals in contracts, both private and public, seems to increase—a phenomenon that has occasioned little comment. An explanation for this phenomenon will be reserved for Chapter 5.

Texts Mentioning Marduk-muballiṭ

The *abi ṣābim* in the Dilbat Bureau of Wool Accounts

Another well-attested *abi ṣābim*-official is Marduk-muballiṭ, whose first appearance (*YOS* 13 289) dates in the year A-d 34. This text formally belongs to the " 'Palast'geschaefte" genre and specifically to the "bureau of wool accounts" texts discussed in connection with Utul-Ištar.

YOS 13 289

13 (gur) 3 (PI) 5 (bán) še gur
šà šám síg *ša* é-gal-*lim*!
ki ^{d}*marduk-mu-ba-lí-iṭ a-bi* erén
⸢I⸣*i-na-pa-le-šu* dumu *a-lí-wa-aq-rum*
⸢I⸣*a-wi-il-*^{d}*i-šum* dumu *i-lu-ni*
⸢*ù* ^{I}*be*⸣*-el-šu-nu* dumu *i-lu-ni*
[šu ba-an-ti]-e-eš
[u_4]-$buru_x$-šè
[*a-na*] é-ì-dub *il-qu-ú*
še-am gur-ru-dam-e-eš

---

igi *i-din-ištar* ugula mar-tu
igi lugal-zi-ma-an-sum dumu *ì-lí-i-ri-ḫa-am*
igi ^{d}*marduk-mu-ba-lí-iṭ* dub-sar
iti áš-a u$_4$-28-kam
m[u *am-mi-di-ta-na* lugal-e]
alam n[am-ur-sag-gá]
sa-am-su-i-lu-na pa$_5$-bil-[ga-na] (A-d 34)

Seal: lugal-zi-ma-an-sum
dumu ì-lí-e-ri-ba-am

Inapalêšu, son of Ali-waqrum, Awīl-Išum, son of Iluni, and Bēlšunu, son of Iluni, received 13 kor, 110 liters of grain out of the wool accounts of the crown from (the bureau of) Marduk-muballiṭ, *abi ṣābim.* At harvest time they will return the grain to the storehouse where they received it.

Another Marduk-muballiṭ text, *VS* 7 72, was already catalogued by Kraus in his discussion of the topic "Gerstedarlehen aus Dilbat."[35] For sake of comparison with the new *YOS* 13 document that text may be recapitulated here:

VS 7 72

4 še gur
šà šám síg *ša* é-gal
ki ^{d}*marduk-mu-ba-lí-iṭ a-bi* erén^{meš}
^{I}*i-din-*^{d}uraš PA.PA
dumu *šu-mu-um-li-ib-ši*
šu ba-an-ti
u$_4$-buru$_x$-šè
a-na na-ši! ka-ni-ki-šu
še-am ì-ág-e
igi ^{d}te-eš-šu-ub-*a'-ri*
igi *a-wi-il-*^{d}uraš PA.PA
igi *i-din-*^{d}uraš dumu *i-din-*^{d}*la-ga-ma-al*
igi ìr-*ku-bi* dumu *ìl-šu-ba-ni*
iti kin-^{d}inanna u$_4$-25-kam
mu *am-mi-ṣa-du-gá* lugal-e
mu gibil (erasure?) egir
sipa ⸢burun-na⸣ an ^{d}en-líl-
bi-da-aš (A-ṣ 3)

Iddin-Uraš, PA.PA, son of Šumum-libši, received 4 kor grain out of the wool accounts of the crown from (the bureau of) Marduk-muballiṭ, *abi ṣābim.* At harvest time, he will weigh out the grain to the bearer of his tablet.

The terms of *YOS* 13 289 differ slightly from those of *VS* 7 72—there is no "Inhaberklausel" in the former—but the nature of Marduk-muballiṭ's activities with the bureau of wool accounts is identical. As was seen in *VS* 7 72 (and *VS* 7 78, the other text from Dilbat cited by Kraus, but not mentioning Marduk-muballiṭ) the Dilbat bureau of wool accounts did not specifically mention the intermediary parties who actually disbursed the grain, as the Sippar texts regularly did. Nevertheless, we may translate ki = *itti* as, "from the bureau of," implying the existence of such minor functionaries. The date of A-d 34 in *YOS* 13 289 shows the more than temporary association of Marduk-muballiṭ with the bureau in Dilbat, as *VS* 7 72 is dated 7 years later.

The *abi ṣābim* in agricultural management

Another text concerning Marduk-muballiṭ, dated to A-d, but lacking the exact year, is *YOS* 13 309. This text is a harvest-labor contract of the type discussed in detail by Lautner:[36]

YOS 13 309

1 (gur) [x]
a-na e-⸢ṣi-di-im⸣
ki ^{d}*marduk-mu-ba-lí-i⸢ṭ a-bi⸣* erén
^{I}*e-til-pu* x[x]
šu ba-an-ti
u_4-buru$_x$-šè ⸢*e*⸣-[*ṣi-dam i-il-la-ak*]
ú-ul i-l[*a-ak-ma*]
ki-ma ṣi-im-da-at [lugal]
igi *ḫu-zi-rum*
igi *e-til-pi*$_4$-^{d}*na-bi-um*

---

iti áš-a u_4-25-kam
mu *am-mi-di-ta-na* lugal-e
[x]

1 kor (+) of grain, for a harvest-laborer, Etel-pû [ ]
received from Marduk-muballiṭ, the *abi ṣābim*-official.
At harvest time he will furnish a harvester (to the field);
if he does not, then it is according to the *ṣimdat šarrim*.

This type of document will be discussed again in the next chapter, where we shall see that although many harvest labor agreements appear to be private contracts,[37] often there are indications that the work is to be performed in fields owned by the crown and supervised by crown officials.[38]

In Szlechter, *TJM* p. 93, A-d 37, Marduk-muballiṭ is again engaged in hiring harvesters. This contract follows the same form as *YOS* 13 309 except for the clause KA dub-a-ni nu-me-a in line 3 after *ana ēṣidim*. Szlechter interpreted this clause, "la parole [reading inim] de sa tablette n'existe pas *ou* sans parole de sa tablette,"[39] and he translates simply, "sans tablette écrite." In a rather complicated explanation Szlechter supposed that the sum mentioned in the contract to be paid at the end of the work period had in fact already been paid at the *oral* negotiation of the contract. Thus the phrase "without written tablet" was added to the written version of the contract to show that the payment had previously been made. This explanation has little to recommend it since there was nothing standing in the way of writing a tablet as soon as the conditions were agreed upon. Philologically, KA probably stands for Akkadian, *pî*, and the entire phrase is a Sumerianized counterpart of the formula *ezub pî kanīkišu pānî*, "apart from the conditions of his former contract." This phrase, then, merely implies that there was no previous account outstanding at the time of drawing up of the present contract, and the phrase can be simply translated, therefore: "there being no outstanding account (tablet)."

The fact that a clause of this sort was written into documents shows that multiple harvest-labor contracts were registered by Marduk-muballiṭ. In this document, there was no outstanding payment to be made by the party promising to bring harvesters, but as there had been previous transactions with this person, this fact had to be duly noted. (Or, alternatively, this was the first account of the contracting party.) This technical accounting procedure should alert us that many "simple" harvest-labor contracts may in reality be records of agricultural enterprises kept by the crown bureaucracy.

The basic manner of paying for labor to be performed in a certain administrative district was to disburse grain to captains of work-gangs, always including in a contract the standard injunction of a penalty for non-performance. This was the subject of the administrative document *TCL* I 158, discussed above. In many harvest-labor contracts we may have similar types of administrative transactions, although their nature is sometimes difficult to ascertain without further knowledge of the participants mentioned in them. In one type,[40] the *abi ṣābim*-official authorized grain payments that were disbursed by subordinates to work-managers, who thereupon contracted to supply the labor for crown agricultural enterprises.

The Career of Marduk-muballiṭ

There are several documents in which Marduk-muballiṭ, with the title *abi ṣābim*, plays a role that does not seem related to official crown activity. *CT* 8 3b (*HG* 3 633), dating to A-ṣ 3, is a land rental agreement whereby Marduk-muballiṭ rents ab-sín land and kankal land from a member of the family of a *nadītum*. At the behest of one of her brothers (*ana qabê* PN), Marduk-muballiṭ rents the ab-sín land for cultivation and the kankal land for plowing. He pays rent on the former immediately and on the latter in the year when it becomes productive. There are five witnesses, of whom the second is a judge and the third the scribe Šumum-līṣi. There is also the document *W* 33 (date lost), in which Marduk-muballiṭ buys a (young) ox. Six witnesses are noted, the last being the scribe Šumum-līṣi.

One final document that mentions Marduk-muballiṭ, *abi ṣābim*, actually concerns his son. The use of the title of Marduk-muballiṭ in the patronyn is in itself unusual, the more so since Marduk-muballiṭ, as we shall presently see, was not active in that office at the time. The document, *YOS* 13 262[42] (dated to Samsu-ditana 2), concerns the sale of a cow belonging to the son of Marduk-muballiṭ, who bears the title dub-sar-zag-ga (in the seal simply dub-sar) = *zazakkum.*[43] This was also the title of a Marduk-muballiṭ in the year A-d 15 (*TCL* I 152),[44] a text that was also concerned with the purchase of animals. Lautner had already speculated about various offices held by Marduk-muballiṭ in his career,[45] but, of course, could propose only a tentative reconstruction since the name is one of the commonest in the OB period. Moreover, he had fewer documents citing Marduk-muballiṭ, and did not include *TCL* I 152, having had no reason to suppose that the rank dub-sar-zag-ga might also be connected with this same Marduk-muballiṭ who held the titles ugula mar-tu, *abi ṣābim* and *ṭupsarrum.* Nevertheless, the following table offers impressive testimony to the fact that one man, in a regular order, bore all those titles:

Table IV: The Career of Marduk-muballiṭ

A-d 7	*VS* 7 50	dub-sar
A-d 11	*VS* 7 51	dub-sar
A-d 15	*TCL* I 152	dub-sar-zag-ga[46]
A-d 21	*BE* 6/1 90	dub-sar
A-d 32	*VS* 7 59	dub-sar
A-d 34	*YOS* 13 289	*abi* erén
A-d, date lost	*YOS* 13 309	*abi* erén
A-d 37	*TJM* p. 93	*abi* erén
A-ṣ 3, 5th month	*VS* 7 72	*abi* erén^{meš}
A-ṣ 3, 7th month	*CT* 8 3b	*abi* erén
date lost	*W* 33	*abi* erén
A-ṣ 3, 12th month	*VS* 7 75	ugula mar-tu
A-ṣ 4	*VS* 7 76	ugula mar-tu
A-ṣ 10	*VS* 7 89	ugula mar-tu
A-ṣ 11	*VS* 7 94	ugula mar-tu
A-ṣ 12	*VS* 7 96	ugula mar-tu
A-ṣ 16	*VS* 7 122	ugula mar-tu
S-d 2	*YOS* 13 262	*abi* erén (in patronym)
Summary:		
A-d 7 – A-d 34	27 years	(26 years, not more than 27 years, as "scribe")
A-d 34 – A-ṣ 3	7 years	*abi ṣābim*
A-ṣ 3 – A-ṣ 16	14 years	ugula mar-tu
	48 years	

One might be able to add to this table other documents and especially letters mentioning persons named Marduk-muballiṭ, but the implications of the present compilation are sufficiently striking. The analysis of single economic/administrative documents can yield only static information about the actors in that document. Only by assembling documents into "artificial archives" through assumptions of the significance of titled individuals in these texts as constituting segments of an administrative hierarchy and then testing these assumptions with detailed prosopographic investigations could the vicissitudes of Marduk-muballiṭ's career be reconstructed.

Finally, the long and carelessly written letter *PBS* 7 108 referring to Marduk-muballiṭ must be mentioned in this collection of texts that attest his activities in the rank of *abi ṣābim*. According to Table IV, the letter may be dated between A-d 34 and A-ṣ 3, although it is also possible that Marduk-muballiṭ held the title before A-d 34.[47] The letter concerns the looting of a threshing-floor. The owner of the threshing-floor went before the honorable Marduk-muballiṭ, *abi ṣābim* (1. 28-29), who then issued a document about the matter to the party addressed in the letter (the "father" of the writer). The remainder of the letter contains further instructions and admonitions from the writer to the addressee concerning the future maintenance of the threshing-floor and of fields for which he was responsible. The particulars of the affair, as is often the case with letters when we have no knowledge of their antecedents, are not evident. The participation of Marduk-muballiṭ, however, has been described by Krueckmann[48] as testimony of the duties of the *abi ṣābim* as a civilian police official, this letter having to do with the disposition of a criminal case.[49] Although Marduk-muballiṭ obviously gives instructions in the affair of the looting of the threshing-floor, his decision seems to refer primarily to the situation after the theft, the accumulation of grain and the jurisdiction of the fields belonging to the writer. This letter is actually more tantalizing than informative, and the nature of Marduk-muballiṭ's participation is unclear. In other contexts the *abi ṣābim* was basically interested in the apportionment and collection of grain, and it is probable that Marduk-muballiṭ participated in this case for this reason, and not because he was a professional law-enforcement officer.

Ili-iqīšam as *abi ṣābim*

From the examination of the various ranks held in sequence by Marduk-muballiṭ, it is evident that officials were promoted and demoted, though the reasons for these changes cannot be ascertained. That one person held several titles does not indicate that these titles were in any way equivalent (thus, it would not be proposed that *ṭupšarrum* was the same as *abi ṣābim* because Utul-Ištar held both titles). The *CAD*'s reasoning in 1963 that *abi ṣābim* might be the Akkadian equivalent for gal-unken-na on the grounds that the official Ili-iqīšam held both titles is, therefore, a very fragile argument; and with discovery of syllabic spellings of *mu'errum* in the OB period confirming the later lexical equivalence gal-unken-na = *mu'errum*, the *CAD*'s suggestion must now be rejected.

In comparison with the large number of documents attesting (an) Ili-iqīšam[50] with the rank of *mu'errum* in the last years of Ammi-ditana and early years of Ammi-ṣaduqa, there are only a few texts that mention Ili-iqīšam as an *abi ṣābim*-official. The document mentioned by the *CAD* was *CT* 8 21c dating to A-ṣ 10.

CT 8 21c

2 gín kù-babbar *ka-an-kum*
e-zu-ub ½ gín kù-babbar *ka-an-kum*
ša sanga^{meš} *ki-ma še gi-ir-ri*
id-di-nu
igi-sá ^{d}*marduk-mu-ba-lí-iṭ* nar-gal
ša a-na ì-li-í-qí-ša-am a-bi erén
ès-ḫu
mu-DU
^{I}*šu-mu-um-li-ib-ši*
    pa ti gi a ti (?)
nam-ḫa-ar-ti
^{Id}*marduk-mu-ba-lí-iṭ*
ù ^{d}*sîn-na-ṣi-ir*
    di-ki-i

---

iti apin-du$_8$-a u$_4$-2-kam
mu *am-mi-ṣa-du-qá* lugal-e
sipa zi-še-ga
^{d}utu ^{d}marduk-bi-da

2 shekels stamped silver, apart from ½ shekel stamped silver, which the "priests" gave as grain for the caravan–(this is) the *igisû*-tax of Marduk-muballiṭ, the "chief singer," which was assigned to Ili-iqīšam, *abi ṣābim,* (for collection). Brought in by Šumum-libši, the x (?), received by the *dēkû*-officials, Marduk-muballiṭ and Sîn-nāṣir.

The *CAD*[51] reports that the *igisû*-tax was usually collected from "priests and merchants."[52] In *VS* 7 70 the *igisû*-payment was received by a *dēkûm*-official, a "summoner (for tax and corvée work)." In *CT* 8 21c, the relationship between the payment of the "priests" and the *igisû*-tax of Marduk-muballiṭ, the "chief singer," is not made clear. The above interpretation assumes that the *igisû*-tax was given to Ili-iqīšam for collection, following the example of *ed-Dēr* 30, in which an *isiḫtum*-tax[53] was given to Utul-Ištar for collection. Accordingly, the *dēkû*-officials may be seen as subordinates of Ili-iqīšam responsible for the receipt of the tax. The *CAD* took a different point of view, however, in their translation "the license-fee of the chief singer PN, who has been assigned to the *abi ṣābi* PN$_2$."[54]

The two other texts mentioning Ili-iqīšam with the title *abi ṣābim* are land rental contracts. In *CT* 4 17a,[55] A-ṣ 9 (?), Ili-iqīšam rents land from a shepherd for one year agreeing to pay the *bilat eqlim.* The last of three witnesses is Šumum-līṣi, dumu-é-dub-ba-a. In *CT* 8 19b,[56] A-ṣ 11, land previously rented by Ili-iqīšam, *abi ṣābim,* at the behest of PN, is rented by three people in a partnership agreement, among them a *gallābum*-official. The four witnesses include a PA.PA and Šumum-līṣi, dumu-é-dub-ba-a. This is actually a case of sub-leasing, since the land did not belong to Ili-iqīšam, and the phrase *ana qabê* ("at the behest of")[57] implies that the subordinate of Ili-iqīšam actually effected the transaction. This is probably to be seen as an instance of a benefice granted by the crown to an important official then sub-let for a share of the produce of the land, while a future payment to the crown as the ultimate owner of land was still to be made.[58] The scribe (dub-sar) and "archivist" (dumu-é-dub-ba-a) Šumum-līṣi appears in many transactions of crown officials during the early years of Ammi-ṣaduqa, documents that otherwise may appear to be private contracts.

Various *abi ṣābim*-officials, Chiefly During the Reign of Samsu-ditana

There are several new documents from *YOS* 13 mentioning the *abi ṣābim* Nabium-mālik, who was active during the reign of Samsu-ditana. In *HG* 3-6 there are less than two dozen documents dated to the last king of the "First Dynasty," an amount multiplied several times over with the publication of the texts in *YOS* 13 alone, not to mention other texts published since 1923. These new texts contain features that are not common in texts of the earlier Old Babylonian rulers. Adding to the difficulty in interpreting these features, however, is the problem that many of the texts come from Kish, which has not been well-documented heretofore during the period of the post-Hammurapi kings. At the present time it seems evident that a full-scale study of these materials will be necessary before venturing remarks on the character of the activities at Kish during this time.[59] Nevertheless, the basic functions of the *abi ṣābim* can still be recognized under the reign of the last OB king.

YOS 13 66

2 (PI) 2 (bán) še 1 (PI) gú-gal
ša ^{d}*na-bi-um-ma-lik a-bi* erén
a-na qá-bé-e ^{d}*sîn-i-qí-ša-am* dumu-é-dub? -ba? -a?
a-na na-ṣi-ir-na-pi-iš-ti egir (?)
a-na u$_4$-10-kam *i-in-na-ad-nu*
iš-tu iti apin-du$_8$-a u$_4$-23-kam
2 sìla-ta-a *i-sa-ad-da-ar-ma*
[2 (PI) 2 (bán) še] 1 (PI) gú-gal
(line missing)
[*a-na*] ⌜*na-ši ka-ni*⌝-*ki-šu*
[*i-n*]*a-ad-di-in*

---

igi *ma-ad-du-mu-uq*-^{d}AK (*Nabium*) ⌜x x x⌝
igi *ḫu-za-lum* dumu *tam-la-tum*

igi *i-na*-é-sag-íl-numun dumu *ša-al-lu-rum*
igi *ib-ni*-^{d}*marduk* dumu-é-dub-ba-a

---

iti apin-du$_{8}$-a u$_{4}$-23-kam
mu *sa-am-su-di-ta-na* lugal-e
^{d}pa$_{5}$-nun-an-ki nin-an-ta-gál-la (S-d 14)

(amounts of) barley and chickpeas of Nabium-mālik, *abi ṣābim,* at the behest of Sîn-iqīšam, dumu-é-dub-ba-a, were given to Naṣir-napišti, egir (?), for 10 days. From the 8th month, 23rd day, 2 liters each (day) he shall enter in account. (The amounts of) barley and chickpeas . . . to the bearer of his tablet, he will give.

The function of Nabium-mālik as the proprietor of the storehouse was thus to dispense grain. In *YOS* 13 337 we again see Nabium-mālik playing a role in a grain transaction.

YOS 13 337

5½ gín kù-babbar
a-na šám *še-e*
ki ^{d}*na-bi-um-ma-lik a-bi* erén
a-na qá-bé-e ma-ad-du-mu-uq-^{d}AK
^{I}ìr-*ili-šu* dumu *bi-ga-an*
šu ba-an-ti
u$_{4}$-buru$_{x}$-šè
a-na na-ši ka-ni-ki-šu
ganba *ib-ba-aš-šu-ú*
še ì-ág-e

---

igi ìr-^{d}*na-bi-um* dumu *ib-ni*-^{d}*sîn*
igi *i-na*-é-sag-íl-numun [x]
igi *i-di-ki-it-ta* dumu [x]
igi ìr-^{d}*na-bi-um* um-mi-a

---

iti diri še-gur$_{10}$-ku$_{5}$ u$_{4}$-14-kam
mu *sa-am-su-di-ta-na* lugal
alam-a-ni tuš-bi
aš-te-ta (S-d 13)

Seal: ^{na_4}kisib ìr-*ili-šu*

At the behest of Mād-dummuq-Nabium, Warad-ilišu, son of Bigan,[60] received 5½ shekels silver to acquire grain from (the bureau of) Nabium-mālik, *abi ṣābim*. At harvest time to the bearer of his tablet, at the market price, he will weigh out the grain.

Mād-dummuq-Nabium, the subordinate of Nabium-mālik, who took active part in this transaction, was also the first witness in *YOS* 13 66. We observe from these texts how the bureaucracy that operated the storehouse was recorded in administrative contracts. Far from being persons casually enlisted as the contract was drawn up, witnesses were often precisely those bureaucrats interested in its terms. Mād-dummuq-Nabium was one of several subordinates of the chief of the storehouse, Nabium-mālik; he alternately dispensed grain ("at his behest") or took part as a "notary" in a transaction officially recorded by a bookkeeper attached to the storehouse (as seen in *YOS* 13 337 and *YOS* 13 66 respectively).

A third Nabium-mālik text is *YOS* 13 444, which also deals with agricultural products:

YOS 13 444

5 (bán) še-giš-ì ^{giš}bán-^{d}utu
a-na ṣa-h̬[a-ti]-im-ma
ì-giš [*el*]*-lim*
[ki ^{d}*na-bi-um-ma-l*]*ik a-bi* erén
^{I}[ ]di dumu ^{d}*marduk-mu-ba-lí-iṭ*
šu ba-an-ti
[a]d-ma
a-na 10 u_4*-mi*
1 (bán) ì-giš ^{giš}bán-^{d}utu
a-na ^{d}*na-bi-um-ma-lik a-bi* erén
i-ma-ad-da-ad

šà é-ì-dub *ša pa-ni* ká-gal
iti ne-ne-gar u_4-13-kam
mu *sa-am-su-di-ta-na* lugal-e
^{d}pa$_5$-nun-an-ki
nin-an-ta-gál-la-a-aš (S-d "d" = 14)

From Nabium-mālik, *abi ṣābim,* PN, son of Marduk-muballiṭ, received 5 liters of sesame according to the seah-measure of Šamaš for processing into sesame oil. . . . In 10 days one liter of sesame oil according the *sūtu*-measure of Šamaš he will weigh out to Nabium-mālik, *abi ṣābim.* From (the supplies) of the storehouse before the great gate.

Nabium-mālik is here explicitly identified as the administrator of the storehouse. He gives out 5 liters of sesame to a processor who in 10 days will bring back one liter sesame oil.[61]

CT 8 8e,[62] dating to A-d 35, concerns a similar transaction. There 9 kor of sesame yields a one-third proportion of sesame oil. Three brothers receive the sesame from Utu-šumundab, the *dayānum* whom we met above in the Utul-Ištar file (Ch. 2). These three brothers contract to process the sesame and to weigh out the oil within one month. We may conclude that both *CT* 8 8e and *YOS* 13 444 were official procedures. The storehouse contained various sorts of agricultural products, and its director in *YOS* 13 444, Nabium-mālik, was in charge of their disposition.

Also from *YOS* 13 comes document no. 428, which concerns the *abi ṣābim*-official Ibni-Šamaš. This text also dates to the time of Samsu-ditana.

YOS 13 428

½ ma-na kù-babbar
KA dub-a-ni nu-me-a
ša ib-ni-^{d}utu *a-bi* erén
a-na qá-bé-e ^{d}*marduk-mu-ša-lim*
dumu *ri-iš*-^{d}*na-bi-um*
a-na ta-ri-bu dumu *el-li-lum*
id-di-nu
a-na iti-l-kam
a-na na-ši ka-ni-ki-šu
kù-babbar ì-lá-e
igi *pir-ḫi*-^{d}*mar-tu* dumu ^{d}*na-bi-um-mu-ša-lim*
igi *i-na*-é-sag-íl-numun kù(?)-dím(?)
igi *i-na*-é-sag-íl-numun ì-šur
igi *e-til-pi*$_4$-^{d}utu um-mi-a

Seal: NI BA [ ] ^{na_4}kišib
BE EL E KI [ ] *i-na*-é-sag-íl-numun
^{d}BI [ ]

iti sig$_4$-a u$_4$-26-kam
mu *sa-am-su-di-ta-na* lugal-e
alam-a-ni tuš-bi aš-te-ta
in-da-ra-gar-ra (S-d 13)

½ mina silver, there being no prior account of his, which Ibni-Samaš, *abi ṣābim,* at the behest of Marduk-mušallim, the son of Rīš-Nabium, gave to Tarību, son of Ellilum. In one month to the bearer of his tablet, he (Tarību) will weigh out the silver.

This text is not different from other documents concerning the activities of the *abi ṣābim*-officials that we have already seen. We may note, however, that the "loan" is phrased without the šubanti-clause and only states that the silver was "given" to Tarību. The technical phrases *ana qabê* and KA dub-a-ni nu-me-a together almost certainly denote an administrative bookkeeping procedure.

YOS 13 142 is an undated memorandum with reference to the *abi ṣābim* Ea-awīlim, the administrator of a storehouse, who disbursed quantities of barley to various people:

10 še gur
íb-tag$_4$ Ì.DUB.É *a-wi-lim a-bi* erén
ša uš-ta-an-nu-ú
sag-níg-ga šà-bi-˹ta˺
etc.

(amt.) grain
remainder of the storehouse of the honorable *abi ṣābim,*
which has been calculated:
Out of this capital . . .

The remainder of the text records the allotments of grain mostly to people connected with the brewing process: the maltster, the brewer, the head-brewer, those associated with the barrels of mash, slaves and hirelings.[63] The relationship between these people and the administrative function of the *abi ṣābim* must lie in the fact that the crown was supplying provisions to its workshops. The technical terms sag-níg-ga, šà-bi-ta, and íb-tag$_4$ are well-known from the bureaucratic records of Ur III times. For a similar text see *YOS* 13 43, whose date of S-d 13 may be an indication of the date of *YOS* 13 142.

The last document from *YOS* 13 that mentions an *abi ṣābim*-official (name broken) is no. 33, dating to A-d 33:

YOS 13 33

2/3 ma-na kù-babbar
˹*a-na* šám˺*še-e*
[ki]-*mu-ša-lim a-bi* erén
^{I}[me-a-im]-ri-a-mu
[*ù* x]-nu?-ni?-ru
(erasure) dumu^{meš} ^{d}utu/iškur-zi-mu
šu ba-an-ti-meš
u$_4$-buru$_x$-ka!
ganba *ib-ba-aš-šu-ú*
i-na kiš$^{\text{˹ki˺}}$
a-na pí-i é-ì-dub
˹*a-na*˺ *na-ši ka-ni-ki-šu-nu*
še ì-ág-e-meš

igi ^{d}*sîn-ni-šu* dumu ^{d}*sîn-šar-ma-tim*
igi *ì-lí-*[*x*]*-ha-na-ti*
dumu *ib-ni-é-a*
igi ^{d}*marduk-mu-ša-lim*
dumu ^{d}⌜*marduk*⌝ *mu-ba-al-li-iṭ*
igi *i-din-*^{d}[*sîn*] dub-sar

---

iti bara-zà-gar u$_4$-18-kam
mu *am-mi-di-ta-na* lugal-e
nam-á-gál-la
^{d}marduk-ke$_4$
nam-zalág-SÍR-da-bi-šè (A-d 33)

This text simply notes the involvement of an *abi ṣābim*-official who loans an amount of silver "to buy" grain, which is to be paid back at the storehouse in Kish.

Letters Mentioning Unnamed *abi ṣābim*-officials

Having concluded the survey of documents and letters mentioning named *abi ṣābim*-officials, we may observe that the *abi ṣābim* was basically concerned with the management of agricultural affairs, and more particularly with the supervision of crown granaries. Let us now briefly examine the few letters referring to unnamed *abi ṣābim*-officials to see whether they confirm the *abi ṣābim's* service to the crown.

First, in *AbB* 2 90[64] the subject is a complaint lodged by a clerk against a person who had previously assigned certain fields to *rēdû*-soldiers but who was now trying to claim otherwise. The clerk, who had enrolled the soldiers' names in a list, had informed the "honorable *abi ṣābim*" of the situation, but this action was not a critical part of the investigation and is mentioned only in passing. Little information about the role of the *abi ṣābim* can be gleaned from this letter, but his involvement in a matter concerning the determination of lands and provisions fits the general picture of his agricultural duties. The "clerk" (no title is given) concludes his report by adjuring his lord not to give even one liter of grain to the PA.PA who was claiming the rights to the grain from the disputed fields.

The very brief letter *AbB* 2 104[65] records that a complaint of unspecified nature had been brought before the *abi ṣābim*. Hardly more helpful is the letter *VS* 7 195,[66] a request to bring animals to Babylon, to which the remark *šakān awīlī abi* erén^{meš} *qurrub* ("the installation of the *abi ṣābim*-officials is at hand")[67] is appended. This is an intriguing statement, but not very revealing as to the role of the installed officials. *VS* 16 202 rs. 4 mentions an unnamed *abi ṣābim* (*ṭuppi awīlim a-bi* erén), but the context is too broken to allow any determination of his function.

Although letters can often shed important light on the activities of officials, they are not so helpful in establishing the basic duties of an office. Leemans has stressed the complementarity of letters and documents[68] in studying events and actions in Old Babylonian times, but was willing to conclude solely on the basis of letters that *abi ṣābim*-officials were specifically concerned with cases pertaining to thievery.[69]

Conclusion

The matter of role in Old Babylonian society, as in other societies, cannot be discussed in terms of only a specific, unidimensional function. We have tried to show in this chapter that the *abi ṣābim* was not a police officer, a leader of troops, or a specialist for the investigation of certain wrongs. He was rather, a crown official whose basic duties lay in the area of agricultural administration—the procurement and storage of resources, and then in the utilization of these resources in profit-making financial activities. These duties naturally involved certain relations with those elements of the populace not directly dependent on the crown, especially when those duties took on larger public significance. Thus, the legal authority of the *abi ṣābim* was recognized in cases when "community" members owed service to the state—for example, military service. The *abi ṣābim* not only supplied provisions to the military, but also enforced decisions made by the community about whether certain of its members were obliged to serve. The *abi ṣābim* would not be expected, however, to preside in cases that were properly the jurisdiction of local authorities.

The various "chains of authority" need to be clearly demarcated when analyzing legal sanctions in Old Babylonian juridical documents. Nevertheless, the individual networks of legal authority cannot be studied as if each behaved in isolation from the larger social system in which all are embedded. We shall return to these points and venture a few comments on the changing nature of interdependent institutions of authority in the Old Babylonian period after a discussion in the next chapter of another crown official, the *mu'errum.*

NOTES

[1]There are 17 new texts in the *YOS* 13 volume alone; see Table II, p. 55ff.

[2]Walther, *Gerichtswesen,* pp. 158-59.

[3]"Leutevater nur teilweise behandelt," *Gerichtswesen,* p. 158, n. 2.

[4]Walther, *Gerichtswesen,* p. 158, "dass ihre Taetigkeit verschiedene Seiten hat."

[5]*BB*, p. 251.

[6]*UAZP,* p. 309.

[7]*HG* 3, p. 221 and passim, 1909.

[8]Goetze, *AS* 16, p. 211, n. 3.

[9] *Studies Oppenheim,* p. 124.

[10] *TJG,* p. 38

[11] *BB,* p. 252.

[12] *Personenmiete,* p. 151.

[13] *Beamtennamen,* passim.

[14] *TJG*, passim.

[15] Cf. *MSL* 12.

[16] See Table II. Its use seems to have been limited to the period of the last three kings.

[17] *UAZP* 37; older literature, Daiches, *ZA* 18, 202ff; Pinches, *JRAS* (1899), 109ff.

[18] *ellēta* is a technical term in the vocabulary of the Mesopotamian manumission. The usual pattern in the northern OB manumission documents is first to adopt the slave, cleanse his forehead (*pūtam ullulum*) then turn him toward the east. The slave in turn guarantees to look after his master in his old age and goes free when his master's god summons him (i.e., when the master dies). The cleansing ritual often represented the entire act of the manumission (a metonym) and some commentators have simply translated *ellēta*, "you are free," (e.g. Schorr, *UAZP* 37). In documents from southern OB proveniences the tablet recording a manumission agreement is occasionally called kišib-nam-sikil-la, "a document of purification."

In the southern texts there is no mention of an adoption. Koschaker, in *Griechische Rechtsurkunden* (1931), p. 71ff, placed great store by this difference in northern and southern types, while Driver and Miles, *Babylonian Laws,* p. 227, stressed the similarity in both types and that the act of purification was essentially the act of manumission. Both these sets of documents, however, were essentially contracts whereby the slave undertook the care of the aged master, gaining freedom upon the latter's death. The exact nature and stipulations of this freedom could take several forms, one of which was full equality with the natural children of the master.

[19] *HG* 6 1428.

[20] Cf. n. 18 above and *HG* 6 p. 5 to *HG* 6 1428.

[21] Specifically he would be adopted into the nuclear family of his manumittor with provisions for receiving a share in the inheritance of the family estate. Such status may also have included membership in a larger community organization, the character of which is very much an open question in Old Babylonian times.

[22] Cf. Evans, The Incidence of Labour Service in the Old Babylonian Period, *JAOS* 83, 20ff.

[23] *Studies Oppenheim,* p. 124.

[24] Lines 27-31:

> (amt.) še gur
> ^{giš}ba-rí-ga ^{d}marduk *ša nam-ḫar-tim*
> *ši!.i-iq me-še-qi-im bi-ru-yi-im*
> *a-na* šuku erén-^{giš}gigir$^{\text{ḫi-a}}$ *ù* erén-gìr
> šà *i-na* UD.KIB.NUN^{ki}*-am-na-nim wa-aš-bu*
>
> grain according to the *parsiktum*-measure of Marduk customary for receipts, according to the 'mean' standard, for the provisions of the charioteers and infantry living in Sippar-Amnānum.

[25] Lines 4, 9, 11:

> šà *li-tum* PN *a-bi* erén
>
> from the administrative precinct of PN, *abi ṣābim.*

These three lines are cited in the *AHw* (p. 562) under "*luītum* (unbekannter Herkunft) (L. Adv?), PN," the word occurring only in these three lines in *CT* 45 48. This hapax, however, is to be deleted. Hirsch (*ZANF* 24, 1967, p. 332) construed the lines, "*li-tum* PN a-bi erén" without being able to understand the first sign. He translated the well-known word *lītum*, "zur Verfuegung," and suggested that perhaps the first sign was DIB, translating, "Fassung, zur Verfuegung von . . . ." This first sign, however, can be interpreted more easily as a cursively written OB šà (although one would be happier then with a genitive, *lītim*). The phrase šà *lītim*, is indeed, already attested, cf. *AHw*, under *lītum*, (p. 557 1 b), OA and OB *i-li-ti-šu*, šà *li-(i)-tim*, "Verwaltungsbereich." That šà was an optional element in the phrase is shown in *CT* 45 54, see below n. 27.

[26]zi-ga zì *še-e na-at-ba-ak* UD.KIB.NUN[ki]*-ya-aḫ-ru-rum*

expenditure of meal (and) barley of the storehouse of Sippar-Yaḫrurum.

[27]Line 13:

lītum Marduk-lamassašu abi ṣābim

The functions of an *abi ṣābim*, Nanna-mansum, in his administrative district (*lītum*) are further seen in *CT* 45 61. In this text Nanna-mansum accounts for 1685 head of cattle which are at the individual dispositions of 5 "generals" (ugula mar-tu).

[28]Lindl, *Beamtennamen*, p. 283, nr. 1140, ventured the date A-d 36, but this is by no means certain.

[29]Cf. *HG* 5, p. 122.

[30]Lautner, *Personenmiete*, p. 151 and nn. 459-60.

[31]Ibid., p. 151.

[32]Ibid., p. 187.

[33]Ibid., p. 123. Maria deJ. Ellis in a study of *ṣimdat šarrim* (*JCS* 24 (1972) 74ff) discusses the entire semantic range of *ṣimdatum* and questions Lautner's translation, "tarif," for the term. She agrees, however, that some kind of payment was made for non-compliance with the terms of the contract. The texts do not indicate whether this payment was to be a proportional sum calculated according to the original terms of the document, but presumably some such situation was implied and understood by all parties.

[34]Cf. Chapter 2, p. 32ff.

[35]*Edikt*, pp. 100-01.

[36]*Personenmiete*, pp. 142-44; see Ch. 4, p. 101ff. + note 76.

[37]Their basic character was interpreted as private contracts by Lautner, *Personenmiete*, p. 157.

[38]If the traces in line 4 after the name Etelpû can be restored ⌜PA!⌝[TE.SI]= ensí, Etel-pû was playing the role of a manager in agricultural enterprises with which Marduk-muballiṭ was connected.

[39]*TJG* p. 106 n. 2.

[40]*TCL* 1 158; *TJM* p. 93; *YOS* 13 309.

[41]*AJSL* 29, p. 188; *HG* VI 1648.

[42]*YOS* 13 262:

1 áb mu-3
áb ^d^*sîn-iš-me-a-an-ni* dub-sar-zag-ga
dumu ^d^*marduk-mu-ba-lí-iṭ a-bi* erén
ki^d^*sîn-iš-me-a-an-ni* dub-sar-zag-ga
5 *be-el* áb
^I^*ú-túl-istar* išib an-^d^inanna
dumu *ì-lí-i-qí-ša-am*
in-ši-in-šám
šám-ti-la-bi-šè

18 gín kù-babbar
in-na-an-lá
ù ⅓ gín kù-babbar diri-ga
iš-ku-un
a-na ba-aq-ri-ša
ki-ma ṣi-im-da-at šar-ri
iz-za-a-az

---

igi ^{d}*na-na-a-e-ri-iš* išib an-^{d}inanna
igi *ri-iš-*^{d}*marduk* gala-maḫ an-^{d}inanna
igi *ta-ri-bu* dumu ^{d}*i-šum-mu-ba-lí-iṭ*
igi *be-el-šu-nu* dumu ^{d}*sîn-na-di-in-šu-mi*

---

iti še-gur$_{10}$-ku$_{5}$ u$_{4}$-30-kam
mu *sa-am-su-di-ta-na* lugal-e
mu gibil egir inim-maḫ-a
lugal bal-a-na bí-in-g[e-en]

Seals:	^{d}*sîn-iš-me-an-ni*	^{d}*na-na-a-e-ri-iš*
	dub-sar	išib an-^{d}inanna
	dumu ^{d}*marduk-mu-ba-lí-iṭ*	dumu *ab-di-*[*e-ra-aḫ*]
	ìr-^{d} [ ]	ìr-*am-mi-ṣa-du-qá*

43 *CAD* Z, p. 75. dub-sar was probably employed generically to designate several types of bureaucratic specialists who possessed advanced scribal degrees.

44 *TCL* I 152:

4 gín igi-6-gál kù-babbar
a-na šám 5 udu-nita$^{ḫi\text{-}a}$
ki ^{d}*marduk-mu-ba-lí-iṭ*
dub-sar-zag-ga
^{I}sig-*an-nu-ni-tum* enku (ZAG.ḪA)
a-na qá-bé-e ugula dam-gàr
ù di-ku$_{5}$^{meš}
šu ba-an-ti
u$_{4}$-um sig-*an-nu-ni-tum*
i-ir-ru-ba-am
4 gín igi-6-gál kù-babbar
a-na na-ši ka-ni-ki-šu
ì-lá-e
iti gan-gan-è u$_{4}$-19-kam
mu *am-mi-di-ta-na* lugal-e
^{urudu}ki-lugal-gub-gal-gal-la
[x x x x]
[kur]-ḫur-sag-gá i$_{7}$-i$_{7}$-gal

45 *Personenmiete,* pp. 157-58.

46 Cf. n. 43 above.

[47]Ungnad, *BB* 108. Ungnad thought the text came from Sippar (p. 5), but most of the texts referring to Marduk-muballiṭ come from Dilbat.

[48] *RlA* I, p. 448.

[49]Cf. Leemans, *RSO* 32, p. 666 and n. 2.

[50]On the possiblity that two individuals named Ili-iqīšam are concerned, see Ch. 4, note 54.

[51]Vol. I, p. 41f.

[52]Cf. Fish, *LFBD* 1 (p. 6) where a "priest" (gala) pays an *igisû*-tax.

[53]Same root as *esḫu*, line 7, *CT* 8 21c.

[54]Vol. A/1, p. 51. Why a "chief-singer" would be assigned to an *abi ṣābim* is not explored.

[55]*HG* 3 578.

[56]*HG* 3 653.

[57]See Ch. 4, p. 110ff.

[58]See Ch. 2, p. 31.

[59]For now, see Finkelstein, "Introduction" to *YOS* 13; Yoffee, "The Old Babylonian Texts from Kish: A First Report," in press for a memorial volume honoring Prof. J. J. Finkelstein.

[60]The name Bigan is a "Gutian" name, cf. Hallo, "Gutium," *RlA* 4, p. 716.

[61]*CAD* cites ì-giš = *ellu*, "sesame oil (of a specific quality)," vol. E, p. 106. This definition is defended by Kraus and Landsberger against Helbaek (Kraus, *JAOS* 88 (1968), p. 112ff; Landsberger, *Festschrift David*, p. 69ff; Helbaek, in Mallowan, *Nimrud and its Remains*, vol. 2, Appendix I: The Plant Remains, p. 113-120). *ellu* in line 3 is taken here as a gloss for ì-giš, rather than as an adjective referring to the quality of ì-giš.

[62]Cf. *UAZP* 165: *HG* 3 188.

1 9 gur še-giš-ì
2 bára-ga *ša-lu-uš-ti* ì-giš
10 še-giš-ì *i-ṣa-ḫa-tu-ma*
11 ì-giš ì-ág-e-meš

[63]"Maltster" = munu$_x$ (dim$_4$)-sar, Akkadian, *bāqilum* Line 11); "brewer" = bappir, (line 10); "head-brewer" = sag-bappir (line 12); "Mahlkasten" = *metēnum* (line 5). Cf. Roellig, *Das Bier*, pp. 38, 48 and n. 184. Other texts concerning the munu$_x$-sar are *YOS* 13 43 and *TLB* 1 60. For the reading munu$_x$, see *TCS* 1, p. 154, n. 493.

[64]*CT* 4 19a; *BB* 228.

[65]*CT* 6 8; *BB* 253.

[66]*BB* 251.

[67]*CAD* A/1, p. 51.

[68]*JESHO* 11, p. 171ff; see Ch. 1, p. 8ff.

[69]*PBS* 7 108, see above p. 68; Leemans, *RSO* 32 (1957), p. 666 and n. 2. Leemans also discussed there *TCL* 1 164, for which see the commentary, Ch. 4, pp. 126-27.

CHAPTER 4

The *mu'errum*

On the basis of the fact that one Ili-iqīšam held two titles, *abi ṣābim* and gal-unken-na (erén-ká-é-gal), the *CAD* (in 1964), in its article *abi ṣābim,* suggested that *abi ṣābim* may have been the Akkadian equivalent of the Sumerian gal-unken-na. This line of reasoning posited that no other Akkadian equivalent for gal-unken-na appears in Old Babylonian texts, though *mu'errum* was written in later syllabaries as the Akkadian translation of gal-unken-na. The *CAD* also pointed out that men bearing either the title *abi ṣābim* or gal-unken-na were often addressed with the term *awīlum,* "the honorable x-official." However, these suggestions of the possible equating of *abi ṣābim* and gal-unken-na were based on insufficient information and specious reasoning (cf. pp. 54 and 84ff.).

The reference to the "palace" as part of the title of the gal-unken-na (erén-ká-é-gal) has not unnaturally been assumed by investigators to be an expression of the crown's interest in the duties of that official. In this chapter we shall test this assumption and attempt to isolate the specific range of official activities performed by the gal-unken-na. First, though, we must consider the various opinions on the spoken (Akkadian) representation of the official whose title was written with the Sumerogram gal-unken-na and the generally held views of his functions in Old Babylonian society.

The Reading and Etymology of GAL.UNKEN.NA

In examining the native lexical traditions for interpreting the reading of the signs GAL. UNKEN.NA, it is imperative to clearly demarcate the temporal and geographical levels in the several lexical series and in contemporary texts. It is frequently impossible to determine the Sumerian and Akkadian equivalents of a title in one period on the basis of the lexical lists composed in another. The history of the title ensí = *išš(i)akkum* provides perhaps the best example of the varying importance of an official designation and the need to examine carefully and sequentially contemporary textual usages of titles.

The GAL.UNKEN(.NA) is an historic title well-attested in lexical series before the OB period. In *MSL* 12, the collection of lexical texts dealing mainly with professions and occupations and centering on the series lú = *ša* and related texts, GAL.UNKEN is found in the Early Dynastic lists.[1] In OB proto-lú, the forerunner of the late canonical series lú = *ša*, there is again a reference to gal-unken-na.[2] Both occurrences appear early in the lists near other prestigious titles. The canonical series itself, compiled in the first millennium, is presented as a composite of numerous sources in *MSL* 12[3] as follows:

(1)	110.	gal-unken	=	*mu-'-i-ru*
	111.	kin-gal	=	MIN
(3)	112.	kin-gal-unken-na	=	MIN
	113.	á-gal[3a]	=	MIN
	114.	$^{\text{e-ra}}$GÁ x ME.EN	=	MIN
	115.	gal-GÁ x ME.EN	=	MIN
	116.	gal-zu	=	MIN
	117	gal-zu-unken-na	=	*rab pu-uḫ-ru*

Source "P" in *MSL* 12 is *STT* 2 373 and may be compared with *MSL*'s composite edition especially with regard to entries (1) and (3):

(1)	111.	$^{\text{kin-gal}}$gal-unken	=	*mu-'-[ir]-ru*
	112.	kin-gal	=	*mu-'-[ir]-ru*
(3)	113.	[kin-ga]l-unken-na	=	*a rab pu-uḫ-ri*
	114.	[á]-gal	=	*mu-'-e-ri*
	115.	[ ]	=	*mu-'-e-ru*
	116.	[ ]	=	*mu-'-e-ru*
	117.	[ ]	=	*[mu-']-e-ru*

In the S^b Vokabular,[4] we read across three columns: kin-gal, gal-unken, *mu-'-ir-ru.* Translation there: "Oberster der Buergschaft." Finally, in the Emesal vocabulary,[5] the listing is edited: [a-ma-]al: á-gal = *mu-'-ir-ru,* "sheriff."

The ancient compilers of these texts thus translated GAL.UNKEN into Akkadian *mu'errum,* and, unlike some modern commentators, never confused this equivalence with the purely etymological translation of the component parts gal and unken yielding *rab puḫri.* This latter is properly the Akkadian equivalent of the gal-zu-unken-na, a totally different official who acts within a separate "chain of authority" and in a different range of time.[6]

Even the Sumerian reading of the signs GAL.UNKEN.NA is problematic. Falkenstein proposed[7] that kingal be the reading for the signs gal:unken. This he based on the *MSL* 3 vocabulary, which reads kin-gal 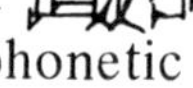 for the signs 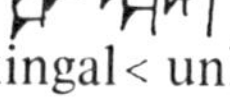. To account for this reading, Falkenstein proposed a phonetic development, kingal< unken-gal with a nasal assimilation and a loss of the first syllable because the accent was placed on the second (thus, the reading of unken or unkin instead of ukkin). The school of Falkenstein has followed this lead. Van Dijk, for example,[8] noted the reference in lú = ša, GAL$^{\text{kin-gal}}$ UNKIN,[9] but expressed reservations whether kingal could be derived from GAL.UKKIN since ukkin-gal (> kingal) would mean "great assembly," not "great one [van Dijk: "leader"] of the assembly." Falkenstein himself was bothered about the reading of kingal for GAL.UNKEN because of the complement -na[10] following the ideogram. This -na would, of course, ordinarily indicate a reading of the sign preceding the -na ending in n. For his part, van

Dijk[11] simply thought that GAL.UKKIN.NA = *mu'errum* was just a by-form or later substitution for gal-(zu-)ukkin-na = *rab puḫri.* He therefore set up an equation *mu'errum* = *rab puḫri,* assuming that GAL.UKKIN.NA, when used in OB letters, was read *rab puḫri.* This solution, however, did not take account of the listing of *mu'errum* as the equivalent for gal-unken(-na) in the lexical tradition and of the separate lexical citations of *rab puḫri.*

Sjoeberg[12] follows Falkenstein's understanding of kingal < unkengal, and notes that GAL. UNKEN was already a title in Fara texts. He states, "I interpret kin-gal as a (syllabic) writing for GAL.UNKEN = kingal = *rab puḫri, mu'erru.*" Sjoeberg was thus not troubled by any etymological difficulty nor was he disposed to account for the -na complement in the OB writings of the term (but which only rarely appears in lexical texts).

In lú = *ša*, gal-unken and kingal are listed in successive entries and once gal-unken is glossed kin-gal. There is also the phrase kin-gal-ukkin-na which is given with different Akkadian equivalents, although the scribe of the Sultantepe tablet seems to have made a false start in one entry.[13] With the exception of line 113 of the *STT* text, however, the equivalent of GAL.UNKEN in all these variations is *mu'errum.* By this last simple observation we may attempt to cut through some of the etymological speculations that have obfuscated any attempt to discuss the gal-unken-na without introducing assemblies into the argument. *rab puḫri* is not a synonym of *mu'errum*; there is, therefore, no necessity for individual etymologies combining gal and unken, that is, *rabu* and *puḫru,* nor are they relevant to the explanation of *mu'errum,* the Sumerogram of which was written GAL.UNKEN.NA. The translations of GAL.UNKEN, based on the assumption that *rab puḫri* was the Akkadian translation of that term, are, therefore, incorrect.

If it is agreed, then, that the Akkadian translation of the signs GAL.UNKEN.NA is *mu'errum,* we may return to the previous discussion of the reading of those signs, which, according to the lexical glosses, is kingal. If the reading is kingal, however, we must also return to Falkenstein's paradox: why the writing of the complement -na?

We might consider that the Babylonian scribes, though they knew that *mu'errum* was the equivalent in Akkadian of GAL.UNKEN, automatically added a Sumerian grammatical explanation, -na *i.e.*, gal-unken-a(k), when writing a Sumerogram. They wrote it thus even though they knew well that this grammatical explanation made no etymological sense (from the Akkadian point of view) and that the Sumerian reading of GAL.UNKEN was kingal! Obviously there was plenty of confusion on the matter, for the lexical lists sometimes combined reading and writing into kin-gal-unken-na. It is important to note, however, that the Sumerian equivalents of *mu'errum* and *rab puḫri* (= gal-zu-unken-na) were never so confused.[14]

If GAL.UNKEN was in fact read kingal, it seems we have another example of the "petrified" historic wirtings of words such as EN:ZU (su'en) and ZU:AB (abzu).[15] The Akkadian scribes saw no conflict, apparently, in realizing that the Sumerian expression GAL:UNKEN should be pronounced kingal and had nothing to do with *rab puḫri* (since they wrote in lexical lists *mu'erru*); at the same time, when writing a Sumerogram, they constructed a hypercorrect Sumerian form, namely gal (substantive) -unken-a(k)! The phrase in

Akkadian—and this is the crucial point—was never translated according to this "correct" Sumerian grammar, but simply as the Akkadian word *mu'errum*. Thus, the problem for the Babylonian lexicographers was not to find an Akkadian equivalent for a Sumerian term, but to find *and write* an appropriate Sumerian translation for an Akkadian term.

GAL.UNKEN was a venerable title already by the OB period, but the time-honored petrified writing of the title seems to have been at least as important as its Sumerian pronunciation. When the title was read in a letter or document, it was read *mu'errum*, and the hyper-correct Sumerian gal-unken-na never led the scribes to think that *rab puḫri* was intended. The equivalence gal-unken-na = *mu'errum* is, simply, not based on etymology. The scribal academies preserved for centuries the knowledge of the reading kingal for GAL.UNKEN.NA, but were too impressed by the historic form of the writing—that is, the visual appearance and order of the signs in their historic form—to ever want, or need, to write kingal, kin-gal. The -na was added as a gratuitous grammatical misunderstanding, based apparently on the historic order of the signs gal-unken, and reflected neither the Sumerian pronunciation nor an etymological understanding of its constituent elements. Therefore, the transcription gal-unken-na (in lower case) will be utilized here under the assumption that kingal-na is an impossible reading.[16] Whether gal—unken—na or simply *mu'errum* was dictated to scribes writing letters and documents in the OB period, we may never know for certain. For the purposes of examining the social and economic role of the official whose title was written gal-unken-na, however, we shall speak, as did the Babylonians, of the *mu'errum*.[17]

OB Syllabic Writings of *mu'errum*

The word *mu'errum* itself is a participle from the D-stem verb (*wârum*) *wu'urum*, "to send, to order, command." The initial/waw/is regularly lost already in the OB period (but for the appearance of *muwerrum* see below). In 1964 the *CAD* claimed that "no Akkadian equivalent for GAL.UNKIN.NA is known from OB texts,"[18] but in 1967 the *AHw's* lemma *mu'erru(m)* listed four syllabic writings from the OB period.

First, there is the OB personal name *mu-we-er-ru-um*.[19] This name is briefly discussed twice in Stamm's *Namengebung*. Initially Stamm grouped it under the rubric "abbreviation through omission of the theophoric element," but he offered no translation in this section.[20] The name was also mentioned in the section on bodily defects,[21] but only as being morphologically similar to certain other participles that described these defects. *muwirrum* was again not translated. Actually there is nothing against considering the name as a kind of abbreviation for "the god is my commander"; unfortunately, though, this full name is not attested. Against an emendation to the common name *munawirrum* is the fact that this latter name is invariably spelled with the last syllable *-rum*.

The second OB reference to the term is in a three column "Silbenvokabular A."[22]

The third instance of an OB syllabic writing is the letter *CT* 43 52.[23] A certain Ištar-išmešu wrote his father (*abum*: a term of respect for a powerful individual with whom I.

had to deal) about an affair with which he had previously been charged by his superiors. I., however, had bungled the matter, not properly detaining the *rabi'ānum* and elders of a certain city. He now pleaded with his "father" to seize these four men after dark and hold them for later disposition; otherwise, I. would be killed by his superiors.[24] I. apparently tried to excuse his negligence by complaining that the *muwerrum* had responsibility for the four men.[25]

Kraus's translation of *muwerrum* in *AbB* 1 52 as "Versammlungsvorstand" is a learned misconception. Kraus knew the lexical equivalent of *mu'errum* was gal-unken-na but then proceeded to connect the gal-unken-na with *rab puḫrim;* this, though a good explanation (etymologically) for the Sumerian gal-unken-na, is not its Akkadian equivalent (translation). The syllabic writing here is clearly *mu'errum*, and the Akkadian etymology for *mu'errum* has, of course, nothing to do with assemblies. Perhaps the references to *rabi'ānum* and *šībūt ālim* misled Kraus. Admittedly, however, the removal of the confusing reference to "Versammlungvorstand" does not help in the understanding of the significance of the role of the *mu'errum* in this text. Though the circumstances of the affair are completely unknown, it seems that I. was trying to get off the hook by contending that a crown official had improperly intervened in the matter, thereby relieving him of his responsibility for guarding the four men.

The fourth instance of a syllabic writing of *mu'errum* in the OB period is in a court deposition.[26] The text, part of the Ubarum archive, is analyzed by Landsberger in the following context: Ubarum and his brother, both soldiers, fulfill military obligations alternately and while Ubarum is away his brother must take care of his field. This particular document, however, shows that the brother had to be brought to court before he would agree to do the plowing, and then only with the stipulation that Ubarum would guarantee the expenses therein involved. Landsberger expresses his surprise that a court had to be convened and that a simple order by the "general" (ugula mar-tu) and "captains" (PA.PA) was not enough to get the brother of Ubarum back to his field. Line 12, in connection with the investigation of the case, reads *a-na ṣ[e-er mu]-er-ri-im it-ru-ni-iš-šu-ma,* "they brought him to the *mu'errum.*" Landsberger translated *mu'errum* "city-officer," and made the interpretation that "a mixed court had to assemble, consisting of a municipal authority, the *mu'irrum,* and the military set."[27] He also noted that *mu'errum* was the Akkadian correspondent of the "gal-unkina, 'chairman of the assembly'." The proceeding in this document, however, may be analyzed without resorting to explanations of a "mixed court" if we do not regard the *mu'errum* as a municipal officer. The *mu'errum* was involved in this case because he was a crown official in charge of the administration of fields that were ultimately owned by the crown and that were leased to certain beneficiaries of the state—in this case, soldiers. The general and the captains convened with the *mu'errum* precisely because of his supervision of these fields.

Previous Opinions on the Role of the *mu'errum*

We have already seen that the most common translations of gal-unken-na were based on the supposed equation with Akkadian *rab puḫri*. *mu'errum*, even when correctly understood as the Akkadian equivalent of gal-unken-na, was analyzed as if it were *rab puḫri*. Thus, we have seen that Kraus translated "Versammlungsvorstand," and Landsberger, "city-'officer' " (and the latter in *MSL* 3, "Oberster der Buergschaft"). The *AHw* translated "Versammlungsleiter."[29] Other commentators have followed these notions of connecting the *mu'errum* to a position in the assembly: Frankena (1966),[30] "Vorsteher der Versammlung"; Harris (1962),[31] "head of the assembly." Oppenheim (1967)[32] thought that the GAL.UNKIN was a municipal authority in charge of certain affairs in the city of Sippar.

There have also been translations that paid less attention to the –unken– "assembly" part of the title than to the rest of the title in OB documents, -erén-ká-é-gal (which is indiscriminately appended to gal-unken-na as space and inclination allow). Szlechter, for instance, submitted "chef des gens de la porte du palais,"[33] going back to the tradition of Ungnad, who variously tried "Oberinspektor? des Palasttores"[34] and "Vorsteher;"[35] Lautner also translated " 'Vorsteher' des Palasttores."[36] Ungnad contributed "Vorsteher der Truppen des Palasttores,"[37] apparently taking erén = *ummānum* as he had done in the title *abi* erén. Klengel has recently offered an original translation on this ká-é-gal theme: "Chef der Torhueter."[38]

The ká-é-gal, "gate of the palace," has been dealt with by Falkenstein, translating ká-é-gala$_8$ as "Trakt des Palastes."[39] This interpretation of *bāb ekallim* is certainly more realistic than literal "gate of the palace" translations. Kraus agreed with Falkenstein that the more general the translation the better, and himself wrote "Wirtschaftstrakt des Palastes," although once he translated "Oekonomiegebaeude."[40] In the text *AbB* 4 8[41] ensí's do service (*izzazū*) at the ká-é-gal. We shall see below that ensí's are often administrators of agricultural lands over which the gal-unken-na exercised superior authority. In letter 43 of *AbB* 4, *bārû*'s also do service at the ká-é-gal. These "divination priests," however, were submitting complaints regarding their rights in certain fields—in other words no specific gate is referred to, and the matter concerns no religious practice but simply fields farmed by *bārû*'s. In *AbB* 2 17, 2 ensí's and a máš-šu-gid-gid (*bārûm*) are described together as 3 erén šà erén-ká-é-gal, well translated by Frankena as "drei Angehoerige des Palastpersonels." Renger cited Falkenstein's opinions of the erén-ká-é-gal in his discussion of the *bārûm* in service to the state.[42] Renger concluded that the "ERÉN *ša bāb ekallim*" (a phrase not actually attested in Akkadian) included the priests among their number. The sources for this statement were the royal correspondence cited above (*AbB* 4 8) and especially Mari letters. Renger thought that the priests' service to the state (i.e., palace) was based on performing divinations that aided the state in various decision-making processes. According to Renger, in payment for these services the *bārû*'s received land from the palace. However, the role of the *bārûm* in OB economic and administrative documents was not a subject undertaken by him.

We agree with Falkenstein and others that *bāb ekallim* refers to crown land holdings and not to a particular "gate of the palace." The erén = *ṣābum*, in *ṣāb bāb ekallim*, worked on these lands, but it is not clear whether the term referred only to those dependents of the crown who worked on crown land or also included those higher officials who received benefices of land from the crown. Those receiving benefices and those contracting with the state for land had to pay "taxes;" and since the state contracts were effected by certain officials, it is often difficult to ascertain which documents are concerned solely with management, as opposed to rental, of crown lands.

The notion that the *mu'errum* was some sort of royal official has usually been founded on the mention of the palace (*ekallum*), which was usually written as part of the title gal-unken-na erén-ká-é-gal (see table below). The new article of the *CAD*[43] simply defines *mu'errum* as "a high official of the royal household in charge of personnel, commander." Klengel considered that he "was active within the royal economy."[44] This opinion follows Diakonoff, who wrote that "practical administration of the royal estates fell within the province of the *mu'irrum ša bāb ekallim.*"[45]

Earlier commentators made substantial contributions to the understanding of this title. Unger in 1931 wrote about the "*mu'irru*-Beamte der 'Palast-Pforte' . . . worunter wohl die koenigliche Hofhaltung zu verstehen ist, vielleicht aber auch die Vertretung des Koenigs im Palaste";[46] and Schorr translated "Direktor" and "Verwalter" (1913),[47] implying some official position.

To date the two longest treatments of the title are those by Walther (in 1917), who devoted eleven pages to the *mu'errum,*[48] and by Krueckmann, in *RlA* I (1932), who made good use of Walther's pioneering work. Walther considered the *mu'errum* to be a high state official, or at least of reasonably high rank ("zu den angeseheneren Verwaltungsbeamten zu rechnen"). He thought, however, that the references to the *mu'errum* were too disparate to attempt to put together a consistent picture of his duties. Presciently, Walther surmised that even in texts mentioning the *mu'errum* and not referring to explicit administrative functions but to certain putatively private business enterprises, the *mu'errum* was involved in them in the role of "official inspector" ("Aufsichtsbeamter"). He cited a "vokabularische Uebersetzung" of gal-ukkin-na as *rab puḫri,* which he connected to one of the powers accorded Marduk in *enūma eliš, mu'errūt puḫri,* "leadership of the assembly."[49] Although the substantive *mu'errūtu* is, of course, etymologically related to *mu'errum,* in itself it tells us nothing about the nature of the title *mu'errum.*

Walther quoted the longer form of the title as *mu'irrum ša bāb ekallim,* but the *ša* was read incorrectly on the basis of the broken texts *VS* 7 119:3 and *VS* 7 56:7[50] (gal-unken-na *šá* ká-é-gal). The sign read by Walther as *šá* is erén, but commentators (see above) still refer to *mu'errum ša bāb ekallim,* not to **mu'er ṣāb bāb ekallim.* Walther defined *ekallum* as "administration," especially of finances, and the "gate of the palace" as the place or "concept" of concluding business transactions.[51] These definitions of terms are, in my opinion, essentially correct, though Walther was too rigorous in trying to separate the *mu'errum* from the *mu'errum*-of-the-(men-of-the-)gate-of-the-palace.[52] These two terms stand in free variation with each other, and the addition of the erén-ká-é-gal to gal-unken-na seems to depend on the amount of room available in the line as much as anything else. In terms of duties, Walther was inclined to the view that the "two" titles were often identical, but the necessity for orderly philological bookkeeping impelled him to keep them separate.

Krueckmann's contribution to the *RlA* I (p. 448) has been largely, if not completely, ignored by later literature on the subject, yet his treatment, utilizing the basic insights provided by Walther, contains an excellent analysis of the subject as well as some salient observations on the structure of the society within which the *mu'errum* functioned. The *mu'errum* is the first official under Krueckmann's category, "Beamte in der Verwaltung des Krongutes," and his first major point was that the ideogram GAL.UKKIN has nothing to do with the *puḫrum*. These two evaluations are crucial for the proper analysis of the function of the *mu'errum* and the range of his activities.[53] Krueckmann stressed Walther's analysis that the *mu'errum* was interested in agricultural management and often had the *iššiʾakkum* as his practical administrative subordinate, but he added the notion that these agricultural lands were crown estates. Krueckmann noted that the *ṣāb bāb ekallim* were "Hilfskraefte" of the *mu'errum,* but did not take into consideration the use of this phrase outside the title. Unfortunately, Krueckmann's opinion that the *mu'errum* had nothing to do with the assembly found little favor among later commentators, or, more commonly, was simply not consulted. It will be the function of the remainder of this chapter to elaborate the most important of Krueckmann's conclusions, that the *mu'errum* was essentially in the service of the crown's agricultural bureaus, and to study more specifically the exact nature of that service. This can best be elucidated by an examination of the texts mentioning individuals who held the title.

Table V: Texts Mentioning the *mu'errum*

Latest Edition	Name of *mu'errum*	Date of Text
AbB 1 52 (*CT* 43 52)	unnamed; *mu-we-er-ri*	letter
AbB 2 66 (*LIH* 2 84)	Sîn-mušallim gal-unken-na	letter from Abi-ešuḫ
ARN 169	Nanna-mansum gal-unken-na erén-ká-é-gal	A-ṣ 16
BE 6/1 79	Ilum-damiq gal-unken-na	A-e
BE 6/1 99	Ibni-Sîn gal-unken-na	A-ṣ 12
BE 6/1 119	Ilum-damiq gal-unken-na	A-e–A-d
BIN 7 211	Nanna-mansum gal-unken-na erén-ká-é-gal	A-ṣ 17+a
CT 4 8b	dam gal-unken-na	A-d 13
CT 8 19a	x gal-unken-na erén-ká-é-gal	A-ṣ 5
CT 45 55	Nabium-nāṣir gal-unken-na erén-ká-é-gal	A-d (seal)
JCS 2 p. 104, no. 6	Marduk-muballiṭ gal!-unken!-na!	A-e year after "0"
JCS 5 p. 85 = *JCS* 7 p. 96, no. 24	*a-na ṣ[e-er m]u-er-ri-im*	A-e
JCS 5 p. 89 = *JCS* 7 p. 85, no. 7:20	igi *e-ṭi-rum* dumu gal-unken-na	A-e

Table V (cont.)

Latest Edition	Name of *mu'errum*	Date of Text
JCS 11 35 26	dumu-munus gal-unken-na	undated
PBS 7 82	Apil-ilišu gal-unken-na	letter
PBS 7 100	unnamed gal-unken-na	letter
PBS 7 121	*awīlum* gal-unken-na erén-ká-é-gal	letter
RA 12 115	Ibni-Adad gal-unken-na	Rīm-Sîn
Riftin, SVJAD 48	Ina-palêšu gal-un[ken-na]?	S-i 10
TCL 1 29	gal-unken-na	letter
TCL 1 164	Ibni-Sîn gal-unken-na	A-ṣ 9
TCL 1 166	Sîn-iqīšam gal-unken-na	A-ṣ 13
TCL 1 167	Sîn-iqīšam gal-unken-na	A-ṣ 13
TCL 17 34	gal-unken-na	letter
TCL 18 104	gal-unken-na erén-ká-é-gal	letter
TJG 16 536 p. 27	Ili-iqīšam gal-unken-na erén-ká-é-gal	A-ṣ 2
TJG 16.448 p. 108	Ili-iqīšam gal-unken-na erén-ká-é-gal	A-d 37
TJG 16.148 p. 110	Ili-iqīšam gal-unken-na erén-ká-é-gal	A-ṣ 1
TJG 16.508 p. 111	Ili-iqīšam gal-unken-na erén-ká-é-gal	A-ṣ 1
TJG 16.346 p. 112	Ili-iqīšam gal-unken-na erén-ká-é-gal	A-ṣ 1
TJG 16.381 p. 113	Ili-iqīšam gal-unken-na erén-ká-é-gal	A-ṣ 1
TJG 16.374 p. 114	Ili-iqīšam gal-unken-na erén-ká-[é-gal]	A-ṣ 1
TJG 16 305 p. 118	Ili-iqīšam gal-unken-na erén-ká-é-gal	A-ṣ 1
TJM p. 11	Awīl-Nabium dumu Abalumur gal-unken-na	A-d 33
TLB 1 195	Sîn-iddinam gal-⌜unken!⌝-na	S-i 7
VS 7 56	Ili-iqīšam gal-unken-na erén-ká-é-gal	A-d 24
VS 7 60	Ili-iqīšam gal-unken-na erén-ká-é-gal	A-d 34

Table V (cont.)

Latest Edition	Name of *mu'errum*	Date of Text
VS 7 90	son of Ina-palêšu gal-unken-na	A-ṣ 10
VS 7 119	Nanna-mansum gal-unken-na erén-ká-é-gal	A-ṣ 16
VS 16 181	Ili-iddinam gal-unken-na ša Is[in](?)	letter
Waterman 28 = *AJSL* 29 180	Rīm-Adad gal-unken-na	S-i 8 (?)
Waterman 50 = *AJSL* 29 297	Awīl-Nabium gal-unken-na	A-d 6
[*YOS* 12, see p. 130]		
YOS 13 41	Igmil-Sîn gal-unken-na erén-ká-é-gal	S-d 2
YOS 13 48	Ili-iqīšam gal-unken-n[a]	A-d 36
YOS 13 50	Ili-[iqīšam]	date lost
YOS 13 56	Ili-iqīšam gal-unken-na erén-ká-é-gal	A-d 37
YOS 13 59	Ili-iqīšam gal-unken-na erén-ká-é-gal	A-d 33
YOS 13 79	Ili-iqīšam gal-unken-na erén-ká-é-gal	A-d 34
YOS 13 98	*ana awīlim* gal-unken-na unnamed	letter
YOS 13 173	unnamed	S-d 10 in text
YOS 13 181	dumu gal-unken-na; dumu-meš gal-unken-na	A-ṣ 17+b
YOS 13 207	witness: Nabium-mušallim dumu dumu-é-dub-ba-a *ša* gal-un[ken-na]	A-ṣ 5
YOS 13 222	Ili-iqīšam gal-unken-na erén-ká-é-gal	date lost
YOS 13 231	Ili-iqīšam [ ]	A-ṣ 1
YOS 13 242	Awīl-Nabium gal-unken-na	S-d 1
YOS 13 287	Ili-iqīsam gal-unken-na erén-ká-é-gal	A-d 27
YOS 13 302	Ili-[iqīšam gal-un]ken-na erén-ká-é-gal	A-d 36
YOS 13 330	Marduk-mušallim gal-unken-na erén-ká-é-gal	S-d 2

Table V (cont.)

Latest Edition	Name of *mu'errum*	Date of Text
YOS 13 333	Marduk-mušallim gal-unken-na erén-ká-é-gal	S-d 3
YOS 13 334	Warad-Ilabrat gal-unken-na erén-ká-[é-gal]	date lost
YOS 13 352	Ili-iqīšam gal-unken-[na]	A-d 34
YOS 13 357	Warad-Ilabrat gal-unken-na erén-ká-é-gal	A-ṣ 13
YOS 13 396	Ili-iqīšam gal-unken-na erén-ká-é-gal	A-d 29
YOS 13 399	Warad-Ilabrat gal-unken-na erén-ká-[é-gal]	date lost
YOS 13 482	Warad-Ilabrat gal-unken-na erén-[ká-é-gal]	A-ṣ 13
YOS 13 525	Nanna-mansum gal-unken-na erén-ká-<é>-gal	A-ṣ 16

Table VI: Names of *mu'errum*-officials

Name	Text	Date
Abalumur	*TJM* p. 11	A-d 33
Apil-ilišu	*PBS* 7 82	letter
Awīl-Nabium	*W* 50 (= *AJSL* 29, 297)	A-d 6
	YOS 13 242	S-d 1
Ibni-Adad	*RA* 12 115	Rīm-Sîn
Ibni-Sîn	*TCL* 1 164	A-ṣ 9
	BE 6/1 99	A-ṣ 12
Igmil-Sîn	*YOS* 13 41	S-d 2
Ili-iddinam	*VS* 16 181	letter
Ili-iqīšam	*VS* 7 56	A-d 24
	YOS 13 287	A-d 27
	YOS 13 396	A-d 29
	YOS 13 59	A-d 33
	YOS 13 352	A-d 34

Table VI (cont.)

Name	Text	Date
	YOS 13 79	A-d 34
	VS 7 60	A-d 34
	YOS 13 48	A-d 36
	YOS 13 302	A-d 36
	TJG p. 108, 16.448	A-d 37
	YOS 13 56	A-d 37
	(*TJG* p. 138, 16.218 (no title))	A-ṣ 1
	TJG p. 118, 16.305	A-ṣ 1
	TJG p. 113, 16.381	A-ṣ 1
	TJG p. 110, 16.148	A-ṣ 1
	TJG p. 111, 16.508	A-ṣ 1
	TJG p. 112, 16.346	A-ṣ 1
	TJG p. 114, 16.374	A-ṣ 1
	YOS 13 231	A-ṣ 1
	TJG p. 27, 16. 536	A-ṣ 2
	YOS 13 222	date lost
	YOS 13 50	date lost
Ilum-damiq	*BE* 6/1 79	A-e
	BE 6/1 119	A-e–A-d
Ina-palêšu	*VS* 7 90	A-ṣ 10
Ina-palêsu(?)	*Riftin, SVJAD* 48	S-i 10
Marduk-muballiṭ	*JCS* 2 p. 104, no. 6	A-e year after "0"
Marduk-mušallim	*YOS* 13 330	S-d 2 '
	333	S-d 3
Nabium-nāṣir	*CT* 45 55	A-d (seal)
Nanna-mansum	*ARN* 169	A-ṣ 16
	VS 7 119	A-ṣ 16
	YOS 13 525	A-ṣ 16
	BIN 7 211	A-ṣ 17+a
Rīm-Adad	*W* 28 = *AJSL* 29 150	S-i 8 (?)
Sîn-iddinam	*TLB* I 195	S-i 7
Sîn-iqīšam	*TCL* 1 166	A-ṣ 13
	167	A-ṣ 13

Table VI (cont.)

Name	Text	Date
Sîn-mušallim	*AbB* 2 66	A-e letter
Warad-Ilabrat	*YOS* 13 334	date lost
	357	A-ṣ 13
	399	date lost
	482	A-ṣ 13

Texts dealing with Ili-iqīšam

By far the best attested *mu'errum*-official is Ili-iqīšam. As mentioned in Chapter 3, he was also an *abi ṣābim*, but Tables III and V, giving the dates of Ili-iqīšam's activities, show that the two titles were not freely interchangeable. Ili-iqīšam became an *abi ṣābim* in A-ṣ 9, whereas he was last attested as *mu'errum* in A-ṣ 2.[54] The references to his activities as *abi ṣābim* are few and show barely more than that he held that title; references to his activities as *mu'errum*, on the other hand, are plentiful and informative.

The earliest text mentioning Ili-iqīšam, *VS* 7 56[55] (A-d 24), shows him interceding in a dispute. Three brothers contest the estate of PN before Ili-iqīšam, *mu'errum*, and Elmēšum, the *šandabakkum*-official:

6 *ma-ḫar a-wi-lim el-me-šum* $ša_x$-dub-ba
7 *ù ì-lí-i-qí-ša-am* gal-unken-na erén-ká-é-gal
8 *id-bu-bu-ma*

The tablets concerning the hearing by Elmēšum and Ili-iqīšam were then ordered to be brought to an official in Kish where the case would finally be settled:[56]

9 *ṭup-pí a-wi-lim el-me-šum* $ša_x$-dub-ba
10 *ù ṭup-pi ì-lí-i-qí-ša-am* gal-unken-na erén-ká-[é-gal]
11 *a-na* ᵈutu-*la-ma-sà-šu* dub-sar-zag-ga[57]

We do not know the exact nature of the depositions given by Ili-iqīšam and Elmēšum, who were probably located in Dilbat (if the provenience of the *VS* 7 texts is accepted as being Dilbat). Presumably the case was decided in Kish and a record of its disposition was brought back to Dilbat. We cannot conjecture what the role of these two officials was in this case or the reason that the initial investigation of the matter took place under their jurisdiction.

In year A-d 27 Ili-iqīšam had at his disposal sheep and cattle which he administered for the purpose of making certain transactions. The text is *YOS* 13 287.

4 gín kù-babbar
šám 12 u_8-udu$^{hi\text{-}a}$

ša ^{d}*sîn-i-din-nam* sipa
dumu ^{d}iškur-*ra-bi*
ša i-na qá-ti ì-lí-i-qí-ša-am
gal-unken-<na> erén-ká-é-gal *i-*⌈*il-qú-ma*⌉
⌈ug⌉u ^{d}*na-bi-um-mu-ša-lim*
[dumu *e-*⌉<*ri*>*-ba-am-*^{d}*marduk*
⌈*i*⌉*-šu-ú*
a-na iti-1-kam
[*a-na na-ši ka-ni-k*]*i-šu*
[4 gín] kù-babbar šám 12 u_8-udu^{hi-a}
i-na-ad-di-in

---

igi ^{d}*sîn-ib-ni-šu*
dumu a-wi-il-^{d}*sîn*
igi *ib-ni-*^{d}*marduk* dumu ^{d}*sîn-iš-me-a-ni*

---

iti gan-gan-è u_4-1-kam
mu *am-mi-di-ta-na* lugal-e
^{d}uraš ur-sag-gal
urudu-mah-a

Seal: ^{d}AK-mu-ša-lim (A-d 27)

Sîn-iddinam, the shepherd, son of Adad-rabi, has to the good of (is owed by) Nabium-mušallim, son of Erībam-Marduk, 4 shekels of silver, the price of 12 sheep, which he (Sîn-iddinam) received from Ili-iqīšam, the *mu'errum*-official. In one month to the bearer of his tablet he (Nabium-mušallim) will give 4 shekels of silver, the price of 12 sheep.

Ili-iqīšam here plays a secondary role as the superior of the shepherd who actually had negotiated the animals. This simple text provides a very good indication of the status of Ili-iqīšam and of the functioning of a segment of the "bureau of agricultural resources" as we may provisionally term it.[58] Under the jurisdiction of Ili-iqīšam, the chief of the bureau, 4 animals were made over to the disposition of the shepherd, who then "loaned" them to one Nabium-mušallim. Presumably the tablets of that transaction specified the stipulations of the loan, but this text was written only as a bureaucratic memorandum of the individuals involved in the affair.

The *mu'errum* in the Bureau of Agricultural Affairs: the Hiring of Field Laborers

The next text introduces the type of activity in which Ili-iqīšam seems to have been most involved—if sheer quantity of extant material is any index. The first example of that activity is dated to A-d 29:

YOS 13 396

1 (PI) 3 bán ŠE.MUŠ$_5$
KA dub-ba-ni nu-me-a ša [ ]
a-na še-gur$_{10}$-ku$_5$
ki *ì-lí-i-qí-ša-am*
⸢gal-unken-na erén-ká-⸣é-gal
^{Id}*sîn-ḫa-zi-ir*
dumu *i-na-pa-le-šu*
šu ba-an-ti
u$_4$-buru$_x$-šè
erén še-gur$_{10}$-ku$_5$ *i-il-la-ak*
ú-ul i-il-la-ak-ma
ki-ma ṣi-im-da-at lugal

---

igi *be-la-nu-um* dumu *ka-ma-nu-um*
igi *a-pil-ì-lí-su* dumu *a-pil-ì-lí-šu*
igi *gi-mil-*^{d}*marduk* dub-sar

---

iti ab-è u$_4$-9-kam
mu *am-mi-di-ta-na* lugal-e
^{d}lama ^{d}lama
máš-sù-ga-ke$_4$ (A-d 29)

Seal: be-la-[nu-um]
dumu ka-[ma-nu-um]
ìr-^{d}[ ]
ù-^{d}[ ]

Sîn-ḫāzir, son of Inapalêšu, received from Ili-iqīšam, the *mu'errum*, 90 liters of "late grain"—there was no previous document of his—for (a) harvester(s). At harvest time he will furnish (a) harvester(s);[59] if he doesn't, then it is according to the royal *ṣimdatum*.

The text is one of a common type of "Erntearbeitervertraege" discussed at length by Lautner,[60] and termed "harvest-labor contracts" in Finkelstein's catalogue of *YOS* 13. An amount of grain is given by Ili-iqīšam to Sîn-ḫāzir as rations for harvest workers. For our purposes, it is sufficient to note that this was part of a series of transactions relating to harvesting grain on land that was under the administrative jurisdiction of Ili-iqīšam.

We meet for the first time in A-d 33 another type of harvest-labor contract of which there are a great many examples. These documents attest Ili-iqīšam's role as the administrative authority over large amounts of land, and particularly over numbers of people who do harvest-labor on those lands. They also show that Ili-iqīšam did not have direct control over a force of people that he could simply assign to do the tasks of harvesting and field-work.

YOS 13 59

1/3 gín kù-babbar
a-na e-ṣi-di-im
ki *ì-lí-i-qí-ša-am* gal-unken-na erén-ká-é-gal
a-na qá-bi-e ^{I}ir-*ì-lí-šu*
^{I}ta-ku-lu-ur-^{d}utu
šu ba-an-ti
u$_4$-buru$_x$-šè
i-na a-šà *pí-ḫa-at*
^{I}*uṣ-ri-ya ensí*
še-gur$_{10}$-ku$_5$ *i-la-ak*
ú-ul i-la-ak-ma
ki-ma ṣi-im-da-at lugal

---

igi *a-wi-il-*^{d}iskur dumu ^{d}iskur-*ri-im-ì-lí*
igi *ib-ni-*^{d}*marduk* dumu *be-la-nu*

---

iti ab-ab-è u$_4$-5-kam
mu *am-mi-di-ta-na* lugal-e
mu gibil *ša* egir
bàd *iš-ku-un-*^{d}*marduk* (A-d 33)

Takulur-Šamaš, at the behest of Warad-ilišu, received from Ili-iqīšam, the *mu'errum*, 1/3 shekel silver for a harvester. At harvest time he will furnish a harvester to the field(s) in the precinct of Uṣriya, the the *iššakkum;* if he doesn't, then it is according to the royal *ṣimdatum.*

An amount of silver (probably the standard for a payment made in grain) was dispensed under the authority of Ili-iqīšam by Warad-ilišu to Takulur$^{(?)}$-Šamaš. This individual then had the responsibility to supply a harvest worker to the precinct of the *iššakkum* Uṣriya. There are some instances, commented upon below, in which we can identify the function of this contracting party more specifically,[61] but we know that Uṣriya was the field administrator of Ili-iqīšam in charge of the actual harvesting process. It will also be shown that the witnesses are not disinterested observers but have a professional interest in this affair.

YOS 13 59 is the earliest example of a group of texts from Dilbat mentioning Uṣriya and Ili-iqīšam. In the year after that text was written *YOS* 13 79 and *VS* 7 60 document further activities of this pair.

YOS 13 79

½ ⸢gín⸣ kù-babbar
e-zu-ub pí-i ka-ni-ki-šu pa-ni-i
a-na e-ṣi-di
ki *ì-lí-i-⸢qí-ša-am* gal-unken⸣-na erén-ká-é-gal
^{I}*a-ḫu-um-ṭà-bu ra-bi-a-nu*
^{I}*a-⸢wi-il⸣*-^{d}iškur dumu ^{d}iškur-*ri-im-ì-lí*
^{I}*ib-ni-⸢^{d}marduk* dumu⸣ *be-la-nu*
ù ri-⸢x-x-x-⸣tum
šu ba-an-ti-e-meš
u$_{4}$-buru$_{x}$-šè
i-na a-šà *pí-ḫa-at*
^{I}*uṣ-ri-ya* ensí
erén še-gur$_{10}$-ku$_{5}$ *i-il-la-ku*
ú-ul i-il-la-ku-ma
ki-ma ṣi-im-da-at šar-ri

---

iti apin-du$_{8}$-a u$_{4}$-30-kam
mu *am-mi-di-ta-na* lugal-e
sa-am-su-i-lu-na
pa$_{5}$-bil-ga-na (A-d 34)

Aḫum-ṭābu, *rabi'ānu*, Awīl-Adad son of Adad-rīm-ili, Ibni-Marduk son of Bēlānu, and Ri . . . tum received ½ shekel silver, apart from his (sic) earlier transaction, for harvesters, from Ili-iqīšam, *mu'errum.* At harvest time, they will furnish harvesters to the precinct under the responsibility of Uṣriya the *iššakkum.* If they do not, it is according to the royal *ṣimdatum.* (No witnesses).

VS 7 60

igi-4-gál kù-babbar
a-na erén še-gur$_{10}$-ku$_{5}$
ki *ì-lí-i-qí-ša-am* gal-unken-na erén-ká-é-gal
^{I}*ar-du* dumu ^{Id}iškur-*še-mi*
šu ba-an-ti
u$_{4}$-buru$_{x}$-šè
i-na a-šà *pí-ḫa-at*
^{I}*uṣ-ri-ya* ensí
erén še-gur$_{10}$-ku$_{5}$ *i-la-ak*
ú-ul i-la-ak-ma
ki-ma ṣi-im-da-at šar-ri
igi *a-ḫu-ṭà-bu ra-bi-a-nu*
igi *a-wi-il*-^{d}iškur dumu ^{d}iškur-*ri-im-ì-lí*
igi *ib-ni*-^{d}*marduk* dumu *be-la-nu*

---

iti gan-gan-è u$_4$-30-kam
mu *am-mi-di-ta-na* lugal-e
alam nam-ur-sag-gá
sa-am-su-i-lu-na pa$_5$ -bil-ga-na

Seal: *a-ḫu-ṭà-*[*bu*]
dumu ^{d}utu-[ ]
[ ] (A-d 34)

Ardu, son of Adad-šemi, received ¼ shekel silver for (a) harvester(s) from Ili-iqīšam, *muerrum.* At harvest time, he will furnish (a) harvester(s) to the precinct under the responsibility of Uṣriya, the *iššakkum.* If he does not, it is according to the royal *ṣimdatum.* Witnesses: Aḫu-ṭābu, *rabi'ānu*; Awīl-Adad, son of Adad-rīm-ili; Ibni-Marduk, son of Bēlānu.

These two documents differ from *YOS* 13 59 in omitting any reference to a "middleman" who dispensed the silver (or products) to the parties contracting to supply the laborers. It should not, however, be inferred from the absence of this official that there was no intermediary and that the amount of silver was received from Ili-iqīšam himself; in the shorthand of administrative documents not every step was always recorded, and we have to put together our knowledge from a combination of documents.

Within the differing structures of the last three documents we note the presence of two individuals, Awīl-Adad, son of Adad-rīm-ili, and Ibni-Marduk, son of Bēlānum, in each document; and the presence of the *rabi'ānum* Aḫum-ṭābum in the latter two. In *YOS* 13 59 and *VS* 7 60, Awīl-Adad and Ibni-Marduk are witnesses; in *YOS* 13 79, where there are no witnesses, those two and the *rabi'ānum* are the persons who receive the silver from the bureau (= *itti*) of Ili-iqīšam. Obviously, the distinction between witnessed and unwitnessed documents has nothing whatever to do with the administrative vs. private nature of these texts. It does show, on the other hand, that the witnesses were deliberately selected for their particular interest in the transactions. In fact, the choice of witnesses was a matter of careful concern in most, if not all, economic and legal documents. The reasons for their inclusion are seldom perceived in isolated texts, but when collections of materials are accumulated, the nature of the interest of the witnesses becomes more intelligible.

The following explanation may be proposed to account for the presence of the *rabi'ānum* and two other individuals who appear mostly as witnesses, but also in other capacities (cf. *YOS* 13 79), in the Ili-iqīšam harvest-labor contracts: The harvesters who were recruited to work on the crown fields under the jurisdiction of Ili-iqīšam and administered by his manager, Uṣriya, were not crown dependents, but free members of the community. The presence of the *rabi'ānum* and two other witnesses reflects their status in relation to the people who were to serve as harvesters. As leaders of the community, they were empowered—indeed their presence was necessary—to sanction the hiring of community members to work on state lands. Workers could apparently be hired in two ways: they could be contracted for by crown officials directly from the communal leadership (as in *YOS* 13 79); or they could be hired by a third party, who then needed the sanction of community officials in the form of notarizing witnesses (the case in *YOS* 13 59 and *VS*

7 60). The reference to the *rabi'ānum* is, of course, the key in this analysis. *rabi'ānum* is usually translated "mayor," "headman," or the like, and Walther has pointed out the connection between the *rabi'ānum* and the council of elders in OB legal and economic documents,[62] but there is no modern study of the socio-economic role of the *rabi'ānum* in OB society.[63] Without undertaking a long digression here, our opinion is that the *rabi'ānum* was most probably a high-status member of the community who exercised leadership functions, perhaps on a periodic basis.[64] The structure of the local community organizations[65] in Mesopotamia is unfortunately very poorly understood, mainly because the "community" did not maintain an extensive bureaucracy and bookkeeping system. Nonetheless, community leadership can often be detected in the records of the crown's interactions with the local power structures. The harvest-labor contracts of the crown bureau under the jurisdiction of Ili-iqīšam reflect one aspect of this interrelationship between crown and community.

Lautner[66] and Walther,[67] in their respective studies of *VS* 7 60, concluded that the land being harvested probably did not belong to Ili-iqīšam but was "royal domain" over which the *mu'errum* was administrator. Lautner based his opinion upon the mention of Uṣriya as the subordinate responsible for the work to be done on land under Ili-iqīšam's jurisdiction. Walther assumed that the land was part of the estates of the crown not only because of the relationship of the *mu'errum* and his "Verwalter," but also simply because of the *bāb ekallim* part of Ili-iqīšam's title and the *ṣimdat šarrim* clause.[68]

Similar harvest-labor contracts from the *YOS* 13 volume are the texts 48 (A-d 36?), 56 (A-d 37), and 222 (date lost).

YOS 13 48

[ ] + 1 gín kù-babbar
[*a-n*]a *e-ṣi-di-im*
[ki]*i-lí-i-qí-ša-am* gal-unken-na
^{I}*ib-ni-*^{d}*marduk* dumu *be-la-nu*
šu ba-an-ti
u$_4$-buru$_x$-šè
i-na a-šà *pí-ha-at*
[*u*]*ṣ-ri-ya* ensí
[*e-ṣi*]*-da i-la-ak*
[*ú-ul i-l*]*a-ak-ma*
—rest destroyed—
[ ] i$_7$-me-^{d}en-líl-lá

Ibni-Marduk, son of Bēlānu, received (an amt.) silver for a harvester from Ili-iqīšam, *mu'errum*. At harvest time, he will furnish a harvester to the precinct under the responsibility of Uṣriya, the *iššakkum*. If he does not . . . (rest destroyed).

YOS 13 56

½ gín kù-babbar
a-na erén še-gur$_{10}$-ku$_5$
ki *ì-lí-i-qí-ša-am* gal-unken-na erén-ká-é-[gal]
^{I}*a-wi-la-tum* dumu *a-lí-ba-nu-šu*
šu ba-an-ti
u$_4$-buru$_x$-šè *i-na* a-šà *pí-ḫa-at*
^{I}*uṣ-ri-ya* ensí
e-ṣi-[*i-d*]*i i-la-ak*
(rev. destroyed except for date)
iti ab-è u$_4$-?-kam
mu *am-mi-di-ta-na* lugal-e
bàd bàd^{ki}-ma
dam-qí-ì-lí-šu-ke$_4$ (A-d 37)

Awīlatum, son of Ali-bānûšu, received ½ shekel silver for harvesters from Ili-iqīšam, *mu'errum*. At harvest time, he will furnish harvesters to the precinct under the responsibility of Uṣriya, the *iššakkum*. (rest destroyed).

YOS 13 222

igi-6-gál kù-babbar
a-na erén še-gur$_{10}$-ku$_5$
ki *ì-lí-i-qí-ša-am* gal-unken-na erén-ká-é-gal
^{Id}iškur-*mu-ša-lim* dumu ^{d}*sîn-iš-me-a-ni*
šu ba-an-ti
u$_4$-buru$_x$-še *i-na* a-šà *pí-ḫa-at*
^{I}*uṣ-ri-ya* ensí
erén še-gur$_{10}$-ku$_5$ *i-la-ak*
ú-ul i-la-ak-ma
[*ki-ma ṣi-im-da*]*-at šar-ri*
[igi ^{I}*a-ḫu-ṭà-bu*]*ra-bi-a-nu*
[igi]*-na-ṣi-ir*
rest lost

Adad-mušallim, son of Sîn-išme'anni, received $^1/_6$ shekel silver for (a) harvester(s) from Ili-iqīšam, *mu'errum*. At harvest time, he will furnish (a) harvester(s) to the precinct under the responsibility of Uṣriya, the *iššakkum*. If he does not, it is according to the royal ṣimdatum.

In *YOS* 13 48 Ibni-Marduk, son of Bēlānu, received an amount of silver from Ili-iqīšam for the purpose of supplying a harvester to the fields of Uṣriya. We do not know whether this tablet was witnessed or whether Ibni-Marduk himself had the power of sanction to allow community members to be hired as workers. In *YOS* 13 56 Awīlatum, son of Ali-bānûšu, received silver for the same purpose, and again the remainder of the document is destroyed. In *YOS* 13 222 a *rabi'ānum* whose name is not perserved, but probably Aḫum-ṭābum, witnessed a similar document.

Other documents pertaining to the harvest-labor contracts issued from the bureau administered by Ili-iqīšam have been published by E. Szlechter.[69] These tablets are all witnessed and all contain the clause showing that the field work was to be done in the district administered by Uṣriya, the *iššakkum.* Sîn-ḫāzir, son of Inapalêšu,[70] appears as the person who receives the payment from Ili-iqīšam in A-ṣ 1, an appearance that makes evident his longtime association with Ili-iqīšam–cf. *YOS* 13 396, dated to A-d 29. We also note the mention of Ibni-Marduk,[71] son of Bēlānu, as the contracting party in a contract witnessed by Aḫu-ṭābu, *rabi'ānu.* Both Ibni-Marduk and Aḫu-ṭābu, therefore, could contract with Ili-iqīšam in the body of the text or appear as witnesses, either instance indicating a sanction for the hiring of community members to work on crown estates.

In three of Szlechter's *TJG* texts, Warad-Ikulam, ugula-martu, appears as a witness: twice as the second witness after Aḫu-ṭābu, *rabi'ānu* (*TJG* pp. 111, 113), and once as the first witness without the *rabi'ānu* (*TJG* p. 112). The presence of the ugula-martu seems to imply the interest of the military in the harvest labor personnel. The exact relationship among the communal, administrative and military interests is not explicit, but we saw above[72] in the case of a returned slave that the military and communal interests occasionally clashed over the *ilkum*-service of some community members.

Szlechter argued[73] that the amount of money or materials received in these contracts (from Ili-iqīšam) was the salary for the people who actually received the payments, and that the translation "to furnish harvesters"–erén še-gur$_{10}$-ku$_5$. . . *alākum*–must be incorrect. In this Szlechter disputed but slightly Lautner's previously stated conclusion[74] that the contract did not oblige the contracting party to personal service but required him to provide a harvester at the proper time, although occasionally the contracting party would have to appear himself. Lautner himself did not reject the notion of "furnishing" harvesters, which Koschaker had previously suggested,[75] but considered that if the person himself were intending to do the harvesting, the Akkadian would have simply read, "he will come at harvest time," **ūm ebūrim illak.*

M. Stol in a recent study proposes that harvesters in the logogram (*n*) $^{\text{lú/erén}}$še-gur$_{10}$-ku$_5$$^{\text{(meš)}}$ are the object of the verb *alākum,* that *alākum* is in fact in this phrase used as a transitive verb. This argument finds support logically in *YOS* 13 79 (above, p. 97) in which three parties contract to supply laborers and the plural verb is used, erén še-gur$_{10}$-ku$_5$ *illakū*; it is assured grammatically in *YOS* 13 56 (p. 100) where the text is syllabically written *e-ṣi-di i-la-ak* necessitating that *ēṣidī* be the object of the verb, and is unambiguous in *YOS* 13 48 (above p. 99, not cited by Stol) where silver is received *a-na e-ṣi-di-im,* "for *a* harvester," followed by [*e-ṣi*]*-da i-la-ak,* "he will furnish *a* harvester."[76]

These arguments are pertinent with respect to the contracts initiated by Ili-iqīšam. In *YOS* 13 79 where Aḫum-ṭābu, the *rabi'ānu,* appears as the contracting party (with others), we assume that Aḫum-ṭābu himself was not working in the fields, but was contracting with Ili-iqīšam to supply harvesters. The relatively small amount of payment, ½ shekel silver, can best be taken as a partial payment on account. Szlechter considered that this part payment was implied by the phrase inim dub-a-ni nu-me-a, "sans tablette écrite."[77] We have already had occasion to observe that KA dub-a-ni nu-me-a is an artificial Sumerianized reflex of *ezub pî kanīkišu pānî,* "according to his former document," the negative formulation of which meant, "there were no prior documents on his account." These two conditions appear as "distinctive features" in *YOS* 13 396, "he had no prior transactions," and in *YOS* 13 79, "apart from his prior transaction(s)."

The presence of Ibni-Marduk, son of Bēlānu, as the contracting party in *TJG,* p. 108, a tablet witnessed by Aḫu-ṭābu, does not imply that Ibni-Marduk might go into the fields himself (since he was evidently an important figure in the community and most often witnessed contracts along with the *rabi'ānum*). Awīlatum, son of Ali-bānûšu, appears as the contracting party in *YOS* 13 56 (witnesses not preserved), whereas in *TJG,* p. 113, the same person is himself a witness along with Aḫu-ṭābu, *rabi'ānu,* and Warad-Ikulam, ugula-martu. As already noted, in the document *YOS* 13 396, dating to A-d 29, Sîn-ḫāzir, son of Inapalêšu, contracts with Ili-iqīšam to hire harvesters, and 10 years later in A-ṣ 1 (*TJG*, p. 114), he performs the same function. The exact role of these individuals within the community, however, cannot be ascertained without lengthy prosopographic analysis and without constructing a more detailed model of the communal structure than is possible at this time.

Ili-iqīšam commissioned the disbursements of money or provisions (contracts mention both, but probably only provisions were ever given as ration payments) to the people who undertook to provide harvesters. Ili-iqīšam did not, however, actually disburse the materials himself, but delegated this responsibility to a subordinate, as is shown in *YOS* 13 59 (and in *YOS* 13 231). The operative phrase in *YOS* 13 59 denoting the activity of this subordinate was *itti Ili-iqīšam / ana qabê* PN_1 / PN_2 (the party contracting to supply harvesters) *ilqi.* The inclusion of this phrase was apparently optional in most of the harvest-labor contracts; however, its occasional presence is sufficient to indicate the complexity of the transaction. The omission of the *ana qabê*-phrase in the majority of the Ili-iqīšam documents shows that the position of this subordinate (PN_1) and the execution of his duty was taken largely for granted, and that, in any event, he was not required to be a party to the hiring of the harvesters. In other kinds of transactions, however, a subordinate official might play a more important role, and his duties had to be spelled out in the conditions of the contract. We have already seen an instance of this in the Utul-Ištar texts dealing with slaves.[78]

UṢRIYA, THE *IŠŠAKKUM*

In reference to the Utul-Ištar texts we commented on the phrase *pīḫat* PN.[79] PN in those texts was Bulaṭatum who was the field administrator of Utul-Ištar, particularly responsible for paying laborers and charged with the duty of maintaining the copper implements used in the harvest. His precinct was described as *eqel pīḫat Bulaṭatum,* "the field(s) under the responsibility of B," or, more explicitly, *eqel Utul-Ištar abi ṣābim ša pīḫat Bulaṭatum,* "the field(s) of U., *abi ṣābim*, that were under the responsibility of B." Uṣriya, the *iššakkum,* occurs in the above harvest-labor contracts as Ili-iqīšam's field manager, the person to whom the harvesters had to report at the time of the harvest. The phrase used to denote this responsibility was, as in the documents concerning Utul-Ištar and Bulaṭatum, *eqel pīḫat Uṣriya,* "the field(s) under the responsibility of Uṣriya."

Since all *VS* 7 texts presumably come from Dilbat,[80] the mention of Ili-iqīšam and Uṣriya in *VS* 7 60 indicates that the district managed by Uṣriya was near that city. Thus, the *YOS* 13 texts concerning Ili-iqīšam and Uṣriya should also be from Dilbat. In addition, some of the texts Szlechter published in *TJG* also come from Dilbat, though Szlechter's reasons for this assignment[81] are less convincing than are the internal criteria of the texts themselves.

When we first met Uṣriya he was an associate of a certain Utul-Ištar. We saw in *VS* 7 53 that in A-d 20, Uṣriya son of Warassa, bought a "Mesopotamian" slave from Utul-Ištar, son of Sîn-iddinam, and some other persons. Utul-Ištar bore no title in this document, although an Utul-Ištar with the title dub-sar did, in fact, take an active part in the importation of "Mesopotamian" slaves. If Uṣriya, son of Warassa, was associated with both Utul-Ištar and Ili-iqīšam, we may then perceive a connection between these two very well attested crown officials—a connection that in itself does not occur explicitly in any one document. Both men, it will be recalled, held the same title—*abi ṣābim*—during the same period, ca. A-ṣ 10 (see Table III for exact dates).

This connection between Utul-Ištar and Ili-iqīšam, if correctly perceived, allows us an oblique glimpse into the relations between important personages at various locations and with various responsibilities within the crown's bureaucracy. Utul-Ištar, in particular, seems to have been rather mobile, having begun his career in Dilbat before going on to assume the administration of "the bureau of wool accounts" in Sippar. From royal correspondence, it seems evident that activities of the crown's bureaucracy in larger centers (e.g., Babylon and Sippar) and in smaller settlements (e.g., Dilbat) were directed with a common purpose. As more OB documents are published and studied as groups within specific temporal and geographic units, the present picture of a confusing welter of titles among a disparate officialdom will no doubt be gradually resolved into a more coherent picture of the nature of the crown's hierarchical administration.

That Uṣriya, son of Warassa, mentioned in *VS* 7 53 with Utul-Ištar, is the same man as the *iššakkum* Uṣriya, mentioned in the Ili-iqīšam texts (but rarely with his patronym), may be demonstrated from the following documents:

YOS 13 74

^{I}*mu-úḫ-ra-ga-mil*
ki *il-šu-na-ṣi-ir* šeš-ni
^{I}*uṣ-ri-ya* dumu ìr-*sà*
a-na e-ra-šu-tim
a-na iti-2-kam in-⌜ḫun⌝-*šu*

á-bi iti-2-kam-*šu*
1 (gur) 3(PI) še gur ì-ág-e
2 sìla ta-àm NINDA.PAD-*šu*[82]
4 sìla ta-àm kaš *ma-aš-ti-is-su*
i-na iti-1-kam 3 u_4-*mi*
qá-tam i-ṣa-bat
mi-im-ma i-na qá-ti-šu in-nam-mar-ma
i-na á-bi *i-te-el-li*
igi *ib-ni-*^{d}*marduk* dumu *be-la-nu*
igi^{d}*sîn*-šeš-*i-din-nam* dumu *ip-qá-tum*
iti ne-ne-gar u_4-14-kam
mu *am-mi-ṣa-du-qá* lugal-e
^{d}en-líl nam-en-na-ni (A-ṣ 1)

Uṣriya, son of Warassa, hired Muḫra-gamil from Ilšu-nāṣir, his brother, to do seeding for two months. As the wages for his two months, he will weigh out 480 liters of grain; 2 liters daily bread-rations; 4 liters daily beer-rations. In each month he will have three free days. If anything is found in his possession he will forfeit his wages. Witnesses, date.

Of particular interest here is the presence of Ibni-Marduk, son of Bēlānu, as a witness. We have been able to identify Ibni-Marduk as an influential person who had the power to sanction the hiring of workers from the community. Sîn-aḫam-iddinam, the other witness, is known from *TJG*, p. 108, as one of a number of people receiving an amount of silver from Ili-iqīšam to hire laborers for the precinct of Uṣriya, the *iššakkum*. The connection of these three figures in this text, then, is very strong evidence that the Uṣriya, son of Warassa, mentioned in *VS* 7 53 is the same person as Uṣriya, the *iššakkum* (without patronym), who managed fields for Ili-iqīšam. That Uṣriya, the *iššakkum*, is Uṣriya, son of Warassa, is explicit in the following text. Though Ili-iqīšam does not appear in this document, there is still reason to include it as part of the study of the "bureau of agricultural affairs" in Dilbat.

YOS 13 64

1 gín kù-babbar
šà gú-un a-šà-*šu*
ša mu *am-mi-di-ta-na* lugal-e
    alam nam-ur-sag-gá *sa-am-su-i-lu-na*
    pa_5-bil-ga-na
mu-DU
^{I}*uṣ-ri-ya* ensí
dumu ìr-*sà*
nam-ḫa-⌜*ar*⌝-[*ti*]
[ ]-qum(?)
[*a-wi-il-*^{d}iškur dumu ^{d}iškur-]*ri-im-ì-lí*
[iti u_4- x-kam]
[mu *am-mi-di-ta-na* lugal-e]

[alam nam-ur-sag-gá *sa-am-su*]-*i-lu-na*
[pa$_5$-bi]l-ga-na (A-d 34)

1 shekel silver from his field-tax due in A-d 34, was brought in by Uṣriya, the *iššakkum,* son of Warassa. Received by PN and Awīl-Adad, son of Adad-rīm-ili.

In this document, Uṣriya, described both as an *iššakum*-official and as the son of Warassa, brings in the "rental payment" of a field. The probably restoration of line 11,[83] introducing a character named Awīl-Adad, already known to have taken part in harvest-labor contracts, implies that this document concerns the agricultural activities that Uṣriya administered under the jurisdiction of Ili-iqīšam. If this interpretation is correct, then the personal pronoun *his* (*bilat eqlim*-payment)[84] indicates that the *biltum*-tax was not owed by Uṣriya from *his* personally owned and cultivated field, but rather was collected by him as part of his official agricultural duties. The same phrase, *bilat eqlišu,* appears again in *YOS* 13 479, a transaction similar to that of *YOS* 13 64.

YOS 13 479

½ gín kù-babbar
šà gú-un a-šà-*šu*
i-na qá-ti
^{I}*uṣ-ri-ya* ensí
^{I}*šum-ma-il* dumu *be-el-šu-nu*
ma-ḫi-ir

---

igi *a-ḫu-ṭà-bu ra-bi-a-nu*
igi *ib-ni-*^{d}*marduk* dumu *be-la-nu*

---

iti du$_6$-ku$_3$ u$_4$-8-kam
mu *am-mi-di-ta-na* lugal-e
bàd bàd-*dam-qi*$^!$ (A-d 37)

Šumma'il, son of Bēlšunu, received ½ shekel silver from his field-tax from Uṣriya, the *iššakkum.*

In this text Uṣriya again makes a payment of "his *bilat eqlim*" to a certain party. The same witnesses have appeared repeatedly in the affairs of Uṣriya. In this transaction they represent the community since the field-tax was collected by Uṣriya apparently from fields cultivated by community labor. The yield of these fields was then divided between the laborers (as payments) and the crown (as a tax).

An interesting, though very broken and schematic, document pertaining to these same parties is *YOS* 13 352.

YOS 13 352

20 s[ar] ⸢tùr⸣ [ ]
bal-ri i$_7$ [x]
uś-sa-du an-ta sa ba/zu? [x]
ús-sa-du ki-⸢ta x-x⸣ dumu-meš [x]
sag-an-ta i$_7$ [^{d}EN] [ZU]
sag-ki-⸢ta x⸣- ^{d}[x]e x⸢x⸣ [ ]
ù zu-um-ba-bu dumu-meš ^{I}*pir-ḫi-ì-lí-šu*
é[ ]da *ì-lí-*[*i-qí-ša*]*-am* gal-unken-[na]
é[ ]da [ ]^{d}utu$^{(?)}$ [ ]
[ ]
ša [x]
i-na [x]
ṭup$^{(?)}$-[pi$^{(?)}$]
[x]
a-na ra-bi-[a-ni]
ù lú [x]
30 [ ]
l.e. [x] uṣ-r[i-ya]
[i]d-[di-in]

r. šum?-[ ]
a-na pí-i ṭup-⸢*pi*⸣ [*ì-lí-i-qí-ša-am*]
gal-unken-n[a]
20 sar tùr [ ]
^{I}*a-ḫu-ṭà-bu r*[*a-bi-a-nu*]
^{I}*i-la-kum* dumu *a-l*[i?-]
^{d}*sîn-na-di-in-*šu-m[i]
^{I}ìr-^{d}*i-ku-lam* [ ]
^{I}*ib-ni-*^{d}*marduk* dumu [ ]
^{Id}*na-bi-um-na-ṣir* [ ]
^{I}*a-wi-il-*^{d}iškur [ ]
^{I}*šu-mu-um-li-ib-ši* [ ]
^{I}*el-me-šum* dumu *ì*[*-lí*]
^{I}ìr-^{d}utu dumu gi-[mil-]
^{I}*ri-mu-um* dumu *a-*⸢*na*⸣-[ ]
^{d}nin-šubur-*a-bi* dumu *šu-ma-*[ ]
ù ^{I}*sîn-ḫa-zi-ir* dumu *i-na-pa*[*-li-e-šu*]
a-na uṣ-ri-ya dumu ìr-*sà id-di-nu*

---

iti du$_6$-kù u$_4$-22-kam
mu *am-mi-di-ta-na* lugal-e
alam nam-ur-sag *sa-am-su-i-lu-na*
giš nam-ti-la-šè i-ni-in-ku$_5$-[ra] (A-d 34)

The subject is apparently a transfer of real estate, the location of which is described in lines 1-9. In lines 10-20, which are mostly destroyed, presumably the conditions of the transfer were laid out. In lines 20ff., "according to the tablet of [Ili-iqišam?] *mu'errum,*" the transfer was apparently verified. The restoration of Ili-iqīšam, though not assured, is likely, in view of the reference to him in line 8. The list of thirteen individuals that follows in lines 24-36, who "give the property to Uṣriya," includes Aḫu-ṭābu, the *rabi'ānu,* Ibni-Marduk, [son of Bēlānu] and Warad-Ikulam [ugula martu], important leaders of the community who took part in the harvest-labor contracts initiated by Ili-iqīšam. The nature of this property "transfer," if it were known, would presumably go far toward explaining the previous three contracts in which *bilat eqlim* payments were witnessed by community leaders.

As noted, the operative phrase describing those payments of Uṣriya was not *bilat eqlim* but *bilat eqlišu.* "His" *biltu* field does not describe the field of Uṣriya himself, for *bilat eqlim* would have been sufficient to describe that situation. The person, then, to whom the *bilat eqlim*-payment refers is the person to whom Uṣriya delivers that payment. Uṣriya was an agricultural manager in the harvest-labor documents of Ili-iqīšam, and was presumably acting in the same function in these records.

EXCURSUS ON TEXTS RECENTLY PUBLISHED BY M. BIROT

A comprehensive treatment of the *biltum*-payment will constitute a chapter of M. de J. Ellis's forthcoming book on taxation and land revenues in the Old Babylonian period. In it she will also discuss the role of the *iššakkum* in making these payments and will examine the important group of texts recently published by M. Birot.[85] Since these texts provide supplementary (though indirect) information concerning the duties of (Uṣriya as) a manager of agricultural land, however, a brief excursus devoted to these interesting texts is also included here.

The first eleven texts in Birot, *Tablettes,* refer to calculations of the products on the estates managed by *iššakkum*-officials. They contain unique descriptions of harvest-divisions, payments of imposts to the owners of the lands and also payments of rations to the people who worked on them. They all date to the thirty-second year of Hammurapi, and all refer to activity done near Lagash. For our purposes the following points may be noted: In each text an ensí notarizes the proceedings: ensí PN kišib-a-ni íb-ra, "the *iššakkum* rolled his seal." The texts themselves are complex calculations of various parcels of land (mostly according to the quality of land–ab-sín, kankal, etc.) and of the amount of grain grown on each parcel. In addition, some parcels of land are marked to denote that their produce is intended as payment for various imposts, e.g., *miksum* (níg-ku$_5$), and for "provisions of the *iššakkum,*" šuku ensí. The total reckoning in each text is called *iškar biltim* (éš-gàr gú-un). In texts 5-11 an additional remark at the close of the texts that further describes the *iššakkum* deserves attention:

ensí PN
(*ša mala īliam šaknu*-texts 5, 6, 7)
gú-un *Elmēšum*

gú *nār* Lagaš^{ki}bal-ri ki-^{d}utu-UD-šú-a
kišib-a-ni íb-ra

Birot's translation:

iššakkum PN
(Rendement de redevance) correspondant à la production totale.
(Chargé) de la redevance: Elmēšum.
(Secteur) des bords du canal de Lagaš, rive occidentale.
Il a opposé son sceau.

The phase *ša mala īliam šaknu* occurs not only in the concluding section of texts 5-7, but also in other texts of this group referring to the total amount of grain, *iškar biltim*. Birot consequently chose to add this phrase, "tax yield," before the phrase "corresponding to the entire production" (*ša mala īliam šaknu*). *iškar biltim*, however, usually follows the name of the *iššakkum*. Therefore, a more appropriate translation for *ša mala īliam šaknu* would be, "set aside to be taxed." This translation, then, would fit the instances referring to the amount of grain itself (i.e., that which was set aside) as well as the person who was in charge of bringing in (i.e., setting aside) the grain-tax.

In this perspective the designation of Elmēšum, "(in charge) of the tax" can be clarified. The *biltum* payment of Elmēšum (*bilat Elmēšum*) is the chief matter of the calculation of all these texts, all other calculations being made in reference to this *biltum* payment. Birot thought that Elmēšum was in charge of the district mentioned and that the *iššakkum* had the personal responsibility for the collection of the harvest.[86] This relationship, then, is essentially the same as that expressed in *YOS* 13 texts in which Uṣriya delivers the *bilat eqlim* payment to the person responsible for its payment (*bilat eqlišu*). Elmēšum (like the various persons in *YOS* 13 texts), who received the *bilat eqlim* from *iššakkum*-subordinates, did not own the land, therefore, but was an official responsible for its management and for the payment of the tax to the ultimate owners.

Birot considered that the land managed by an *iššakkum* was (or could be) administered in two ways.[87] On the one hand, the *iššakkum* could function as a cultivator himself, paying a proportion of the tax to the palace.[88] Birot interprets the phrase (*iškar biltim*) *ša mala īliam šaknu* as denoting this sort of activity. On the other hand, the *iššakkum* could rent out land to other people against a percentage of the crop. The latter practice is not found as commonly in the texts as the former. The people to whom land was rented were described simply as lú-didli, and their share of the crop as *miksum*.[89] Part of the crop was then kept aside as the šuku ensí, "provisions for the *iššakkum*." Birot is unable to determine, however, whether the *iššakkum* was essentially treated as an ordinary farmer who had to pay a proportional tax calculated either on the amount of land cultivated or on the amount of the final crop; or, alternatively, whether he was just a salaried administrator of lands.

With these informative texts added to the *YOS* 13 texts, especially as they pertain to the activities of Uṣriya in the bureau of Ili-iqīšam, the following brief summation may be formulated. In the Old Babylonian period the *iššakkum* was a manager of crown lands, not a private farmer;[90] he could be paid either a fixed wage or a proportional share of the harvest; workers in his precinct were always paid fixed sums. These statements must remain tentative, however, since definitive statements on the role of the *iššakkum* must await a more comprehensive study of all available materials.

THE "CHAIN OF AUTHORITY" IN HIRING LABORERS FOR CROWN LANDS

Walther and Lautner, in their analyses of *VS* 7 60 (cf. above, p. 97ff.), thought that the land being tended in the harvest-labor contracts of Ili-iqīšam dealt with royal domains, and they therefore considered Ili-iqīšam a royal official.[91] Lautner contended that contracting parties in the harvest-labor contracts were not professional "hirers," because the "hirers" did not seem to appear more than once although the contracts tended to come from the same area and at about the same time.[92] These "hirers" were then not "capitalists" (Lautner's word) who profited by serving as middle-men between groups of free workers and land owners. With new publications of texts relating to the latter part of the OB period, however (especially *YOS* 13), we can start to utilize prosopographic data, and indeed we have already seen from the documents presented here that certain figures do reappear in the harvest-labor contracts. In some instances it seems that these persons are high-status members of the community, and that the work to be done was not of "private character,"[93] but that the harvest-laborers were drawn from the community to work on estates managed by the crown bureaucracy. One community "head-man," the *rabi'ānum* Aḫum-ṭābum, often contracted with Ili-iqīšam or his subordinates to supply workers. Against Lautner,[94] who thought such contracts represented an option for the contracting party to work himself or let himself be represented by a worker, it seems improbable that Aḫum-ṭābum ever intended to perform the harvest-labor tasks himself.

Occasionally texts mentioning Aḫum-ṭābum were unwitnessed, since the very mention of the *rabi'ānum* in the body of the contract represented all the sanction necessary for the hiring of laborers. One might ask why the crown did not simply requisition some of its own work-force to do this labor, but the answer to this involves some notion of the resources controlled by the crown during this period, a subject that will receive attention in the next chapter.

Two further documents published by Szlechter, *TJG,* p. 118[95] and *TJG*, p. 27,[96] attest activities of Ili-iqīšam that on first inspection seem to have no connection with the area of harvest-labor contracts although both are witnessed by Aḫum-ṭābum. In the former Ili-iqīšam makes a loan of 1 šekel silver to Nabium-nāṣir "to buy a yoked team." Whenever Ili-iqīšam wishes, Nabium-nāṣir will "perform the services with the oxen[97] in the fields under the responsibility of Uṣriya, the iššakkum." In *TJG,* p. 27, at the behest of Ili-iqīšam's subordinate, a man receives an amount of grain that he will repay at the specified moment to the "bearer of his contract." One of the witnesses in this contract is Nabium-nāṣir, the same individual who, as we have just seen (*TJG*, p. 118),[98] contracted with Ili-iqīšam to provide a team of oxen for use on the fields managed by his agricultural subordinate, Uṣriya.[99] The first witness in both texts is the *rabi'ānum,* Aḫum-ṭābum. It follows, then, that although the document, *TJG*, p. 27, takes the form of a private loan transaction, the presence of Aḫum-ṭābum and Nabium-nāṣir is sufficient reason to consider this text too as part of the records of Ili-iqīšam's management of crown lands.[100]

THE *ANA QABÊ* AND "INHABER" CLAUSES

The phrases *ana qabê* PN and the so-called "Inhaberklausel" were last discussed by Edzard.[101] In the phrase *ana qabê* PN, Edzard contended that the exact relationship between the parties PN_1 and PN_2 (*itti* PN_1, *ana qabê* PN_2 = "from PN_1, at the behest of PN_2) could be ascertained only through a knowledge of the persons involved in the transaction and was not implicit in the order to the parties in the clause. In the texts with which we are dealing and in those previously considered (cf. above, the Utul-Ištar slave-buying texts) no difficulty arises, however, because the structure of the clause in each instance does determine its meaning. The one party, *itti* PN_1, "from PN" bears responsibility for the transaction, commissions PN_2 (to acquire men and/or materials), and supplies the wherewithal for him to effect the transaction. *ana qabê* PN2/PN3 verb, therefore, stands apart from *itti* PN syntactically and indicates that PN_2 is the representative of PN_1. This is, in effect, the opinion of Landsberger, who translated *ana* (he wrote *ina*) *qabê* NN (= PN_2), "NN acting as representative(s) of a public office," in the following context:[102]

(1) *eqel* S. *guzalîm*
(2) *itti* S. *bēl eqlim* (S = PN_1)
(3) *ana qabê* N. *aḫišu* (N = PN_2)
(4) A. . . . *ušēṣi* (A = PN_3)

(4) A. rented
(1) the field of S., the *guzalûm*-official,
(2) from S., the owner of the field,
(3) at the behest of N., his brother.

Landsberger noted in this instance that "the *guzalûm* does not act in person but is represented by his brother, who uses the formula *ina* (sic) *qabê*." Without mentioning the brother relationship, the *ana qabê*-clause would be interpreted simply to indicate that A. had rented some land that was under the responsibility of S. and that was managed by his (S.'s) subordinate N. If, therefore, N. and A. were brothers (which is Edzard's interpretation[103]), the text would have had to read

(3) **ana qabê* N.
(4) *A. *aḫašu . . . ušēṣi*

The ambiguity over who is whose brother is introduced from the fact that the practical renting of the land was carried out between N and A, while S remained above the situation. Nevertheless, the land was in fact rented from S (not N), who held authority over the land. The *ana qabê*-clause is written solely to indicate that the transaction was carried out by S's subordinate. The syntax thus indicates clearly that the subordinate (N) was S's brother.[104]

The significance of the "Inhaberklausel," *ana nāši kanīkišu*, has vexed many scholars and would not be resumed here but for its presence in *TJG*, p. 27, a contact which has elicited particular attention.[105] Edzard thought that uniquely in this text could the clause be considered as "Abholung fuer, nicht Zedierung durch den Glaeubiger," (pick-up for, not ceding [the loan] by the creditor).[106] The essential nature of the clause has been disputed as to whether the "debt" is simply to be collected by a representative of the creditor, or whether a "cession" is implicit, that is, whether the debt could be collected by another party, but with some loss in interest before the actual due date of the loan.[107] The weight of opinion currently seems to lean toward the latter interpretation, as is indicated by statement quoted from Edzard above, although some difficulties cannot be satisfactorily resolved.[108] In *TJG*, p. 27, it seems from the use of *ana qabê* PN_2 etc., that the "debtor," PN_3, must pay the "bearer of the tablet" and that PN_2 is the representative of Ili-iqīšam (PN_1). From our knowledge of this relationship it follows that the transaction was not a private loan, but that PN_2 was the subordinate of Ili-iqīšam charged with making grain loans. One problem with the "cession" theory in general is that a "cessionaire" is never mentioned in the contracts. In this text, however, the "cessionaire" may be regarded as a representative of the creditor, thus obviating the difficulty of seeing *either* a cession of the obligation to another party, *or* a call for its collection by a notarized representative of the creditor. In this contract both parties would be the same person. That is, the obligation would be "ceded" (or diminished) by the creditor, but the proceeds of its collection would still accrue to him. The creditor was willing to accept a small loss in the collection of the loan, but this enabled him to make his collection at a time when he might most need the money. This type of clause is rare in transactions of the palace[109] precisely because the palace would seldom be in such need to collect a debt before the full interest on the loan became due. Thus, Edzard's opinion that the "Inhaberklausel" was a "geniale Erfindung"[110] of the time of Hammurapi, is quite inaccurate, for this measure must have been a sign of grave financial insecurity. Its frequent occurrence in crown business documents dating to the end of the OB period speaks eloquently of the deteriorating economic power of the crown during this time.

Other *mu'errum*-officials

Nanna-mansum

Though Ili-iqīšam is the best-attested *mu'errum* (to date), there were many other *mu'errum*-officials active in the late OB period. Walther described one text, *VS* 7 119, as pertaining to the "royal finance officer," Nanna-mansum:[111]

VS 7 119

2 gín kù-babbar
a-na šám *še-e*
ki ^{d}nanna-ma-an-sum gal-unken! -na erén! -ká-é-gal
a-na qá-bi-e ìl-šu-ib-ni dam-gàr é-gal
^{I}ir-*be-li-ti* dumu ^{d}*sîn-i-din-nam*
šu ba-an-ti
u_4-$buru_x$-šè
a-na na-aš ka-ni-ki-šu
ganba *ib-ba-aš-šu-ú*
še-am ì-ág-e
igi *be-el-šu-nu* dumu *e-ri-bi-ya*
igi *ib-ni-*^{d}*mar-tu* dub-sar

iti áš-a u_4-1-kam
mu *am-mi-ṣa-du-qá* lugal-e
i_7 *am-mi-ṣa-du-qá*
nu-hu-uš ni-ši (A-ṣ 16)

Warad-Bēlti, son of Sîn-iddinam, to acquire grain received 2 shekels silver from Nanna-mansum, the *mu'errum,* at the behest of Ilšu-ibni, the royal *tamkārum.* At harvest time to the bearer of his tablet, according to the current market rate, he will weigh out the grain.

A tablet dating to the same year, A-ṣ 16, *YOS* 13 525, ought to be compared to this text since the two documents together provide complementary information about the activities mentioned in them.

YOS 13 525

6 sìla ì-giš
a-na šám *še-e*
ki *i-din-*^{d}*marduk* dam-gàr é-gal
níg-šu ^{d}nanna-ma-an-sum gal-unken-na erén-ká-< é->gal
^{I}*i-din-*^{d}iškur dumu *ip-qu-*^{d}gu-la
šu ba-an-ti
u_4-$buru_x$-šè
ganba *ib-ba-aš-šu-ú*
a-na na-ši ka-ni-ki-šu
še-am ì-ág-e
igi ^{d}*sîn*-šeš-*i-din-nam* *ra-bi-a-nu*
igi *ì-lí-i-qí-ša-am* nagar
igi *be-ya-a* dumu *be-el-šu-nu*

---

iti gan-gan-è u_4-24-kam
mu *am-mi-ṣa-du-qá* lugal-e
i_7 *am-mi-ṣa-du-qá* ša-x (A-ṣ 16)

Iddin-Adad, son of Ipqu-Gula, to acquire grain received 6 liters of sesame oil from Iddin-Marduk, the royal *tamkārum,* under the disposition of Nanna-mansum, the *mu'errum*-official. At harvest time according to the current market rate, he will weigh out the grain to the bearer of his tablet.

Although there are some differences in the terminology of these two documents, the transactions are identical in essence. In the first place, we may regard the 2 šekels silver in *VS* 7 119 as being a standard against which another product was valued. The explicit mention of the sesame oil in *YOS* 13 525 would seem to bear out this supposition. Next, the respective phrases *itti* Nanna-mansum and níg-šu Nanna-mansum express the same function—they show the ultimate authority and responsibility of Nanna-mansum over the entire procedure of the contract but, at the same time, imply that he personally took no part in the direct exchanges stipulated in the documents. The subordinate who did carry out these transactions was, in each text, a "royal merchant."[112]

Leemans conceded that Ilšu-ibni was a "government agent" but thought that "by his [Ilšu-ibni's] order (*ana qabî*) a loan was granted by the *mu'erru ša bāb ekallim*"; thus he assumed that the *mu'errum* was subordinate to the *tamkār ekallim.* However, when this text is compared with *YOS* 13 525, and our analysis of the phrase *ana qabê* is taken into account, it is clear that the goods were simply given out by the "royal *tamkārum*." *itti* PN *tamkār ekallim,* "from the 'royal merchant'," is therefore identical in effect to *ana qabî* PN *tamkār ekallim,* "at the behest of the 'royal merchant'." We may view these documents, then, as those records of a crown bureau under the jurisdiction of Nanna-mansum, and the "royal merchants" as his subordinates.

A third text concerning a Nanna-mansum, with the title *mu'errum,* also dating to A-ṣ 16, is *ARN* 169:

ARN 169

5 (iku) gana a-šà ab-sín
a-gàr iš-si-gal-ni^{ki}
a-šà *i-din-*^{d}*marduk* dumu *ku-ub-bu-tum*
ki *i-din-*^{d}*marduk* dumu *ku-ub-bu-tum*
be-el a-šà
⌜I⌝^{d}Nanna-ma-an-sum
[gal-un]ken-na erén-ká-é-gal
[*a-n*]*a ir-ri-šu-tim*
[nam gú-u]n nam! mu-1-kam
[*ú-še*]-*ṣi*
rest of obverse lost
[igi *m*]*a-aq-tu-li-zi-iz*
[igi x] dumu ì*r-ku-bi*
[igi] ^{d}en-líl-i-bí-za *u-bar-*⌜?⌝
[igi *t*]*a-ri-bu-um* dumu *ì-lí-a-wi-lim*
[igi]ìr-^{d}*na-bi-um* dumu *ma-aq-tu-li-zi-iz*

---

iti gu$_4$-si-sá u$_4$-10-kam
mu *am-mi-ṣa-du-qá* lugal-e
i$_7$ *am-mi-ṣa-du-qá*
nu-hu-uš ni-ši

The *mu'errum*-official Nanna-mansum, in order to cultivate for one year against a *biltum*-tax, rented plowed fields in the meadow of I. from Iddin-Marduk, son of Kubbutum, the owner of the land.

Nanna-mansum thus contracts to cultivate a rented field for one year in what seems to be simply a private rental contract. Kraus, in his introductory remarks to the *ARN* texts (p. 62), considered that this text originated in Sippar because of the presence of the witness Warad-Nabium, son of Maqtu-lizziz, who was known from Scheil's *Une saison de fouilles à Sippar,* no. 76. Since it is improbable (but not impossible) that there were two individuals named Nanna-mansum who were both *mu'errum*-officials acting in the year A-ṣ 16 in different locations, we would like to reconcile Kraus's conclusion as to the provenience of this *ARN* text with the assumption that the *VS* 7 text concerning Nanna-mansum must have come from Dilbat. Ili-iqīšam, *nagar*, a witness in *YOS* 13 525, appears also in *VS* 7 183: vi 1, which supports the Dilbat location of the *YOS* 13 text, but the connection between these two texts does not in itself challenge the location of the *ARN* text at Sippar. The close connection and flow of official business between Sippar and Dilbat has previously been noted through the activities of Utul-Ištar. It is well-known that the two cities were among the first to be incorporated by Sumu-la'el of Babylon into the burgeoning "empire" he founded. In this little conundrum of locating the sphere of activities of Nanna-mansum, the possibility that texts referring to him may turn up in various administrative archives must be considered. Nevertheless, based on present information to posit such an interconnection among all these texts would be perilous. The likelihood is that there were two individuals named Nanna-mansum, one in Dilbat, one in Sippar (at least two: see Ch. 3, n. 27 for an *abi ṣābim*-official named Nanna-mansum in Sippar in A-ṣ 17 + b).

Warad-Ilabrat and Šumšunu, the *iššakkum*

Four texts from *YOS* 13 concerning the *mu'errum*-official Warad-Ilabrat can best be analyzed together, since the activities in these documents are complementary. Two of the texts are dated to the same year, A-ṣ 13; the dates in the other two are lost.

YOS 13 357

1 (gur) še gur ½ gín kù-babbar
ù $1^{1}/3$ erén še-gur$_{10}$-ku$_{5}$
a-na e-ṣe-di-im
ki ìr-^{d}nin-šubur gal-unken-na erén-ká-é-gal
^{I}*id-da-tum* dumu *gi-mil-ì-lí*
šu ba-an-ti u$_{4}$-buru$_{x}$-šè
i-na <a>-šà *pi-ḫa-at šum-šu-nu* ensí
erén še-gur$_{10}$-ku$_{5}$ *i-il-la-ak*
ú-ul i-il-la-ak-ma
ki-ma ṣi-im-da-<*at*> *šar-ri*

---

igi ^{d}*sîn-na-di-in-šu-mi ra-bi-a-nu*
igi *ib-ni-* ^{d}utu dumu *gi-mil-ì-lí*

---

iti še-gur$_{10}$-ku$_5$ u$_4$-4-kam
mu *am-mi-ṣa-du-qá* lugal-e
^{urudu}ki-lugal-gub ì-maḫ-a (A-s 13)

Seal: ^{d}*sîn-na-di-in-šu-mi*

Iddatum, son of Gimil-ili, received 300 liters of grain and ½ shekel silver from Warad-Ilabrat, the *mu'errum*-official, for 1 ¹/₃ harvesters to do harvest-labor. At harvest time, he will furnish (a) harvester(s) to the fields under the responsibility of Šumšunu, the *iššakkum*. If he doesn't, then it is according to the royal *ṣimdatum*.[113]

YOS 13 482

[ ]1 (gur) 2 (PI) 3 bán še gur
[*a*]-*na e-ṣi-di-im*
[ki ì]r-^{d}nin-šubur gal-unken-na erén-ká-é-gal
[*i*]-*lu-ni* dumu *ib-n*[*a-tum*]
[šu ba-an]-ti ⌜u$_4$-buru$_x$⌝ -šè
[*i-na* a-šà *pí-ḫa*] *-at šum-šu-nu* ensí
[erén še-gur$_{10}$-ku$_5$ *i-il-l*]*a-ak*
úl i-la-ak-ma
ki-ma ṣi-im-da-at šar-ri

---

igi ^{d}*sîn-na-di-in-šu-mi ra-bi-a-nu*
igi *a-wi-il-* ^{d}AK dumu [x-x-x-x]
igi *si*?-*na*?-*tum* dumu *ib-ni-*^{d}*marduk*

---

iti še-gur$_{10}$-ku$_5$ u$_4$-4-kam
mu *am-mi-ṣa-du-qá* lugal-e
^{urudu}ki-lugal-gub ì-maḫ-[ ] (A-ṣ 13)

Iluni, son of Ibnatum, received 450 liters of grain for (a) harvester(s) from Warad-Ilabrat, *mu'errum*. At harvest time, he will furnish (a) harvester(s) to the fields under the responsibility of Šumšunu, the *iššakkum*. If he doesn't, then it is according to the royal *ṣimdatum*.

YOS 13 334

1 (gur) 2 (PI) 3 bán še gur
11 erén še-gur$_{10}$-ku$_5$
a-na e-ṣi-di-im
ki ìr-^{d}nin-šubur gal-unken-na eren-ká-[é-gal]

^{I}*ku-un-zu-rum* dumu *ip-qu-*^{d}*ša-* [*la*]
šu ba-an-ti u$_{4}$-buru$_{x}$-šè
i-na a-šà *pí-ḫa-at šum-šu-nu* en[sí]
e-ṣi-di i-il-la-ak
[*ú*]*-ul i-il-la-ak-ma*

(rev. lost)

Kunzurum, son of Ipqu-Šala, received 450 liters of grain for 11 harvesters to do harvest labor, from Warad-Ilabrat, the *mu'errum*. At harvest time, he will furnish harvesters to the fields under the responsibility of Šumšunu, the *iššakkum*. If he does not, . . .

YOS 13 399

2 (gur) še-gur
a-na e-ṣi-di-im(sic)
ki ir-^{d}nin-šubur gal-unken-na erén-[ká-é-gal]
^{I}*ib-ni-*^{d}utu dumu *gi-mil-ì-lí*
šu ba-an-ti u$_{4}$-buru$_{x}$-šè
[*i-na* a]-šà *pí-ḫa-at šum-šu-nu* ensí
⸢*erén*⸣ *e-ṣi-di i-il-la-ak*
ú-ul i-il-la-ak-ma

(rev. lost)

Ibni-Šamaš, son of Gimil-ili, received 600 liters of grain for a harvester(sic). At harvest time, he will furnish harvesters to the fields under the responsibility of Šumšunu, the *iššakkum*. If he does not, . . .

The two dated documents were written not only in the same year but also on the same day. Although the date for *YOS* 13 399 is not preserved, it clearly belongs with the first two documents, since the contracting party, Ibni-Šamaš, son of Gimil-ili, is the same person who witnessed *YOS* 13 357. These four documents record the same type of harvest-labor transaction that Ili-iqīšam so actively directed. On the authority of Warad-Ilabrat, products (in *YOS* 13 357 silver is recorded in addition to barley) are received by certain parties who agree to supply laborers at harvest time. In the two documents in which the witnesses are preserved, the *rabi'ānum* plays the important role as first witness. We have considered that this probably meant that community members were going to be recruited for harvest work on crown lands, and that a sanction to that effect by the leader(s) of the community had to be included in the document.

Also similar to the case in the Ili-iqīšam texts is the specific reference to the district in which the harvest-laborers shall do their work. The administrator of this land, performing the same function as Uṣriya, is the *iššakkum* Šumšunu. In the Birot texts it was seen that *iššakkū* directed the division of the harvest. Although the procedure by which Šumšunu was assigned to the fields under the authority of the *mu'errum* Warad-Ilabrat is unknown,[114] we can observe some of his responsibilities in agricultural management as revealed in several texts from *YOS* 13:

YOS 13 218

1 (PI) še *qí-iš-ti-ili* dumu *il-šu-ba-ni*
⌈5⌉ bán še *id-da-tum* KA dub-a-ni nu-m[e-a]
1 (PI) 5 bán še *a-na e-ṣi-di-im*
ki *šum-šu-nu* ensí
a-na qá-bi-e ili-ba-aš-ti-il-a-bi
[x-x-x-x] [*id*?]*-da-tum*
[šu ba-an-ti]
[u$_4$ -buru$_x$ -šè]
[erén še-gur$_{10}$-ku$_5$] *i-il-la-ku*
[*ú-ul*]*i-il-la-ku-ma*
[*ki-ma*] *ṣi-im-da-at šar-ri*

[igi *ri-i*]*š-é-i-bi-a-nu* ⌈*ra-bi-a-nu*⌉
[ ]-^{d}*e-ra-aḫ*

---

iti še-gur$_{10}$-ku$_5$ u$_4$-15-kam
mu *am-mi-ṣa-du-qá* lugal-e
sipa-zi še-ga
^{d}utu ^{d}marduk-bi-id-da-bi (A-ṣ 10)

60 liters of grain, Qīšti-ili, son of Ilšu-bani, 50 liters of grain, Iddatum, with no previous account; total: 110 liters grain for harvester(s) Iddatum received from Šumšunu, the *iššakkum,* at the behest of Ili-bāšti-il-abi, (?). At harvest time, they will furnish the harvesters; if they do not, then it is according to the royal *ṣimdatum.*

YOS 13 225

1 (PI) še *a-na* [*e-ṣi-di-im*]
ki *šum-šu-nu* e[nsí]
a-na qá-bi-e ili-ba-aš-[*ti-il-a-bi*]
^{I}*ar-ra-bu-šu*
[š]u ba-an-ti
u$_4$-buru$_x$-šè
⌈erén še-gur$_{10}$-ku$_5$⌉ *i-*[*il-la-ak*]
[*ú-*]*ul i-il-*⌈*la*⌉*-*[*ak-ma*]
[*ki-ma ṣ*]*i-im-da-*[*at šar-ri*]
[igi *r*]*i-iš-é-i-*[*bi-a-nu*]
igi ^{d}*sîn* (XXX)*-ib-ni* dumu *ni-id-n*[*a-at-*^{d}*sîn*]
igi ^{d}*sîn-na-di-in-šu-mi*

iti ab-è u_4-10-kam
mu *am-mi-ṣa-du-qá* lugal-e
sipa-zi še-ga ^{d}[utu]
⸢^{d}marduk-bi-id-da-bi⸣ (A-ṣ 10)

Arrabušu, at the behest of Ili-bašti-il-abi, received 60 liters of grain for harvester(s) from Šumšunu, the *iššakkum*. At harvest time he will furnish the harvester(s); if he does not, then it is according to the royal *ṣimdatum*.

YOS 13 226

1 (PI) 4 bán še *a-na e-ṣi-di*
ki *šum-šu-nu* ensí
a-na qá-bi-e ili-ba-aš-ti-il-a-bi
^{I}*ab-du-*^{d}*e-ra-aḫ* PA.PA dumu *u-bar-rum*
šu ba-an-[ti]
u_4-[$buru_x$-šè]
erén še-⸢gur_{10} -ku_5 *i-il-la-ak*]
ú-ul i-*il-la-ak-ma*
ki-ma ṣi-im-da-at šar-[*ri*]

---

igi *ri-iš-é-i-bi-a-nu* ⸢*ra*⸣*-bi-*[*a-nu*]
igi *ib-ni-*^{d}*e-ra-aḫ* PA.PA
igi *ab-du-*^{d}*e-ra-aḫ*

---

iti gan-gan-è u_4-25-kam
mu *am-mi-ṣa-du-qá* lugal-e
sipa-zi še-ga ^{d}utu ^{d}marduk-
bi-id-da-bi (A-ṣ 10)

Abdu-Eraḫ, PA.PA-official, son of Ubarum, received 100 liters of grain for harvesters at the behest of Ili-bāšti-il-abi from Šumšunu, the *iššakkum*. At harvest time he will furnish the harvester(s); if he does not, then it is according to the royal *ṣimdatum*.

These texts are harvest-labor contracts initiated by Šumšunu, the *iššakkum*. The phrase *ina eqel pīḫat Šumšunu* is unneccessary because the work would obviously be done on the lands administered by Šumšunu. In each case the notation *ana qabê* PN was written, showing that the party contracting with Šumšunu received the payment "at the behest" of Šumšunu's subordinate. Thus the *iššakkum* acquired workers for his administrative districts through two kinds of contractual agreements. Under the first, *his* superior, a *mu'errum*-official, would contract with certain parties to supply harvest-laborers to work in fields managed by the *iššakkum.* Under the second, the *iššakkum* himself contracted for the laborers he needed in order to accomplish the work in his administrative district.

These contracts concerning Šumšunu came from Dilbat. In *VS* 7 81,[115] Šumšunu, the *iššakkum,* disburses grain to a certain Ḫuzalum.[116] In texts published by Szlechter in *TJM* that come from Dilbat,[117] Šumšunu appears in the following harvest-labor texts contracting to acquire laborers: *TJM* p. 94 (H 79) = No. 1; p. 94 (H 34) = No. 2; p. 96 (H 27) = No. 3; p. 97 (H 17) = No. 4; p. 98 (H 19) = No. 5. The first four date all to the year A-ṣ 10, while in the last the date is not preserved. In texts 2, 3, 4 and perhaps 5 an amount of grain to hire harvesters is dispensed according to the formula: *itti Šumšunu iššakkum / ana qabê Ili-bāšti-il-abi / PN ilqi.* Ili-bāšti-il-abi[118] thus appears in these contracts as the subordinate of Šumšunu. In the contracts the witnesses include: no. 1, Sîn-nādin-šumi, *rabi'ānu* (A-ṣ 10); no. 2, Rīs-é-ibbi-anu, *rabi'ānu* (A-ṣ 10); no. 3, witnesses not preserved (A-ṣ 10); no. 4, a PA.PA (A-ṣ 10); no. 5, witnesses and date lost. These texts might benefit from some collations, but in general we can accept them as of the same type as the *YOS* 13 contracts in which Šumšunu hired harvest-laborers. Two other documents published in *TJM*, p. 42 (H 32) and p. 116-17 (H 37), also date to A-ṣ 10 and concern activities of Šumšunu. The former, also attesting *Ili-bāšti-il-abi,* Šumšunu's subordinate, deals with a loan of sesame oil valued in grain; the latter (which needs collation) is similar to Edzard, *ed-Dēr* 30, a "Schulduebernahme."[119]

Sîn-iqīšam and Bēliyatum, the *iššakkum*

Two texts in *TCL* I, nos. 166 and 167, refer to the *mu'errum* Sîn-iqīšam. In no. 166,[120] dated to A-ṣ 13, there is an agreement that a certain Šumum-libši will pasture the herd of Sîn-iqīšam for a set price:

> gu_4 šà gu_4 *ša* ^{d}*sîn-i-qí-ša-am* gal-unken-na
> *i-ri-i* 1 bán še *a-na i-di-šu be-li-ya-tum*
> *iš-ku-šum* (!)
>
> (Šumum-libši) will pasture oxen from among the oxen of
> Sîn-iqīšam, the *mu'errum.* 10 liters grain Bēliyatum set as
> his wage.

The contract continues, "if he (Šumum-libši) flees or goes away, he will forfeit his wages," and further stipulates the day until which he must pasture the herd. The contract concludes with the listing of two gìr-officials, Bēliyatum and Sîn-šemi.[121] Walther considered the possibility that the contract was not a private agreement and that the herd was state property,[122] and Lautner reached the same conclusion.[123] The latter thought that the wages were not paid at the time of the contract, but were assigned by the state financial authority (Sîn-iqīšam), who would pay after the work had been accomplished. Lautner further assumed from the presence of the gìr-officials that Bēliyatum and his colleague drew up the contract.[124]

That Bēliyatum's title as a gìr-official was an *ad hoc* designation, not an official rank,[125] seems indicated in *TCL* I 167.

TCL I 167

82 (gur) 3 bán še gur ^{giš}baneš-é
ša 27 *ki-iṣ-ri*
ù 11 ^{giš}baneš
8 (gur) 3 (PI) 3 bán gur ŠE.MUŠ$_5$
^{giš}baněs-é
ša 2 *ki-iṣ-ri*
ù 27 ^{giš}baneš
90 (gur) 4 (PI) še gur ^{giš}baneš-é
nam-ḫar-ti ši-i-iq me-še-qum kab-rum
qá-du ŠE.MUŠ$_5$
ša a-šà kar- ^{d}utu^{ki}
pí-ḫa-at be-lí-ya-tum
ensí
ša ^{f}*la-ma-sà-ni* lukur- ^{d}utu
dumu-munus ^{d}*sîn-i-qí-ša-am* gal-unken-na
mu-DU *a-na* é-ì-dub
nam-ḫar-ti ^{f}*la-ma-sà-ni* lukur- ^{d}utu
^{d}*sîn-ri-me-ni*
ù ^{f}ba-za
gìr *e-tel-pu* dumu-é-dub-ba-a

---

^{I}*šu-mu-um-li-ib-ši*
ù be-lí-ya-tum ensí
iti šu-numun-a u$_4$ -28-kam
mu *am-mi-ṣa-du-qá* lugal-e
^{urudu}ki-lugal-gub ì-maḫ-a (A-ṣ 13)

item: 24,630 liters barley measured according to the standard 30-liter measure, which is 27 payments of 900 liters plus 11 additional payments of 30-liter measures.
item: 2610 liters "late grain" measured according to the standard 30-liter measure, which is 2 900-liter payments plus 27 additional payments of 30-liter measures.
total: 27,240 liters grain measured according to the standard 30-liter measure. Received according to the "thick" standard, including "late grain," from the fields of Kār-Šamaš under the responsibility of Bēliyatum, the *iššakkum* of Lamassani, *nadītu* of Šamaš, daughter of Sîn-iqīšam, the *mu'errum*-official. Brought in to the granary, received by Lamassani, *nadītu* of Šamaš, Sîn-rīmēni, and Ms. Baza.
overseers: Etel-pû, dumu-é-dub-ba-a, Šumum-libši, and Bēliyatum, *iššakkum*.
date: 28.4.A-ṣ 13

Remarks on this unusual text are few, the most detailed being only Walther's brief corrections of the misunderstandings of Ungnad in *HG* 5 1255. Concerning the standards of measuring grain in the OB period, an obviously important subject in the study of the economics of the period, Goetze's statements in *JCS* 2 (1948) p. 85, must be cited. Goetze itemized a 60-liter measure, the "lean" standard; a 64-liter measure, the "thick" standard; and a 72-liter measure. Goetze also recognized that the grain standard could be expressed by a *sūtum*-standard rather than by the more common *parsiktum,* and that the "thick" standard measure, usually written: *ina* ^{giš}bán- ^{d}utu *ina kabrim ina mešēqim,* could be abbreviated: *ina sūti* ^{d}*šamaš ina mešēqim.* In *TCL* I 167 we can see that there was also a 30-liter measure. The é probably refers to a temple, as an abbreviation for the commonly found *sūt* ^{d}*Šamaš* (or *sūt* ^{d}*Marduk*). Walther considered the *kiṣru*-payment as a standard payment of 3 gur (900 liters), probably a monthly sum, and 30 liters a daily payment. The text, however, does not deal with payments to individual workers (who would receive between 5-10 liters per day) but with receipts from the fields administered by Bēliyatum, the *iššakkum,* and delivered to the owner of the fields, Lamassani. Beliyatum also transported the grain to the granary. *kiṣrum*[127] appears to refer to an "agreed payment," in this case 30 times the 30-liter measure.

Bēliyatum was an agricultural manager of fields in the district of Kār-Šamaš. His duties included the hiring of "shepherds" to care for the herd under the jurisdiction of Sîn-iqīšam (in *TCL* I 166), and the administration of lands for the daughter of Sîn-iqīšam. Harris has twice discussed the *nadītu* Lamassani,[128] citing the above texts and adding some others in which she appears: *TCL* I 168 (A-ṣ 13) and *TCL* I 229-30 (undated), both of these which concern activities of Bēliyatum in the management of agricultural lands and the division of the *bilat eqlim*-payments of those lands. *TCL* I 174[129] mentions many other activities carried on by Bēliyatum, most probably as part of his duties as agricultural manager of, and paymaster for, the rather extensive land holdings under the jurisdiction of Sîn-iqīšam, the *mu'errum.*[130]

TCL I 174

8 erén *ab/p-lu-tum ḫa-ra-ṣum*
3 erén *za-ru-ú*
2 erén *e-si-ip* e$^{\text{hi-a}}$
2 erén lú sita$_5$ ri-ri-ga
10 erén *ma-ṣa-ar e-ri-bu*
36 erén lú a-bal *ša* 6 u_4-mi 4 erén^{meš} *ma-ha-ḫu*
16 erén lú a-bal *ša* 4 *u_4-mi* 4 erén^{meš} *pa-ša-rum*
40 erén lú a-bal *ša* 7 *u_4-mi* 4 erén^{meš} *šu-ul-lu-šu*
25 erén^{meš}
92 erén^{meš} a-bal

---

117 erén^{meš} a-bal

---

8 sìla *su-ki-ip-tum*
2 bán še *si-bu*
1 bán ^{d}*sîn-ri-me-mi*
2 bán šà gu$_4^{\text{hi-a}}$
2 bán *ù* 15 še kù-babbar gìr *be-lí-ya-tum*

1 (PI) 1 bán 8 sìla še

iti gan-gan-è u$_4$-1-kam
mu *am-mi-ṣa-du-qá* lugal-e
alam [ ]x

8 men for cutting furrows; 3 sowers; 2 men for banking dikes; 2 accounters of carcasses; 10 watchmen against ravens; 36 irrigators of 6 days, of whom 4 would prepare the soil; 16 irrigators of 4 days, of whom 4 would "loosen" the soil; 40 irrigators of 7 days, of whom 4 would do the "third plowing." Totals: 25 men plus 92 irrigators—in all, 117 irrigators. 8 liters for PN; 20 liters grain for PN; 10 liters PN; 20 liters for oxherds; 20 liters (grain) and 15 še silver, overseer, Bēliyatum. In all, 78 liters grain.

Marduk-mušallim and Bēlšunu, the *iššakkum*

The *mu'errum*-official Marduk-mušallim is represented in two texts in the *YOS* 13 volume, nos. 330 and 333. These are dated to Samsu-ditana 2 and 3 respectively, and are from Kish (as is stated in no. 330, line 6, where a *šāpirum* of Kish is mentioned, and in 333:9, where *šāpir Kiš* may be restored). These texts are both "rental-partnership agreements."

YOS 13 330

a-šà *ma-la*<*ma*>*-ṣu-ú* ab-sín
a-gàr *a-mur-i-za-nu*
a-šà ^{d}*sîn-iš-me-a-ni* sukkal
a-na qá-bi-e be-el-šu-nu ensí,
^{d}*marduk-mu-ša-lim* gal-unken-na erén-ká-é-gal
^{I}*a-wi-il-*^{d}*sîn ša-pí-ir kiš*^{ki}
ù be-el-šu-nu ensí
a-na tab-ba *a-na ir-ri-šu-tim*
a-na gú-un *a-na* mu-1-kam
ú-še-ṣu-ú
ma-na-aḫ-tam a-wi-lum ma-la a-wi-lim
i-ša-ak-ka-nu

u_4-buru$_x$-šè a-šà *i-ša-ad-da-du-ma*
1 bur-e 6 gur
ì-ág-e-meš
ma-na-aḫ-ta-šu-nu i-ip-pa-lu
še-am ša ib-ba-aš-šu-ú
mi-it-ḫa-ri-iš i-zu-uz-zu
šà-*ba* gú-un a-šà-*šu*
6 gín kù-babbar *ma-ḫi-ir*

---

igi *i-lu-ni-šar-rum* ugula mar-tu
igi *ib-ni-*^{d}*sîn* ugula mar-tu
igi *ib-ni-*^{d}*za-ba*$_4$*-ba*$_4$ dumu *ma-lik*(?)-^{d}utu
igi *e-ri-ba-am-ištar* dumu-é-dub-ba-a

---

iti gu_4-si-sá u_4-10-kam
mu *sa-am-su-di-ta-na* lugal-e
mu gibil egir inim-maḫ-a AN.^{d}Marduk
lugal-bal-a-ni (S-d 2)

YOS 13 333

a-šà *ma-la* [ ]
a-g[àr]
pa_5-e šu-up-pa-x[ ]
a-šà *il-šu-ba-ni ù* ^{d}*marduk-mu*[*-ša-lim*]
dumu *a-wi-il-*^{d}*sîn*
ki *il-šu-ba-ni ù* ^{d}*marduk-mu-ša-lim*
be-el^{meš} a-šà
^{d}*marduk-mu-ša-lim* gal-unken-[na erén-]ká-é-gal
ù a-wi-il-^{d}*sîn ša-pir kiš*^{ki}
a-na tab-ba *a-na ir-ri-šu-tim*
a-na mu-1-kam *a-na* gú-un
a-na 1 bur-e 1-e[ ] še gur
íb-ta-è-a-meš
[ ] še numun *ù ma-na-aḫ-tam*
(rest of obverse, reverse lost)
iti ne-ne-gar u_4-2-kam
mu *sa-am-su-di-ta-na* lugal-e
an ^{d}en-líl-bi inim-zi-bi [-x]
mu-un-na- [ ] (S-d3)

Translation of *YOS* 13 330:

> Field(s), as much as is required, plowed land in the pasture Amurizanu, field(s) of Sîn-išme'anni, *šukkallum* . . . at the behest of Bēlšunu, *iššakkum*–Marduk-mušallum, *mu'errum,* Awīl-Sîn, *šāpirum* of Kish, and Bēlšunu, *iššakkum,* in partnership for purposes of cultivation against a *biltum*-payment rented the land for one year. They will perform the work equally. At the harvest-time they will measure the field(s) (calculate the produce of the fields). For each bur (6½ ha.) of land they will weigh out 6 kor (1800 liters). They will account for their investment, and the grain, as much as there is, they shall divide equally. Out of the *biltum*-payment of his field(s), he (Sîn-išme'anni) has already received 6 shekels silver.

Marduk-mušallim, together with the *šāpirum* of Kish and an *iššakkum,* agree to rent land in partnership. The *iššakkum,* who is one of the partners, is also the agent of the *šukkallum,* Sîn-išme'anni, who is the "owner" of the land. The transaction seems to be a private affair, with the *iššakkum* administering a certain portion of land for an official, but then renting it out to himself and two other important individuals. We do not know whether the land itself had previously been granted to the *iššakkum* and which then might have been his to negotiate further, or whether this was a business transaction of the *šukkallum* in which an "employee" of his took part. In any event, the equal sharing of the work does not necessarily mean that the individuals mentioned were themselves bound to do the work, but rather that their various dependents or hirelings shared in the agreed amount of labor.

YOS 13 333 is a similar transaction in which two of the same partners (without Bēlšunu, the *iššakkum*) rent land. The phrase *ana qabê* does not appear in this contract, but the essence of the rental-partnership agreement may in fact be no different from that of *YOS* 13 330. It is significant that almost everyone mentioned in these texts is titled (in *YOS* 13 330 everyone is an "official" save one witness). But to interpret these texts as official crown documents would be to misunderstand the changes in value these titles underwent through time. We must also note that these texts are from Kish, and that our knowledge of this site in the OB period is, at present, very limited.[131] The *YOS* 13 volume, on the other hand, contains many texts whose provenience is Kish, many dating to the reign of Samsuditana, a time about which we are very poorly informed from all sites.[132] From just a cursory examination of their contents (cf. "Introduction" to *YOS* 13), these texts show quite different (forms of) social institutions from those attested from other sites and in earlier times. We must be circumspect, therefore, in trying to analyze these later texts from Kish on the models of texts from other sites and earlier dates. Nevertheless, during the latter stages of the OB period there seems to be a clear proliferation in the usage of titles in texts from all sites. The implications of this growing "officialdom" at a time of waning political power of the OB dynasty will be dealt with in the next chapter.

Various other *mu'errum*-officials

Another text mentioning a *mu'errum*-official at the time of Samsu-ditana, also in connection with a rental-partnership agreement, is *YOS* 13 41:

YOS 13 41

1 (bur) 12 iku a-šà ab-sín
a-šà BAD *ib-ni-*^{d}*marduk ù kur-di-ištar*
dumu-meš *e-ṭi-rum*
12 iku a-šà ab-sín
a-šà BAD aga-uš^{meš} *um-ma-ti*[133]
níg-šu ^{d}*sîn-i-qí-ša-am* PA.PA
2 (bur) 6 iku a-šà ab-sín a-gàr i$_7$-idigna?
a-na qá-bé-e i-ri-ba-am-ištar dumu-é-dub-ba-a
ù a-wi-il-^{d}*é-a* dumu ^{d}*é-a-na-ṣi- ir*
ig-mil-^{d}*sîn* gal-unken-na erén-ká-é-gal
ù [x-x-x-x-] *ša-pir* kiš^{ki}
a-na (nothing missing?) [tab]-ba
a-na ir-ri-šu-tim
a-na gú-un
a-na mu-1-kam
íb-ta-è-a-meš
ma-na-aḫ-tam a-wi-lum ma-[*la a-wi-lim*]
i-ša-ak-k[*a-nu*]
u$_4$-buru$_x$-šè [a-šà]⸢*i-ša-ad-da-du-*⸣[*ma*]
1 bur-e 6 še gur
gú-un a-šà ì-ág-e-meš
še-am ša ib-ba-aš-šu-ú
mi-it-[*ḫa-ri-iš i-zu-uz-zu*]

---

igi [x x-x-x]
igi *a-pil-ì-lí-su* [x-x]
igi *ìl-šu-na-ṣi-ir* [ ]
igi ìr-^{d}*be-*⸢*le*⸣*–tim* dub-sar
iti šu-numun-a u$_4$- [ ]
mu *sa-am-su-di-ta-na* [ ]
mu gibil egir inim-maḫ- [a]
^{d}*marduk* lugal-ba[1-a-ni] (S-d 2)

Two parcels of land, the first belonging to two brothers, now deceased, the second denoted as land of (unnamed) deceased soldiers under the jurisdiction of the "general," Sîn-iqīšam, both indicated as being "at the behest" (*ana qabê*), of two individuals, were rented by Igmil-Sîn, *mu'errum*, and a *šāpirum* of Kish (whose name is not preserved). The conditions of the agreement are similar to those of *YOS* 13 330. Perhaps the connection between the parcels was that Sîn-iqîšam was the supervisor of various plots of land that had been given to soldiers under his command and that reverted to his authority after their death. These lands could then be rented out by him through his administrative assistants Erîbam-Ištar[134] and Awīl-Ea.

YOS 13 242 is a variation of this kind of rental partnership agreement. This text is also dated to the time of Samsu-ditana and also comes from the area around Kish.

YOS 13 242

1 (eše) 3 iku a-šà ab-sín
a-gàr *ka-al-ba-ta-nu*
a-šà ^{f}*da-an-e-ri-is-sà* lukur-^{d}za-ba$_{4}$-ba$_{4}$
dumu-munus ^{d}*marduk-la-ma-sà-šu*
šu-ṣu-ut
^{Id}*marduk-mu-ba-lí-iṭ* dumu *ìl-šu-ba-ni*
ki ^{Id}*marduk-mu-ba-lí-iṭ* dumu *ìl-šu-ba-ni*
^{I}ìr-*ku-bi* ensí ìr-^{d}*marduk* ensí
ù i-na-šar-^{d}*marduk-a-la-ak* ensí
ša a-wi-il-^{d}*na-bi-um* gal-unken-na
a-na ir-ri-šu-tim a-na mu-1-kam
a-na gú-un 1 bur-e 8 gur
íb-ta-è-a-meš
u$_{4}$-buru$_{x}$-šè
a-šà *i-ša-ad-da-du-ma*
1 bur-e 8 gur
gú-un a-šà še ì-ág-e-meš

---

igi *ib-ni-* ^{d}za-ba$_{4}$-ba$_{4}$ sanga-^{d}za-ba$_{4}$-ba$_{4}$
igi *e-til-pi*$_{4}$-^{d}*za-ba*$_{4}$*-ba*$_{4}$ ugula-lukur-^{d}za-ba$_{4}$-ba$_{4}$
igi ^{d}*sîn-na-di-in-aḫ-ḫi* dumu *ib-ni-*^{d}*marduk*
igi *i-na*-é-sag-íl-numun dumu ^{d}*sîn-be-el-ap-lim*
iti ne-ne-gar u$_{4}$-9-kam
mu *sa-am-su-di-ta-na* lugal-e
inim-maḫ-a marduk-ke$_{4}$
lugal-bal-a-ni (S-d 1)

This is a case of the sub-rental of land. A certain amount of arable land belonging to a *nadītu* of Zababa was rented to Marduk-muballiṭ, who then rented it out to (or had it managed by) three *iššakkum*-officials. The last of these (or perhaps all three?) was in the service of Awīl-Nabium, the *mu'errum*.

abi ṣābim and *mu'errum*-officials appear together in *TCL* I 164.[135] Lines 1-7 are an introduction to a legal inquiry into a theft of oxen:

Concerning 5 oxen of Ilšu-ibni, shepherd of Ašar-Mama, which were lost and then turned up in the possession of Ibni-Marduk, son of Sîn-iddinam, the shepherd, Ibni-emaḫ-tila, and Atamu, son of Sîn-erība:

ṭup-pí a-wi-le-e a-bu erén
a-na ib-ni-^{d}*sîn* gal-unken-na
ù ip-qu-^{d}*na-bi-um* šu-i
il-li-ka-am a-na ká-dingir-ra^{ki}
ú-še-lu-šu-nu-ti
ma-ḫar a-wi-le-e a-bu erén
[awātam][136] *da-ab-ba-a-ma*
[gu$_{4}^{hi\text{-}a}$] *ri-a-ba-am*
[*iq-ta-*]*bu-šu-nu-š*[*i-im*]

A document from the honorable *abi ṣābim*-officials to Ibni-Sîn, *mu'errum,* and Ipqu-Nabium, the *gallābum*-official, arrived here. They (the *abi ṣābim*-officials) summoned them (the thieves) to Babylon. The cases have been pleaded before the honorable *abi ṣābim* officials, and they decreed the replacing of the oxen for them.

The remainder of the text records, as a result of this decree, that one ox belonging to Ibni-Marduk, one of the thieves, has already been given over to a dub-sar-erén, a bookkeeping assistant of the *abi ṣābim*-officials, for later disposition to Ilšu-ibni. The witnesses are Awīl-Ištar, son of Ibni-Šamaš; Ilima-aḫi, son of Ilšu-abušu; Ibni-Erra, son of Marduk-mušallim; Sîn-mušallim, son of Eṭīrum; and Šumum-iīṣi, dumu-é-dub-ba-a. The text dates to the ninth year of Ammi-ṣaduqa.

On the basis of this text Walther[137] concluded that the *mu'errum* played a subordinate role to the *abi ṣābim*-officials in Babylon. The interest of the *mu'errum* in this case apparently proceeds from the fact that investigation concerned animals that were used for agricultural purposes. The *mu'errum* was consulted because he was a state authority in the management of agricultural enterprises. It may be plausible that the theft of oxen from the shepherd Ilšu-ibni called for the "judicial review" of the *mu'errum* and *abi ṣābim,* because the oxen were owned by the crown and Ilšu-ibni was a shepherd in the crown's service.

There is further evidence that Ibni-Sîn, the *mu'errum*, was associated with land-management activities and the distribution of the products of the land. In *BE* 6/1 99[138] amounts of grain from shepherds, "generals," etc. are brought in (mu-DU) to the granary at Sippar-Amnānum, and received (*namḫarti*) by five people: Ibni-Sîn, *mu'errum;* Ibni-Sîn, son of Sîn-iddinam; Sîn-išme'anni, *dayānu*; Ipqu-ilišu, *dayānu*; and the *kārum* of Sippar-Amnānum. The year is A-ṣ 12, only 3 years after *TCL* I 164.

The *biltum*-payment of a *mu'errum* is the subject of a text, *CT* 45 55, that may be dated to Ammi-ditana (the date is completely lost, but the seal mentioning A-d is probably contemporary with the document).

CT 45 55

-broken-
ù x še x x x
šà-*bu* gú-un ^{d}*na-bi-um-na-ṣi-ir*
gal-unken-na erén-ká-é-gal
ensí *ta-ri-ba-tum*
ša [*iš-tu*] *pa-di-du-um*^{ki} (?)
a-na sippar *ya-ah-ru-rum*
ib-ba-ab-lam-ma
i-na na-at-ba-ki-im ša i-ta ká-gal- ^{d}a-a
iš-ša-ap-ku
kaskal *a-bi-e-šu-uḫ-li-di-iš*
^{I}*gi-mil-*^{d}*marduk*
ù ^{d}*iškur-*<*ì*>*-lí-šu*(?) rá-gab
lú-meš ú-ru-uš lú ba x
nam-ḫa-ar-ti
^{I}*ìl-šu-ib-ni* ugula-dam-gàr-meš
^{I}sippar^{ki}*-li-wi-ir* dam-gàr
ù aḫ-ḫi-šu dumu-meš *ta-ri-ba-tum*
^{I}ìr-*i-lí-šu* di-ku$_{5}$
ù aḫ-ḫi-šu dumu-meš *i-bi-*^{d}utu
^{I}*ib-ni-*^{d}iškur di-ku$_{5}$
ù aḫ-ḫi-šu dumu-meš *nu-úr-*^{d}utu
^{I}*ìl-šu-ba-ni* di-ku$_{5}$ *ù aḫ-ḫi-šu* dumu-meš *a-wi-il-*^{d}utu
^{I}dumu-meš *ìl-šu-ba-ni* di-ku$_{5}$
^{I}dumu-meš ^{d}*sîn-i-din-nam* ugula-dam-gàr-meš
^{I}*i-din-*^{d}nin-šubur dumu ^{d}*sin-ḫa-zi-*[ir]
^{d}utu-*na-ṣi-ir* dumu *ìl-šu-ba-ni*
^{I}*ta-ri-ba-tum* dumu *ib-na-tum*
^{Id}*marduk-na-ṣi-ir* dumu ^{d}*sîn-i-din-*[*nam*]
dumu-meš *sà-ni-iq-pi*$_{4}$-^{d}utu
ù kar sippar^{ki} *-ya-aḫ-ru-rum*

---

gìr *šu-ì-lí-šu* dub-sar-erén
u$_{4}$-10-kam
(rest of date lost)

seal: *ìl-šu-ib-ni*
ugula dam-gàr
dumu *ìr-ra-*[ ]
ìr *am-mi-di-*[*ta-na*]

(First two lines broken and/or missing)
From the *biltum*-payment of Nabium-nāṣir, *mu'errum*-official
–*iššakkum* Tarībatum–which was brought from GN (?) to Sippar-

> yaḫrurum and was poured out into the granary which was by the great gate of Aya. The caravan of A, G, and A, the *rābikum,* men of GN (?), was received by Ilšu-ibni, *wakil tamkārī;* S, *tamkārum,* and his brothers, sons of T; I, *dayānum,* and his brothers, sons of I. etc.. Overseer: Šu-ilišu, *ṭupšar ṣābim.*

It is unfortunate that the first two lines are damaged, for they might have given some information on the origins of these payments and how they came to be connected in this text. Were the receivers of the products of the business caravan representatives of social units, extended families or the like (as might be indicated by "brothers"), that had capitalized the venture?

From the time before Ammi-ditana, two documents mention the *mu'errum* Ilum-damiq (AN-damiq), *BE* 6/1 79 and *BE* 6/1 119.[139] The former text refers to animals that were received by Ilum-damiq, *mu'errum,* son of Zimri-Šamaš, from Nergal-ibbi, son of Ipqu-Annunītum. This laconic note is followed immediately by a date of Abi-ešuḫ. A much longer document, but hardly more informative as to the activities of Ilum-damiq, is *BE* 6/1 119, which contains 5 columns, 156 lines. It records real estate transactions of Ilum-damiq and his family in the times of Abi-ešuḫ and Ammi-ditana. Many of these transactions were made by Lamassani, daughter of Ilum-damiq and a *nadītu* of Šamaš. One of these transactions, however, mentions neither of these people, but does refer to a certain Nergal-ibbi (r. col. iv. line 6), who may be the same person we met in *BE* 6/1 79. In rev. col. v:16 it is interesting to find that Ilum-damiq, son of *zi-im-ri-*^{d}utu, is titled ugula mar-tu—an indication of mobility at this time among certain official positions, but, of course, with no clue to the direction or nature of this mobility. One son of Ilum-damiq held a PA.PA rank (col. iii:11-12), and another son was named Sîn-mušallim. Walther[140] surmised that the latter might be the *mu'errum* of that name in *AbB* 2 66, a letter from the time of Abi-ešuḫ.

A possible earlier reference to a named *mu'errum,* dating to Samsu-iluna 10, occurs in a text published in Riftin, *SVJAD,* no. 48. The document reads in translation:

> Concerning the marriage-gift (*zubullûm*) that Sîn-ašared, *šāpir mātim,* and his brothers brought as a marriage-gift to the estate of Bēlaniya: Since they did not give in marriage the daughter of Bēlaniya, they brought suit against Lamassum, wife of Bēlaniya, to recover the gift. Ina-palêšu, *mu'errum* (?), Awīl-Ištar, *šāpirum,* Ibbi-Sîn and PN examined their case, and they repaid to them his marriage-gift (that is, they ordered repayment of Sîn-ašared's marriage-gift to him and his brothers). They will not return to court; Lamassum, wife of Bēlaniya, will not sue. If his (Sîn-ašared's) old document should turn up, it will be broken. Oath of Šamaš, Marduk, and Samsu-iluna. Witnesses and date.

This text may be the only instance in which a named *mu'errum* exercises a judicial function unconnected with his primary duties as an administrator of lands. The passage (line 10) mentioning Inapalêšu, however, is broken and the restoration gal-un[ken-na] is uncertain.

The earliest of all the texts in which a *mu'errum* is named, and the only published text mentioning a *mu'errum* from the south, dates to the reign of Rīn-Sîn.[142] The text itself, however, adds little to our understanding of the role of the *mu'errum* in this time period, although it has occasioned some interest since *hab/piru*-soldiers are mentioned in it.

RA 12, p. 115

4 (or 5) túg-gú-è
a-na aga-uš^{meš}
lú *ḫa-bi-ri*
šu-ti-a *ib-ni*-^{d}iškur gal-unken-na
[zi-ga]
šà níg-ŠID é-^{d}utu
šu *i-lí-ip-pa-al-sà-am*
[iti bara]-zà-gar u_4-11-kam
mu *ri-im*-^{d}*sîn* lugal-e

4 (or 5) "red-cloths"[142a] received by Ibni-Adad, *mu'errum*-official, for the *rēdû*-soldiers, *ḫapīru;* disbursed from the accounts of the temple of Šamaš by Ili-ippalsam.

Seven texts from the yet unpublished *YOS* 12 volume, six dating to Samsu-iluna 23, the other to S-i 10, mention the *mu'errūm* Marduk-mušallim and Sîn-rēmēni, respectively. Six texts (nos. 411, 412, 415, 416, 422, 425) refer to *zabbilū* (laborers) who are among gardeners from Malgium performing agricultural tasks on *biltum*-fields of Marduk-mušallim.[143]

Another recently edited text dating to Samsu-iluna (from the south) *TLB* 1 195:6,[144] refers to one Sîn-iddinam, gal-⸢unken!⸣-na. The *mu'errum* appears in broken context but apparently in charge of calculations of land and workers.

In addition to these numerous documents, a few letters refer to activities of *mu'errum*-officials. One of the earliest of these is a letter written by king Abi-ešuḫ.[145] The king writes to Marduk-nāṣir, to the *kārum* of Sippar, and to the judges of Sippar, that certain people are to be sent to the *biltum*-field[146] of Sîn-mušallim, *mu'errum.* The king attended to this affair because he was interested in the collection of the *biltum*-tax due on fields administered by the *mu'errum.* As Ellis points out,[147] the same field could be viewed in two perspectives, both as the subsistence field of the person cultivating it (or having it cultivated), and at the same time as the source of income for the person or institution that ultimately owned the property. From both views, the field could be called a *biltum*-field, though the formulations *eqel biltim* and *bilat eqlim* may not necessarily reflect these different perspectives.

Letters and Documents Mentioning Unnamed *mu'errum*-officials

Several letters that do not mention a *mu'errum* by name merit a brief review. The text *TCL* I 29[148] provides an example of the kind of information that can be gleaned from letters. Anatum writes Ḫabil-ili about "his brother" Ilabrat-tayyār, who refused to have anything to do with him. Anatum then goes to his *šāpirum* (also called his "helper,"*ālik idiya*), who convenes legal proceedings. Ilabrat-tayyār tells the *šāpirum* that Anatum and Ḫabil-ili are houseborn slaves (*i-li-id bītim,* l. 14), at which point the whole matter is brought to the *mu'errum.* Ilabrat-tayyār is incarcerated in the house of the *mu'errum* for 4 days before deciding not to slander Anatum further—presumably he has called him a *wilid bītim*[149]—and is released. Thus, we observe an unnamed *mu'errum* playing a "judicial" role, but we are ignorant as to the basis of his judicial authority. Perhaps the matter at question is one of service to the administration—a requirement that Anatum to fulfill some obligation based on his status as *wilid bītim,* and one that he could escape if he could prove that he was not a houseborn slave. If so, this text can be compared to *CT* 6 29,[150] in which an *abi ṣābim* helped to decide the obligations of service of a runaway slave. The *mu'errum* in *TCL* I 29 may have derived his "judicial" authority from similar circumstances: his position as an administrative officer of the crown allowed him the right to make a decision in case of conflicting claims about the social obligations and status of a community member vis-à-vis his duties to the state. Though the relationships between crown and community are not explicit in this letter, the presence of the *mu'errum* can best be explained in terms of functions in which we have seen this officer associated. Methodologically, approaching the analysis of the role of officials in letters through a general understanding of their activities as described in economic texts, is, I believe, more fruitful than accepting the isolated functions described in each letter as defining the social and legal roles of these officials.

In the letter *PBS* 7 100 Ilšu-bani writes to his master (*awīlum,* not to be identified with the *mu'errum* mentioned later in the body of the letter, who is called *awīlum mu'errum* "the honorable *mu'errum*"). The sister of Ilšu-bani, the wife of a *mu'errum*, had reported that she gave the purchase price for 3 female slaves to a *tamkārum* of Sippar-Annunītum, but received only two slaves. Labištum, the *gallābum*-associate of the *mu'errum,* was sent to get the third slave, but the *tamkārum* did not hand her over. Ilšu-bani, whose role in this affair seems limited to dealing as his sister's agent (apparently because the *mu'errum,* his brother-in-law had died), now writes to the *awīlum* that he should order the third slave girl to be delivered. The resolution of the conflict between the widow and the *tamkārum* remains unknown.

The brief letter *PBS* 7 121 has been translated[151] in full as follows:

> The honorable magistrate of the palace personnel (gal-unken-na erén-ká-é-gal) has embarrassed me before the troops (erén^{meš}). Take charge of your troops and in the first day of the seventh month, come here quickly. Don't put this off.

Both Ungnad[152] and the *CAD* assume erén (= *ṣābu*) and *pāni ṣābim* refer to military troops, but the text might just as plausibly refer to crown dependents, workers of a certain sort. In either case our knowledge of the role of the *mu'errum* cannot be elucidated further from this brief letter, but to assume a military function for the *mu'errum* goes against everything we have already observed.

In the letter *TCL* 17 34 one Dada writes to his *šāpirum* to explain why he (Dada) has been unable to fulfill his *girrum* (probably a responsibility concerning a business-caravan) while he was in Isin in consultation with the *mu'errum* there, an associate of the *šāpirum*.[153] The *mu'errum* had informed Dada that no business-caravans had appeared in Isin, which information Dada now relays to the *šāpirum*, hastening to add that the needs of the *šāpirum* will be taken care of when the *šāpirum* himself reaches Isin. Dada concludes his letter by pleading for the well-being of his pledges. About the function of the *mu'errum* we learn only that he was in a position to know about business-caravans and was perhaps performing some administrative function pertaining to them.

In *TCL* 18 104 a certain Sîn-imguranni writes to certain gentlemen (*ana awīlē*) concerning the matter of the sesame of the *mu'errum* presently held by another man, and he asks the gentlemen to come to Babylon to settle the affair. We again observe the involvement of the *mu'errum* with agricultural products.

Several references to unnamed *mu'errum*-officials also occur in *YOS* 13 texts, one of which is an unaddressed letter, *YOS* 13 98:

YOS 13 98

^{d}utu *li-ba-al-li-iṭ-ka*
lu ša-al-ma-ta
i-nu-ma iš-tu kiš^{ki} *ú-še-li-*[*ku*]
aš-šum it-ti ì-lí-i-qí-ša-am dumu ^{d}iškur-ma-an-sum
ù it-ti ì-lí-i-qí-ša-am lú-kúrun-na
šu-ta-ti-im-ma ṭe$_{4}$*-mi ša-pa-ri*
ù uzu(?) *a-na a-wi-lim* gal-unken-na
šu-bu-lim aq-bi-ku
ṭu-ub ù ma-ás-ka
ma-la im-ḫu-ra-ka
ṭe$_{4}$*-em-ka ú-ul ta-aš-pu-ur*
aš-šum ŠE.MUŠ$_{5}$ *ù* ziz-an-na
ša i-na é *a-wi-lim am-ḫu-ru*
ki-ma ^{d}*marduk-mu-ba-lí-iṭ* dumu-é-dub-ba-a
ša gal-unken-na *la im-ḫu-ru*
ṭe$_{4}$*-em ma-la aš-pu-ra-ak-ku*
i-na ṭup-pi-ka pa-nam šu-ur-si-a$^{!}$*-a-am-ma*
šu-up-ra

May Šamaš give you long life and may you be healthy. When I summoned you from Kish on account of the confrontation[154] with PN and PN$_{2}$ the brewer, I ordered you to bring my report and (?) to the honorable *mu'errum*.

> Good and bad, as much as he confronted you, your report you did not make. I wrote you concerning the "late grain" and the emmer which I had received in the house of the gentleman, and, which according to Marduk-muballiṭ the dumu-é-dub-ba-a-official, the *mu'errum* did not receive. The report as much as I wrote you, write in your document, make it clear.[155]

The *mu'errum* acts in an official capacity concerning an amount of grain. A person has written reprimanding his subordinate because he did not report to the *mu'errum*, as he previously had been instructed, concerning a missing amount of grain. The "gentleman" in line 13 probably refers to the *mu'errum* himself, and, if so, it follows that his "house" must refer to the granary. In short, we see here a case in which the *mu'errum* acts not as a judge or policeman, but rather in his well-attested role as administrator of agricultural supplies. We know nothing about the position of the writer of the letter, of course, but perhaps we may read this as a glimpse into the difficulties of repaying a "loan" of grain from the stores of the *mu'errum* (to which we have seen so many references in the economic documents). We may also note briefly the reference to the dumu-é-dub-ba-a as acting in the service of the *mu'errum*, as a recorder of supplies from the granary. As we have already seen, persons bearing this "scribal" rank were often associated with *mu'errūm* and other crown officials.

YOS 13 173, dating to the time of Samsu-ditana, is an accounting of various cereals. Mentioned along with the *šāpirum* of Kish, a šu-i, and a dumu-di-ku$_5$, there is a *mu'errum* (lines 13, 20). The purpose of the accounting is obscure.

YOS 13 181 (A-ṣ 17+b) is another account of expenditures or allotments of grain. In line 3 there is recorded a dumu gal-unken-na and in line 10 dumu^{meš} gal-unken-na.

There are two additional texts that also mention dependents of a *mu'errum.* A dam gal-unken-na is mentioned in *CT* 4 8b, line 19, in a list of allotments of products to women associated with a temple. Similarly, in *JCS* 11, p. 35, 26:13, in a list of objects belonging to certain women, there is a reference to the dumu-munus gal-unken-na. In the latter text it apparently was not necessary to identify the daughter of the *mu'errum* by name—although all the rest of the women were identified by patronym, *mārat* PN.

CT 8 19a[156] records a dispute over property mentioning a *mu'errum* (line 16), a reading that Walther thought questionable,[157] but that can hardly be read otherwise. The name of the *mu'errum* is lost in a break immediately before his title, and his function in the document is altogether unclear. The date is A-ṣ 5.

YOS 13 207, also dating to A-ṣ 5, records the hiring of a worker from his mother to do *šamallūtum*-work.

YOS 13 207

iš-tu iti gu$_4$-si-sá u$_4$-12-kam
^{I}*ib-ni-*^{d}*marduk* dumu *pí-il-ḫa-*^{d}iškur

ki ^{f}*bu-un-na-nu-ša um-mi-šu*
a-na ša-ma-al-lu-ti
a-na mu-1-kam
^{I}*ì-lí-i-qí-ša-am* da[m-gàr]
in-ni-[in-ḫun]
á-bi mu-1-[kam]
6 gín [kù-babbar]
ma-ḫi-⸢*ir*⸣
li-ib-bu á-bi
½ gín kù-babbar
ma-ḫi-ir

---

igi ^{d}*na-bi-um-mu-ša-lim* du[mu$^{(?)}$]
dumu-é-dub-ba-a *ša* gal-unken-[na]
igi *ú-túl-ištar* dumu ^{d}*marduk-mu-ša-lim*
igi ^{d}*sîn-na-di-in-šu-mi* dub-sar

---

iti gu$_4$-si-sá u$_4$-12-kam
mu *am-mi-ṣa-du-qá* lugal-e
alam-a-ni máš igi-du$_8$-a
šu-a an-da-gál-la

Ili-iqīšam, the *tamkārum,* has hired from 12.2 Ibni-Marduk, son of Pilḫa-Adad, from Bunnanuša, his mother, to do *šamallūtu*-work for one year. His wages for one year, 6 shekels silver, he will receive. Out of the wages, he has already received ½ shekel.

Leemans in his discussion of *šamallûm* notes that *šamallūtum* in the meaning of "cultivation" in Nuzi has "an extraordinary, derived sense,"[158] since *šamallûm,* an agent of the *tamkārum,* has nothing to do with cultivating. I cannot suggest, however, what other kind of work *šamallūtum* might imply if not cultivation. Either the first witness was the "son of the dumu-é-dub-ba-a of the *mu'errum,*" or, if we assume a dittography, the title of Nabium-musăllim was "dumu-é-dub-ba-a of the *mu'errum.*" In either case we see a further instance of the connection between a "scribal rank" and the bureaucracy of the crown in the latter part of the Old Babylonian period.

Conclusion

We offer as a provisional synthesis the following brief observations on the status and role of the *mu'errum.* The rank *mu'errum* seems to be lower in the crown's administrative hierarchy than that of *abi ṣābim.* Ili-iqīšam, who held both titles, was first a *mu'errum*, and though this is perhaps not concrete proof that a promotion was involved, such a conclusion is the most likely and is consistent with other data on their respective positions. In *TCL* I 164[159] the *mu'errum* reported to the *abi ṣābim*, a fair indication of their relative status. Both officials were managers of the arable lands of the crown, but the *abi ṣābim* was concerned chiefly with lands directly owned by the crown and cultivated by those workers dependent on the state for their livelihood. He was responsible for their payment (in rations) and for supplying and maintaining the implements with which they worked. His responsibilities also extended into those activities involving the loan of resources from crown fields for profit. The *abi ṣābim*, then, acted frequently as a crown finance officer.

The *mu'errum*, on the other hand, seems to have occupied an intermediate position in the crown bureaucracy concerned with agricultural resources. His prime responsibility, as documented in many harvest-labor contracts, was to recruit laborers. However, since the royal administration had no demand-right of agricultural service on people who were not directly dependent for their subsistence on the largesse of the crown, the *mu'errum* had to contract for these laborers with certain community leaders. This basic function of recruiting laborers for lands is clearly reflected in the *mu'errum*'s title in the phrase erén-ká-é-gal: "*mu'errum* of the workers of the crown's estates."[160] The office of mu'errum was created (or better: greatly expanded) in the latter part of the Old Babylonian period when the crown was unable to remunerate a large number of permanent dependents and therefore had to hire laborers for specific purposes at specific times of the year. In light of this analysis of the office, we may finally offer a translation for the title *mu'errum*: "commander (recruiter) of (part of) the (seasonal) agricultural labor force of the crown."[161]

As part of his duty as a liaison between crown and community, the *mu'errum* often investigated and helped to decide cases that arose when citizens not directly bound to the crown nevertheless owed it certain kinds of services (e.g., in the military). Judicial functions were not characteristic of the office, however, but were rather an outgrowth of the *mu'errum*'s normative spheres of duty. The *mu'errum*'s authority seems to have been limited to activities surrounding the bureaus of agricultural affairs, and in comparison to the duties of the *abi ṣābim*, his subsequent participation in areas of dispute were much less extensive.

As more texts are published and more studies of significant groups of officials and their activities are undertaken, disparate glimpses from isolated texts and individual ranks will be drawn into a more coherent picture of the lines of authority that bind these officials in the crown's bureaucracy. Having examined the internal organization of certain segments of the crown's economic bureaus, it behooves us also to speculate on the purposes behind these bureaucratic affairs. Within the context of the larger socio-economic structure in Old Babylonian times, the crown played only one role, albeit a crucial one. The official ranks of *abi ṣābim* and *mu'errum* were designed as specific responses to changing conditions in late Old Babylonian society. It is to this subject of historical change in the Old Babylonian period, then, that we turn in our final chapter.

NOTES

[1]*MSL* 12, p. 10, no. 16, copy on Plate II, and p. 17, no. 10.

[2]*MSL* 12, p. 33, no. 14.

[3]*MSL* 12, p. 96, nos. 110-117.

[3a]I have been informed by M. de J. Ellis that a text in the collections of the Free Library of Philadelphia mentions an official with the title á-gal. The text will be edited by Ellis in *Ancient Near Eastern Studies in Memory of J. J. Finkelstein* (eds, M. de J. Ellis, J. Cooper, N. Yoffee, Memoirs of the Connecticut Academy of Arts and Sciences Vol. 19, in press).

[4]*MSL* 3, 139, 125.

[5]*MSL* 4, 14, 19.

[6]See the well-known articles by T. Jacobsen now collected in *Toward the Image of Tammuz,* ed. W. Moran, Ch. 8, "Early Political Development in Mesopotamia" and Ch. 9, "Primitive Democracy in Mesopotamia." Compare also Evans, *JAOS* 78, 1-11; Diakonoff, "The Rise of the Despotic State in Ancient Mesopotamia, ed. I. Diakonoff, 173-203; Diakonoff, "On the Sturcutre of Old Babylonian Society," in Klengel, ed., *Beitraege zur sozialen Struktur des alten Vorderasien,* 15-31. Most of the references to the gal-zu-unken-na occur in Sumerian literary texts and particularly in royal correspondence of the Ur III kings and in certain myths. The attestations of this figure have been utilized to indicate the existence of popular assemblies in Mesopotamia (or local, community organs of government) with this official as the leader of the assembly. Mr. Piotr Michalowski, in his dissertation, "The Royal Correspondence of Ur," includes a discussion of the gal-zu-unken-na.

[7]*SGL* 1, p. 67.

[8]*SGL* 2, p. 122ff.

[9]Source A in *MSL* 12 (*BAW* I 80f).

[10]*SGL* 1 p. 67 n. 102; Falkenstein rightly saw no reason to separate GAL.UNKEN from GAL.UNKEN.NA.

[11]*SGL* 2 p. 122-23 and n. 19 also quoting Jacobsen who thought gal-ukkin-na = *rab puḫri.*

[12]*TCS* 3, p. 96ff; numerous references (1969) for GAL.UNKEN, but gal-unken-na is unconsidered (since it does not appear in the genre of literary texts that Sjoeberg compares to the "Haupttext" of *TCS* III).

[13]I am unable to explain [kinga]l-unken-na = *a rab puhri.*

[14]Except in the instance of the Sultantepe Text whose version is properly rejected by the editors of *MSL* 12. The writing kin-gal-unken-na = **mu'er puḫrim* finds an analogue in *enūma eliš,* Tablet I, line 149, *mu'errūt puḫri,* "leadership of the assembly."

[15]GAL appears often graphically as the first element in a word, but not necessarily in its pronunciation. An excerpt from *MSL* 3 (p. 139) shows variation in several instances of "petrified" writings. The first column reflects the Sumerian pronunciation, the second the writing of the term, and the third the Akkadian translation:

123.	ú-šum-gal	gal-ušum	*ú-šum-gal-lu*
124.	ú-kur	gal-ŠAḪ	*ṭa-ri-ḫu*
125.	kin-gal	gal-unken	*mu-'-ir-ru*
126.	ab-zu	zu-ab	*ap-su-u*

[16]A formulation GAL.UNKEN = kingal = *rab puhrim,* while GAL.UNKEN.NA = *mu'errum* (or the reverse!) would be a red herring in this discussion and is best passed over rapidly. Literary texts invariably write GAL.UNKEN for which the translation "leader" (e.g., *TCS* 3 , p. 30) or "commander" is most appropriate. OB documents invariably write GAL.UNKEN.NA for which a translation "commander," although too

literal, also conveys something of the sense of the word. In neither case does any equation with *rab puḫrim* seem to be merited. Prof. Hallo suggests that the spelling -na indicates "that there were two different pronunciations, one logographic (kingal), the other syllabic (gal-ukkinna), comparable to ugnim (-ma) and kilubgar(-ra)." (Personal communication).

[17]Is GAL.ERA (lú = *ša,* 114-115) a play on GAL.URI = kindagal (= *gallābum*), which sounds in turn like kingal? This analysis is not more than a guess, but if correct, the connection would not be as random as might be supposed, for the *gallābum,* written ŠU.I in OB letters and documents, is also an important official in the OB period whose duties are far more extensive than those of a mere "barber." For kindagal see Kraus, *Sumerer und Akkader,* p. 61ff..

[18]*CAD* A/1, p. 52.

[19]The text is *VS* 13 28 rs. 6, a house sale dating in the 24th year of Hammurapi. The fourth witness is Ili-abi son of Muwerrum; cf. *HG* 6, 1573.

[20]Stamm, *Namengebung,* pp. 114-16.

[21]Stamm, *Namengebung,* pp. 264-65.

[22]Sollberger, *AS* 16, p. 23, l. 46," written in a small but very neat and elegant 'classical' Old-Babylonian hand," *AS* 16, p. 21.

[23]*AbB* 1 52

[24]I. reports that "the reed fence of death is being adjusted for me" (*gisallu ša mūtim ina muḫḫiya ḫariṣ*).

[25]Lines 26-27: 4 *annūtin mu-*WE*-er-ri iddinam,* "these 4 (men) my *mu'errum* gave me."

[26]Published by Sollberger, *JCS* 5, p. 85 (MAH 15914); edited by Szlechter, *JCS* 7, p. 96ff. (no. 24); re-edited by Landsberger, *JCS* 9, p. 126f.

[27]*JCS* 9, p. 126.

[28]*JCS* 9, p. 126, n. 90.

[29]*AHw*, p. 667.

[30]*AbB* 2 66.

[31]*JCS* 16, p. 9; also *Studies Oppenheim,* p. 123.

[32]*JESHO* 10, p. 6, n. 1.

[33]*TJG*, p. 108.

[34]*BA* 6/5, p. 54 and *HG* 3 55.

[35]*HG* 6 1788.

[36]*Personenmiete,* p. 158 and n. 489.

[37]*PBS* 7 121.

[38]Klengel, *Beitraege,* p. 44, n. 25; "all-league goalie"?

[39]*Bagh Mitt* 2, p. 26, n. 102.

[40]*AbB* 4 8, note a.

[41]*TCL* 7 8.

[42]*ZANF* 25, p. 215, n. 1013.

[43]I have to thank Professors †Oppenheim and Reiner for making available to me the "Wurstmachine" draft of the *mu'errum* article for the M volume of the *CAD* in December, 1971.

[44]Klengel, *Beitraege,* p. 44.

[45]*Ancient Mesopotamia,* p. 200.

[46]*ArOr* 3, p. 42.

[47]*UAZP* 162 and 309 and cf. index, p. 539, where he read kingal for gal-unken-na.

[48]*Gerichtswesen,* pp. 148-58.

[49]See above, note 14.

[50]Walther then misread *VS* 7 60 on the basis of his earlier misreadings of *šá* for erén.

[51]Walther, *Gerichtswesen,* p. 149: "Doch wahrscheinlich ist die oertliche Vorstellung verblast und *ekallum* bedeutet wie sonst die Verwaltung, bes. die der Finanzen."

[52]*Gerichtswesen,* p. 148.

[53]Krueckmann's opinion in regard to the *abi ṣābim*, whom he considered among the "Beamte in der Stadtverwaltung," namely of the *kārum,* is, however, less convincing.

[54]Indications are only circumstantial that Ili-iqīšam, *abi ṣābim,* and Ili-iqīšam, *mu'errum,* are really the same person since no patronym is found among the Ili-iqīšam references. Additionally the *mu'errum* references seem to be mainly from Dilbat while the *abi ṣābim* references are likely from Sippar. Nevertheless, *abi ṣābim* seems to be a higher rank than *mu'errum*, and this, taken together with the sequence of dates, might well imply that one Ili-iqīšam was promoted during the course of his service to the crown.

[55]*HG* 3 726; Walther, *Gerichtswesen,* p. 61f. and p. 149f.

[56]The oath is also sworn in the name of Zababa, patron deity of Kish.

[57]Verb missing, cf. *Gerichtswesen,* p. 62, n. 1.

[58]The terms used by this sort of "bureau" can be found in Kraus, *Staatliche Viehhaltung im altbabylonischen Lande Larsa,* Amsterdam, 1966.

[59]See p. 101f. and n. 76.

[60]*Personenmiete,* p. 142ff.

[61]Cf. *Personenmiete,* p. 148ff. on the role of the "contracting party."

[62]*Gerichtswesen,* pp. 107-08 and passim.

[63]*Gerichtswesen,* p. 107ff. (1917) is still the best treatment of the term which obviously merits a more up-to-date study. Cf. Oppenheim, *JESHO* 10 (1967), p. 6, n. 1.

[64]Cf. Landsberger, *JCS* 9, p. 127, n. 44.

[65]Soviet researchers have often spoken of the "commune" in Mesopotamian history, cf. "The Commune in the Ancient Near East as Treated in the Works of Soviet Researchers," *Soviet Anthropology and Archaeology* vol. II, no. 1, p. 32ff. (from *VDI*, 1963); and the essays by Diakonoff in *Ancient Mesopotamia,* "The Rise of the Despotic State in Ancient Mesopotamia," and in Klengel, *Beitrage,* "On the Structure of Old Babylonian Society."

[66]*Personenmiete,* p. 158.

[67]*Gerichtswesen,* p. 149.

[68]See the brief discussion of *ṣimdat šarrim* above Ch. 3, p. 62.

[69]In *TJG*, p. 108ff (see Table V, above p. 92).

[70]*TJG*, p. 114.

[71]Szlechter read Ṣilli-Marduk, in *TJG*, p. 108, MAH 16558.

[72]Ch. 3, p. 57ff.

[73]*TJG*, pp. 115-16 and ns. 68, 60.

[74]*Personenmiete,* p. 164.

[75]*Personenmiete,* p. 163 for references.

[76]M. Stol, *Studies in Old Babylonian History,* Nederlands Historisch-Archaeologisch Instituut te Istanbul, Leiden, 1976, p. 99ff.. One final difficulty with the use of the word *alākum* as a transitive verb is in the phrase "If he does not go," usually written *ul illak(ū),* but occasionally as *ul illik(ū),* even when there is only one contractor (Stol, ibid., p. 106ff.). Stol suggests that either harvesters is the subject of the verb in this case or a subjunctive is involved. Note in either instance that there is no change in the sense of the clause: the contractor is subject to the penalty whether "if the harvester doesn't go (to the field)" or "if he (the contractor) doesn't furnish (the harvester)."
[I received Stol's book while reading proofs on my own and am happy to acknowledge his acute perception to the general problem of interpreting *alākum*-phrases in harvest-labor contracts. My own conclusions to the issue at hand, namely that Aḫum-ṭābum and Ibni-Marduk did not work in the fields themselves but supplied laborers, was offered in the original version of this manuscript in 1973. In this instance, logic (not only my own, but also Koschaker's and to an extent Lautner's) has been substantiated by grammar (and syllabic orthography).]

[77]*TJG*, p. 115.

[78]Ch. 2, p. 22ff.

[79]Ch. 2, pp. 18, 38ff.

[80]*BA* 6/5, p. 3.

[81]*TJG*, pp. vi-viii, on the basis of fingernail impressions on the edge of Dilbat tablets.

[82]I can only suggest that this bread ration be read ninda-pad = *kusapu,* cf. *CAD* K, p. 583, "bite, small repast." No previous OB attestations.

[83]Cf. *YOS* 13 59: 13 (above p. 96).

[84]See below p. 108ff.

[85]Maurice Birot, *Tablettes économiques et administratives d'époque babylonienne ancienne,* Paris 1969.

[86]Birot, *Tablettes,* p. 39.

[87]Birot, *Tablettes,* p. 44f.

[88]All these texts are assumed to be calculations of work done on crown land; occasionally there is reference to crown ownership of certain materials, e.g., *alpū šarrim*, text 1:9.

[89]Birot's interpretation of *miksum* is based on Landsberger's comment in *MSL* 1, p. 191, that *miksum* was part of the harvest received by the farmer himself.

[90]This against Diakonoff in Klengel, *Beitraege,* p. 27 and n. 41 and opposed to Birot's notion that the *iššakkum* was an ordinary farmer.

[91]Szlechter, however, (*TJG*, pp. 117-18) regarded the lands administered by Ili-iqīšam as a fief granted him by the crown. He reasoned that the presence of witnesses showed that the private character of harvest-labor transaction; and he thought that the responsibilities of the *iššakkum* were not limited to the fields of the palace.

[92]*Personenmiete,* p. 172f.

[93]*Personenmiete,* p. 159.

[94]*Personenmiete,* p. 173.

[95]MAH 16.305.

[96]MAH 16.536.

[97]The *CAD* I, p. 49, translates *ini'āti illak,* "he will perform the services with the oxen," taking *ālākum* as "to do *ilkum*-service." Szlechter had translated "un (des) conducteur(s) avec un (des) boeuf(s) ira (iront)," based on analogy with his interpretation of the harvest-labor contracts.

[98]In both texts the name of his father–in the seal of *TJG*, p. 118, and among the witnesses in *TJG*, p. 27–is broken, only *ib-ni-*[ ]preserved in either instance.

[99]This recalls the mention of oxen in the Birot texts (cf. *Tablettes,* pp. 44-45) that were included in the calculations of the division of the harvest on those fields.

[100]This analysis shows that many OB contracts that have been categorized as private documents on the basis of witnesses, šubanti-clause, etc. may require re-evaluation in the context of the activities of the persons mentioned in those documents.

[101]*ed-Dēr,* p. 58ff.

[102]*JCS* 9 (1955), pp. 128-29 and n. 63 referring to text no. 10.

[103]*ed-Dēr,* p. 69.

[104]One of Szlechter's main arguments that the land for which Ili-iqīšam was contracting to supply laborers was a private benefice and not crown lands was the absence of the phrase *ana qabê* (*TJG,* p. 28). Its presence in *YOS* 13 59 and 231 in the same set of negotiations shows the fragility of this kind of argument. For Szlechter's curious opinion that *ana qabê* implies a guaranteed loan, see *JCS* 7, p. 87ff.

[105]Terms summarized above p. 109.

[106]*ed-Der,* p. 74; cf. Bogaert, *La banque,* p. 97 and Leemans, *JESHO* 2, p. 328.

[107]Cf. Landsberger, *JCS* 9, (1955), p. 130.

[108]Cf. Edzard's discussion, *ed-Dēr,* p. 69ff.

[109]Bogaert, *La banque,* p. 74.

[110]*ed-Dēr,* p. 74.

[111]*Gerichtswesen,* p. 149.

[112]Cf. Leemans, *Merchant,* p. 108, considering *VS* 7 119.

[113]*ana eṣēdim* must here be taken as an infinitive, "to do harvest-labor." The odd number of harvesters must refer to an amount of time that would be remunerated, not, obviously, an amount of men.

[114]The documents concerning Warad-Ilabrat and Šumšunu are dated to three years later than the texts in which Šumšunu alone appears. In these latter texts it is uncertain whether Warad-Ilabrat was the official ultimately responsible for the land managed by Šumšunu. In both classes of texts the harvesters were apparently drawn from the membership of the community as is evidenced by the presence of the *rabi'ānum* in both classes.

[115]*HG* 3 190, dated to A-ṣ 6.

[116]Cf. Huzalum in *TJG,* p. 27 in connection with Ili-iqīšam (H. son of Ēṭirum, cf. *YOS* 13 55).

[117]*TJM,* p. viii, n. 15.

[118]Szlechter read ^{d}Bāšti-il-abi. In *YOS* 13 index (prepared by E. Kingsbury) this name appears as *La-ga-ma-al-a-bi, YOS* 13 218; Ili-bāšti son of Šu-abi, *YOS* 13 225-226. The name Ili-bāšti appears in Stamm, *Namengebung,* p. 308, and cf. *CAD bāštu,* vol. B, p. 143, where the name *abi-bāšti* is cited. Ili-bāšti and abi-bāšti together would yield *Ili-bāšti-abi: The god (or "my god") is the protection of (my) father." The problem concerns the sign *-ıl-* which I take as a "syllabic writing" for AN = *ìl,* thus yielding the name Ili-bāšti-il-abī, "(my) protective god is the god of (my) father."
I have W. G. Lambert to thank for pointing out that Lagamal is not the wife of Uraš, patron deity of Dilbat. This opinion was based on an incorrect interpretation of Rawlinson II R, 60 Nr. 1, lines 14-15; cf. Unger, *ArOr* 3 (1931) p. 36; Deimel, *Pantheon,* (1914) p. 160; Ungnad, *BA* 6^{5} p. 134. Lambert's forthcoming edition of An = *Anum* equates Lagamal as the son of Uraš, and it is with his kind permission that I quote the following portions of Tablet V, "the Dilbat section":

40.	^{d}ú.ra.aš$_{IB}$	šu
41.	^{d}gú.an.né.si.il$^{gu.an.ni.si.il.la.ku}$	MIN

42. ^{d}nin.uru dam.bi.munus
43. ^{d}la-ga-ma-al dumu^{d}uraš.ke$_4$
44. ^{d}ip-te-$^{bi-it}$bīt sukkal^{d}uraš.ke$_4$

119 Discussion, *ed-Dēr*, p. 64ff.

120 *HG* 5 1113.

121 Cf. also *UAZP* 162; Walther, *Gerichtswesen*, p. 152ff.

122 *Gerichtswesen*, p. 155.

123 *Personenmiete*, p. 47, n. 173.

124 *Personenmiete*, p. 114, n. 373.

125 Kang, *Sumerian Economic Documents from the Drehem Archive*, Urbana, 1972, p. 257.

126 *Gerichtswesen*, p. 152, n. 2.

127 *CAD* K, p. 438.

128 *JCS* 16, p. 9, and in *Studies Oppenheim*, pp. 123, 132-33.

129 *HG* 5 1312.

130 Harris considered the text to be an indication of the personal means of Bēliyatum, *Studies Oppenheim*, p. 133.

131 See for the present, Yoffee, "The Old Babylonian Texts from Kish: A First Report," (eds. M. de J. Ellis, J. Cooper, N. Yoffee in *Ancient Near Eastern Studies in Memory of J. J. Finkelstein*, Memoirs of the Connecticut Academy of Arts and Sciences, vol. 19, in press).

132 In *HG* 3-6 in which there are almost 2000 texts, there are not more than 20 dating to the reign of this king.

133 Or *um-ma-*<*na*>*-ti*, "soldiers"?

134 Cf. *YOS* 13 330, 24 where the last witness is Erībam-Ištar, dumu-é-dub-ba-a.

135 *HG* 5 1196; *UAZP* 309; *Gerichtswesen*, p. 151ff.

136 *CAD* A/1, p. 51; D, p. 8.

137 *Gerichtswesen*, pp. 150-52.

138 *HG* 3 121.

139 *HG* 3 107 and 414 respectively; the latter is also in photograph in *BE* 6/1 plate xii.

140 *Gerichtswesen*, p. 157, n. 1.

141 Cf. *CAD* Z, p. 152.

142 Scheil, *RA* 12 (1915), p. 115; cf. *HG* 6 1788.

142a H. Waetzoldt, *Untersuchung zur neusumerischen Textilindustrie*, Rome, 1972, p. 52 and n. 118.

143 I thank Prof. W. W. Hallo for allowing me to cite these texts here, Dr. Mark Cohen who first informed of them and Dr. Maureen Gallery who has supplied recent information on the basis of a more detailed examination of them.

144 Leemans, *Festschrift Boehl*, p. 281ff. Another text mentioning a *mu'errum*, probably in the time of Samsu-iluna (S-i 8?) is *W* 28; Rīm-Adad, gal-unken-na, appears amongst several titled witnesses in a contract concerning exchange of land. The affair pertains to the "king" and the well-known *nadītu*, Bēlessunu.

145 Most recent edition is *AbB* 2 66. In a document dating to the time of Abi-ešuh, year after "0" (*JCS* 2, p. 104, n. 6), Marduk-muballiṭ, probably with the title gal$^{!}$-unken$^{!}$-na$^{!}$, appears as a gìr-official. The document concerns the delivery of lambs to *bārû*-priests for use in a ceremony "when the princess is sprinkled."

[146]a-šà gú-un, not gú-un a-šà.

[147]*Taxation,* manuscript, p. 109.

[148]*BB* 143; *Gerichtswesen,* pp. 150-51.

[149]Cf. Kraus, *Edikt,* p. 172.

[150]Cf. Ch. 3, p. 57ff.

[151]Translation from *CAD* D, p. 44.

[152]Ungnad, *ABPh* 121.

[153]Cf. *TCL* I 29 for these same individuals, and *VS* 16 181, 7 which mentions Ili-iddinam gal-unken-na *ša* ì-s[i-in?].

[154]Cf. *CAD* A/2, p. 520.

[155]This interpretation of *pānam šuršûm* follows Kraus, *RA* 64 (1970), p. 55ff.

[156]*HG* 751.

[157]*Gerichtswesen,* p. 150.

[158]*Merchant,* pp. 29-30.

[159]See above, p. 127ff.

[160]Discussion of ká-é-gal above, p. 86ff.

[161]If the *mu'errum* was the labor recruiter for crown estates, the subordinates assigned to the various fields on which the laborers worked were the *iššakkum*-officials. These officials in the Old Babylonian period were managers of land and not independent, private farmers as is sometimes asserted.

CHAPTER 5

Conclusion

Economy and Society in the Old Babylonian Period: A Résumé of the Presented Evidence

Our knowledge of the history of the Old Babylonian period after Hammurapi is sketchy at best, and the standard history books devote few pages to the last five kings of the dynasty and their 155 years of rule until the sacking of Babylon by the Hittites. After Samsu-iluna there are few royal inscriptions, and, except for a scattered reference or two in late chronicles, the historian must rely solely on date formulae to reconstruct the events that transpired under those rulers. The picture has thus emerged only in broad strokes: Hammurapi was a skillful and resourceful monarch, but already under his son Samsu-iluna, the "empire" began to erode under pressures from the south, northeast, and the west.[1] Over the final century the territory under the political control of the last rulers further contracted, sinking slowly into decline, until the Hittite raid put an end to the dynasty.

There have been investigations of Old Babylonian prices[2] and a number of very good studies dealing with various categories of people, from highborn women[3] to agricultural laborers.[4] In the future we are promised monographs on Sippar[5] and Larsa that will be broader than previous studies in their choice of topics and, at the same time, be more strictly controlled geographically and temporally. But for now our best source for many of the problems of social and economic relations in the latter part of the OB period is Kraus's publication of the Edict of Ammi-ṣaduqa. Although Kraus selected issues only in order to explicate the *Edikt* text, not in order to investigate the overall socio-economic structure of OB society, his analysis nevertheless touched on many terms and problems that had formerly received little attention. One problem, in particular, had to do with the economic role of the palace in the OB period, a subject dubbed by Kraus "the business affairs of the 'palace' " ("Die Geschaefte des 'Palastes' ").

Prior to Kraus's chapters the only study to my knowledge devoted to the role of the state in the economic life of the OB period was an article by Koschaker in the early 1940s concerning what he called the state monopoly of the fishing industry in Larsa;[6] and the chief reference book for titled officials in the OB period continues to be Walther's *Das altbabylonische Gerichtswesen,* written in 1917. Most scholars have tended to regard the OB period as an era of private enterprise *par excellence*, a time when "the private sector of the economy has . . . come to the fore."[7] Indeed, except for the two above-mentioned works, Koschaker's comment in 1923 in the last volume of *Hammurabis Gesetz,* that "administrative documents might as well not have been researched at all," is probably still applicable today.

Since Koschaker's and Walther's days, however, the number of OB texts has at least trebled; and although no order has been given these documents and letters (as Ungnad, Koschaker, and Schorr had done for the earlier materials), it is surely appropriate to reassess some of the previous interpretations of socio-economic relationships in the OB period in the light of these new texts. Then, too, if we are ever to penetrate into the internal history of the decline of Hammurapi's "empire" we must utilize these texts and letters, for we have no other sources.

In 1910 Koschaker proposed that administrative documents could be separated from private contracts on the ground that administrative documents were unwitnessed. This formal criterion has persisted into the 1970s and is probably an important reason why scholars have considered OB administrative texts to be so few in number. Actually, many administrative texts can only be recognized as such from a careful examination of the witnesses, a point that was demonstrated effectively by Landsberger in his study of the archive of Ubarum in *JCS* 9. Koschaker's and Kraus's analyses of administrative activity proceeded only from the explicit reference to the *ekallum* in their texts. As *ekallum* did not denote the royal residence, or any specific edifice, however, it was seen as more useful to translate *ekallum* as "crown," and to place the study of the *ekallum* in a larger context.

In order to undertake a study of the economic role of the crown it was necessary to expand the number of texts attesting the crown's economic activities. This became feasible by following a principle enunciated (but not pursued) by Kraus—that certain officials acted in the service of the crown in texts that did not refer to the palace. Thus, we have seen that many of the activities of Utul-Ištar, whom we knew was a crown official in the bureau of wool accounts, were performed in the crown's service even in cases where the word *ekallum* was omitted from the texts. He was engaged as the manager of crown estates responsible for the maintenance of land, supplying rations for the laborers who worked on the land and also providing the tools with which they worked. His services, moreover, went beyond mere land supervision; they also entailed disbursing the products of the lands, grain and wool. Utul-Ištar acted thereby as a finance officer, since the crown used its agricultural resources in order to function as a credit institution.

We noted that Utul-Ištar held two titles, *ṭupšarrum* and *abi ṣābim*, evidently advancing in rank in the latter stages of his career, although this change in status did not necessarily signal a change in all of his responsibilities. Since the title of "scribe" obviously was not descriptive of Utul-Ištar's duties, we turned to the possibility that the relatively obscure title *abi ṣābim* denoted a rank strictly reserved for crown officials acting within a fairly specific locus of responsibility. Since the longest study of *abi ṣābim* consisted of only one paragraph written by Walther half a century ago, and since the dictionaries only briefly touch upon the rank, it was necessary to re-evaluate the approximately 50 texts now known that mention the title *abi ṣābim* in the light of what had been learned about one of its best-attested holders. It was found that there was no attestation of this title before the reign of Ammi-ditana, and that it was possible both to trace the careers of various *abi ṣābim* officials, and also to follow the roles played by subordinates of these rather important individuals.

In this manner we were able to delimit a complex set of crown economic activities that formed what we termed an "artificial archive." One of the most striking results of this concatenation of documents was the finding that texts that would otherwise have been routinely adjudged private documents when analyzed in isolation could be ordered as elements in a complicated administrative procedure. Often the "chain of authority" of a contract, as Landsberger put it, could be ascertained only through a knowledge of the roles of the participants, and, not exceptionally, of those of the witnesses.

The implications of these procedures, as first enunciated by Landsberger, involve nothing less than an attempt to come to grips with the nature of the socio-economic system of organization, of which individual texts represent only the smallest segments of analysis. We should not categorize these texts simply as "administrative" documents, however, for the activities of crown bureaucrats were not limited to intramural governmental affairs, but, as in any state, also involved interaction with citizens not dependent on the crown and (to continue in Landsberger's idiom) with non-governmental "chains of authority." Without going into any detail on the structure of the "community"—which would in any event be highly speculative, given our limited knowledge of such subjects—it may be said here that just as territorially based, economically based and kin-based groups existed in the 3rd millennium (a point that Gelb and Diakonoff have been making for some years now), so too did they exist in the latter stages of the Old Babylonian period. The characterization of "documents" as economic, private, administrative or even legal texts, then, often begs the question of establishing the particular social and economic context in which that "document" was transacted.

It was seen that the rank of *abi ṣābim,* held by Utul-Ištar when he supervised the activities of a crown bureau of agricultural affairs, was confined to officials who were involved in the procurement and distribution of agricultural resources and were in charge of the storehouses of the crown. We turned then to an analysis of the rank *mu'errum.* The *mu'errum* was also a crown official engaged in agricultural activities, but not at such a high level as the *abi ṣābim.* The duties of the *mu'errum* were more localized, more directly concerned with the recruitment of workers on crown estates, while the *abi ṣābim* was the chief of his bureau.

Politics and Society in the Old Babylonian Period: A Study in Instability

In the course of isolating the range of activities of the *abi ṣābim*, the *mu'errum*, and other officials associated with them, it became apparent that many official ranks were rarely, if at all, attested before the time of Abi-ešuḫ (in the north), and that some titles, attested in earlier periods, had substantially different connotations in the time after Hammurapi. In other words, if we may trust our present sample, it seems that as the political strength and territory of the First Dynasty of Babylon waned, the number of titled officials in the service of the crown expanded and their offices became more highly articulated. To conclude this study, I would like to propose a model that tries to explain this seemingly paradoxical situation in terms of the internal process of the decline of the Old Babylonian "empire."

Excursus on the Methodology of Reconstructing Babylonian History from Non-historical Documents

The process of model-building is employed here in conscious departure from the methods of those Babylonian historians who view their mission as the systematic collection and chronological arrangement of all data formally classified as "historical" in a given time period. These data almost invariably deal with great personages and their deeds and with movements of ethno-linguistically defined populations across a carefully delimited stage. The data referring to historical events have been gleaned from the most varied genres of texts: from obviously biased royal inscriptions, tendentious chronicles and king-lists and even series of omens.[8]

In the period after the reign of Hammurapi to the fall of the First Dynasty of Babylon, however, almost none of the standard sources exist from which a traditional historical account could be written. Certain kinds of data from this period are in fact abundant, but the numerous extant documents and letters have usually been reserved for study within the framework of Mesopotamian legal systems. Thus, historians have passed over these years simply as an epoch of drawn-out economic decline and political weakness. Yet if the history of this period is to be written, it must utilize whatever data are available; and if these "non-historical" data can be used to reconstruct (late) Old Babylonian history, the study of these classes of materials in other times will provide a welcome control for the historical pictures already framed. In order to deal with socio-economic and legal documents as historical sources, however, new techniques of manipulating these data need to be developed, and the methods and assumptions involved must be set down explicitly.

Research into the complex area of Mesopotamian social history and its changing features through time must begin with the assumption that certain elements in Mesopotamian social systems will never be directly observable. This does not mean, obviously, that unattested elements or complexes of elements did not exist in the living culture; nor does it mean that we cannot infer their presence in some way. Just as linguists dealing with obscure languages operate within the framework of linguistic theory, and as scientists analyzing moon rocks utilize conceptual tools developed from the study of terrestrial phenomena, so must Assyriologists occasionally put aside their immediate texts in order to gain a better appreciation of Mesopotamian social institutions.

In spite of the enormous number of published texts, the fantastic quantity of tablets in museums awaiting publication and the untold number of texts still unearthed in the Middle East, it is unrealistic to believe that more than a small fraction of the potentially recoverable material will ever see the light of day. To this consideration of "sample" must be added an assessment of how much of a partly literate and long extinct society's socio-economic and political systems would ever have been recorded and also a recognition of the biases of the social strata who were commissioning the composition of these documents. Even under the most optimum circumstances of preservation, recovery and publication, therefore, texts can offer only disparate and highly focused episodes in the structure of ancient society. Restricting the study of social organization to these textual artifacts alone is to pretend that sampling problems do not exist. No amount of adding together discrete lumps of information will ever provide a coherent explanation of the workings of a Mesopotamian social system.

Cognizant that only some aspects of Babylonian society will be represented in the textual record, we may proceed with the further assumption that Babylonian culture is patterned and systematic and that organizational models derived from a cross-cultural perspective can be used to interpret Mesopotamian texts more efficiently. The theoretical position that bases social reconstruction solely on textual data and pointedly ignores cross-cultural reference leads to a cul-de-sac. On the one hand the limited sample of materials must distort all perceptions of cause and effect, and on the other hand restricting analysis only to extant Mesopotamian data is tantamount to asserting that Mesopotamian society differs from all other known societies. Particular Mesopotamian data are unique, but the circumstances determining their existence (redistributive and market networks of exchange, centralized government, bureaucracies, and so on) do not appear solely in Mesopotamia. Thus, Mesopotamian data are also representative since the operation of the various circumstances in Mesopotamian society can be effectively analyzed by judiciously referring to similar cases in other societies.

The formulation of models in which an analysis of Mesopotamian textual data is combined with bodies of cross-cultural, socio-economic theory will enable the Assyriological historian to employ more rigorously deductive methods that draw texts into specific areas of research. Such models will differ from traditional historical accounts: not only will they reproduce and seriate documented phenomena, but they will also incorporate these phenomena within holistic explanations of cause and effect. These explanations will generate their own test implications, then, as they will attempt to state what evidence would be needed to disprove the model. As disparate perceptions of Mesopotamian social history are unified through the construction of such models, description and categorization of data will become only preliminary occupations to the systematization of these materials into coherent explanations.

The ensuing model, of course, is not to be regarded as a final summation, but as a first attempt to explain the relationship between socio-economic and political changes in the latter part of the Old Babylonian period. As more data become available, or as better interpretations of existing data are realized, the model will be refined. Protestations that not every single idea in the model can be correlated with a single textual "fact," however, will not be regarded as fatal criticisms of the model as a whole.

The Economic Role of the Crown in the Old Babylonian Period: A Processual Model

After the period of petty-states and shifting balanced coalitions following the fall of the Third Dynasty of Ur, northern and southern Babylonia were politically and economically unified by Hammurapi. Economic policies were vigorously regulated by the crown, often by the king himself, as the royal correspondence of Hammurapi and Samsu-iluna shows. But there is no reason to believe that local groups and their elite strata were engulfed by this political system. The crown provided resources to certain social groups and in turn was partly dependent on the traditional institutional spheres of these groups for the inflow of the labor and material resources that it needed for the fulfillment of its regulative functions. Also, in order to implement its goals, and to maintain order, the crown needed to follow traditionally legitimate patterns of interaction, such as the promulgation of "law codes" and *mīšarum*-edicts exemplifying the just concern of the crown for all strata within society.

In spite of the appearance of these time-honored expressions of royal care and piety, the political situation in the south underwent notable and unwelcome change. With Hammurapi's conquest, traditional local authority there was bypassed and administrators from the crown were assigned the duties of strictly policing the agricultural, fishing, and hydraulic resources that were the life-blood of the economy. Taxes were exacted, and most land, whatever its tenure prior to the conquest, seems to have been placed in entail to the Babylonian state. Complaints about the inequity of the system were of necessity directed to Hammurapi himself, since the traditional local authorities were powerless, and the new administrators were mere puppets of the Babylonian king.[9] Ever eager to establish his claim as a just and equitable monarch, Hammurapi would often rule against his overzealous administrators in the face of long-standing rights of an injured party. The point, however, is not to belabor the individual inefficiency of the administrators, but to recognize that the Babylonian crown, in its policy of attempting to co-opt native authority in the newly conquered territory, sowed the seeds of its own destruction.

Political and economic systems with a highly centralized bureaucracy recruited from among inner circles of the administration are tremendously efficient military and economic forces in their initial stages, but are seldom able to institutionalize and legitimize themselves.[10] If certain degrees of autonomy are not built into the various institutions of production and consumption, and if conflicting goals are not channeled into legitimate forms of political struggle, such a highly centralized system will consistently appropriate free-floating resources and redirect them to and for the interests of the administration. In the OB period, this type of administration from the capital in Babylon, proved to be highly oppressive to its subjects, and conquered territory very quickly decomposed into its constitutent elements, each of which re-established its own local autonomy.

During the period of Hammurapi and Samsu-iluna the people who transmitted the political decisions from the crown to the populace were apparently recruited from the officers of the royal houshold (or oikos, as Gelb would put it)–kinsmen and dependents of the royal lineage. This system of "patrimonial bureaucracy" could be perpetuated only in times of strong central rulers, and we know that this condition was quite short-lived in the OB period, with the south already effecting its political independence from Babylon during the reign of Samsu-iluna. In the north, in the time after Samsu-iluna, the power of the crown grew progressively weaker, even as its administrative territory was shrinking. Although the crown still possessed some large estates, these were insufficient to meet the needs of maintaining a fiscally stable regulative framework. As a consequence of this weakened political structure and the loss of revenues because of diminished properties, the crown recruited increasing numbers of officials from "extrapatrimonial sources," probably from important families of the local community, mid- to upper-level elites.

With the crown no longer able to control its bureaucracy, officials were able to establish their offices as hereditary positions and to profit from tax-farming at the crown's expense. No longer in a position to maintain large squads of laborers as palace dependents, the crown had to hire personnel controlled by headmen of local units. The crown also acted increasingly as a credit institution, not only in the attempt to regulate market prices to its own ends, but to acquire resources that its estates were no longer supplying. In the attempt to generate hard cash, the crown often foreclosed on loans early (the intent of the so-called "Inhaberklausel" whereby the loan was to be repaid to the "bearer of the note"), thereby taking a loss in interest in order to have ready cash. This was not a "geniale Erfindung" ("happy discovery"), as one recent commentator has suggested, but a sign of serious fiscal instability.

The empire built by Hammurapi experienced a long decline, not through the personal inefficiency of succeeding rulers, but because Hammurapi's system was too inflexible to adapt to changing social and economic conditions. The highly centralized state had become initially quite prosperous from the tribute and taxes exacted from far-flung provinces. Through this new wealth, the crown in Babylon was able to remunerate its dependents and to undertake massive building and waterworks projects. When the southern, western and eastern provinces were able to break away, however, the resources needed by the crown to maintain its ambitious building projects and to finance its labor and military forces were severely curtailed. Without a drastic change in the idea of government on the part of the crown, the power of the Babylonian state, subject to these negative feedback mechanisms, could only weaken further over time.

It also needs to be mentioned that concomitant with the increasing agricultural demands of the crown was the worsening of an already fragile ecological situation. The greater pressures for increased outputs on diminished lands may well have entailed the abandonment of alternate fallow seasons, and the result (to telescope a complicated process) was serious salinization.[11] This process can be observed in the reduced outputs of barley and concurrently inflated prices toward the end of the OB period. Probably one reason for the proliferation of officials at this time was the desperate attempt by the crown to administer the poorer lands even more intensively, which only exacerbated the problem.

As the late Old Babylonian period progressed, then, bureaucrats no longer directly controlled by the crown, tended to emphasize loyalties to the groups from which they were recruited. The depleted resources of the crown left the rulers little more than figureheads, increasingly dependent on locally controlled goods and services. Finally, the state was formally overthrown by a marauding Hittite king and the bureaucracy simply reverted to the position of a locally based aristocracy, while the institutional framework of the political system, as well as its urban manifestations, collapsed.[12] The ruling house in Babylon fell victim to its own long-standing policies and the resulting internal instability, not to a military defeat by a foreign foe or as a result of mass ethnic disruptions. The Kassites, who succeeded to power, had a leadership structure that was apparently not greatly differentiated from the underlying Mesopotamian social organization consisting of ascribed, local groups and their elites, and as such, the Kassites have been described as having a "tribal" organization.[13] Certain administrative techniques of the Old Babylonian crown persisted, however, and the interactions among local groups gradually asserted themselves and in time found new political forms.

Finally, I believe, like Gelb,[14] that the picture of a complex relationship between the political system and the local social structures, with no one overriding power completely co-opting the others, more accurately characterizes the successive phases of Mesopotamian socio-economic history than does a simple evolution of single, predominant socio-economic forms. For the late OB period the analysis of the functioning of the political system within the overall structure of society and its relation to the parts of this structure has received little attention, but even in this period where we lack standard historical sources, we may still be able to trace the development and decline of specific social and economic conditions.

NOTES

[1]Gadd, *CAH*, vol. 1, pt. 2, Ch. 5 (= fascicle 35, p. 47ff).

[2]Schwenzner, *Wirtschaftsleben* (1915) and Meissner, *Warenpreise* (1936) both badly in need of up-dating.

[3]See Bibliography for several of Harris' studies on the *nadītum.*

[4]Lautner, *Personenmiete* (1936).

[5]The conclusions of Prof. Harris' recently published (1975) and highly useful compendium *Ancient Sippar. A Demographic Study of an Old Babylonian City 1894-1595 B.C.*, do not speak directly to the problems of historical change treated in this study. The analysis of certain ranks herein do challenge the views in *Ancient Sippar* and are deemed to provide a more detailed examination of those ranks.

[6]Koschaker, *ZA* 47 (1942), 136ff.

[7]Edzard, in Fischer Weltgeschichte, *Die altorientalischen Reiche* I, "Die altbabylonische Zeit" (= *The Near East: the Early Civilizations,* English translation, 1967, p. 213).

[8]Finkelstein, "Mesopotamian Historiography," *Proceedings of the American Philosophical Society,* fol. 107 (1963), pp. 461-72.

[9]Leemans, "King Hammurapi as Judge," in *Festschrift . . . David*, 1968 pp. 105-28; cf. comments of Finkelstein, "On Some Recent Studies in Cuneiform Law," *JAOS* 90 (1970), pp. 243-56.

[10]See especially the study of S. N. Eisenstadt, *The Political Systems of Empires,* Glencoe, 1963.

[11]See McGuire Gibson, "Violation of Fallow and Engineered Disaster in Mesopotamian Civilization," p. 7ff, and R. McC. Adams, "Historical Patterns of Mesopotamian Agriculture," p. 1ff., in *Irrigation's Impact on Society,* ed. Gibson and Downing, Tucson, 1974. Both papers controvert the "hydraulic hypothesis" of Wittfogel, which, briefly stated, argues that large scale irrigation systems require central management. Philologically approached, the situation in the late Old Babylonian period confirms Adams' and Gibson's archaeologically-derived opinions. Lower yields of barley and inflated prices along with many new official titles concerned with agricultural management in the latter part of the OB period indicate that state direction of irrigation, for the sake of political expediency, would seem to have placed too great a burden on the land. Over-irrigation results in ecological disaster even as neglect of irrigation systems will. For some interesting documentation of how complex, though smaller scale irrigation systems can be managed without a complex bureaucracy, see R. Netting, "The System Nobody Knows: Village Irrigation in the Swiss Alps," in *Irrigation's Impact on Society,* p. 67ff. The perils of centralizing previously locally controlled irrigation systems are described by S. Lees, "The State's Use of Irrigation in Changing Peasant Society," in *Irrigation's Impact of Society,* p. 123ff., and by K. Flannery, "The Cultural Evolution of Civilizations," in *Annual Review of Ecology and Systematics,* vol. III, 1972, p. 399ff; also Ch. VII, "Changing Patterns of Local Authority: Irrigation," in R. Fernea, *Shaykh and Effendi,* Cambridge, 1970.

[12]Archaeological surveys indicate that in the Kassite period there was "a substantial decline in both the density of settlement and the degree of urbanization," R. McC. Adams, *Land Behind Baghdad,* Chicago,

1965, p. 54. The same picture holds for the southern part of Mesopotamia, Adams and Nissen, *The Uruk Countryside,* Chicago, 1972, p. 39.

[13]J. A. Brinkman, "Foreign Relations of Babylonia from 1600 B.C.–625 B.C.: The Documentary Evidence," *AJA* 76 (1972), p. 280; Brinkman, *A Political History of Post-Kassite Babylonia,* Rome, 1968, p. 253f.

[14]Most forcefully stated in *Studi in Onore di Edoardo Volterra,* vol. VI, p. 154.

REGISTER OF CITED TEXTS

BIBLIOGRAPHY

ADAMS, R. McC.
1965 *Land Behind Baghdad.* Chicago: The University of Chicago Press.
1974 "Historic Patterns of Mesopotamian Irrigation Agriculture," in *Irrigation's Impact on Society,* eds. M. Gibson and T. Downing, pp. 1-6. Tucson: The University of Arizona Press.

ADAMS, R. McC. AND H. J. NISSEN
1972 *The Uruk Countryside.* Chicago: The University of Chicago Press.

ALEXANDER, J.
1943 *Early Babylonian Letters and Economic Texts,* BIN 7. New Haven.

BALL, C.
1907 "A 'Kassite' text; and a first dynasty tablet," *PSBA* 29:273ff.

BIGGS, R.
1967 "Semitic Names in the Fara Period," *OrNS* 36:55ff.

BIROT, M.
1969 *Tablettes économiques et administratives d'époque babylonienne ancienne.* Paris: Paul Geuthner.

BOGAERT, R.
1969 *Les origines antiques de la banque de dépôt.* Leiden: Sijthoff.

BRINKMAN, J. A.
1968 *A Political History of Post-Kassite Babylonia,* Analecta Orientalia 43. Rome: Pontifical Biblical Institute.
1972 "Foreign Relations of Babylonia from 1600 B.C.–625 B.C.: the Documentary Evidence," *AJA* 76:271ff.

CARDASCIA, G. AND J. KLÍMA
1966 *Droits cunéiformes.* Introduction bibliographique à l'histoire du droit et à l'éthnologie juridique, A.2. Paris.

CHIERA, E.
1922 *Old Babylonian Contracts,* PBS 8/2. Philadelphia.

ÇIĞ, M., H. KIZILYAY, AND F. R. KRAUS
1952 *Altbabylonische Rechtsurkunden aus Nippur.* Istanbul

DAICHES, S.
1904 "Zur Erklaerung des Hammurabi-Codex," *ZA* 18:202ff.

DEIMEL, A.
1933 *Šumerisches Lexikon,* part II, Vollstaendige Ideogramm-Sammlung, parts 1-4. Rome: Pontifical Biblical Institute.
1950 *Pantheon Babylonicum, oder Keilschriftkatalog der babylonischen Goetternamen,* ŠL IV/1. Rome: Pontifical Biblical Institute.

DIAKONOFF, I.
1963 "The Commune in the Ancient East as Treated in the Works of Soviet Researchers," *Soviet Anthropology and Archaeology* 2:32ff. (from *VDI*).

DIAKONOFF, I.

1969 "The Rise of the Despotic State in Ancient Mesopotamia," in *Ancient Mesopotamia*, ed. Diakonoff, pp. 173ff.. Moscow: Nauka publishing house.

1971 "On the Structure of Old Babylonian Society," in *Beitraege zur sozialen Struktur des alten Vorderasien,* ed. H. Klengel, Schriften zur Geschichte und Kultur des Alten Orients 1, pp. 15ff.. Berlin: Akademie Verlag.

VAN DIJK, J.

1960 *Sumerische Goetterlieder* II, Abhandlungen der Heidelberger Akademie der Wissenschaften, philosophisch-historische Klasse, 1960/I. Heidelberg: Carl Winter.

1967 "VAT 8382. Ein zweisprachiges Koenigsritual," *Heidelberger Studien zum alten Orient,* ed. D. Edzard, pp. 233-68. Wiesbaden: Otto Harrassowitz.

1968 *Old Babylonian Contracts and Related Material,* TIM V. Wiesbaden: Otto Harrassowitz.

DOSSIN, G.

1934 *Lettres de la première dynastie babylonienne,* TCL 17, 18. Paris. (1933, 1934).

EBELING, E.

1937 "Kritische Beitraege zu neueren assyriologischen Veroeffentlichungen," *MAOG* X/2.

EBELING, E., ed.

1932 *RlA* I, II, Berlin and Leipzig: Walter de Gruyter. (1932, 1938).

EDZARD. D.

1957 *Die "Zweite Zwischenzeit" Babyloniens.* Wiesbaden: Otto Harrassowitz.

1965 "Die altbabylonische Zeit," in Fischer Weltgeschichte, vol. II, *Die altorientalischen Reiche* I, pp. 165ff.. Frankfurt: Fischer Buecherei. (English translation: *The Near East: The Early Civilizations,* eds. Bottéro, Cassin, Vercoutter. London: Weidenfeld and Nicolson).

1971 *Altbabylonische Rechts- und Wirtschaftsurkunden aus Tell ed-Dēr bei Sippar,* TIM VII. Wiesbaden: Otto Harrassowitz.

1972 *Die altbabylonischen Rechts- und Wirtschaftsurkunden aus Tell ed-Dēr im Iraq Museum,* Bayrische Akademie der Wissenschaften, philosophisch-historische Klasse, Abhandlunden, Neue Folge Heft 72. Munich.

EISENSTADT, S.

1963 *The Political Systems of Empires.* New York: Free Press.

ELLIS, M. de J.

1969 *Taxation and Land Revenues in the Old Babylonian Period,* unpublished Ph.D. dissertation, Yale University. (Revised edition, in press, 1976).

1972 "*ṣimdatu* in the Old Babylonian Sources," *JCS* 24:74ff.

EVANS, G.

1958 "Ancient Mesopotamian Assemblies," *JAOS* 78:1-11, 114-15.

1962 "The Incidence of Labour-Service in the Old Babylonian Period," *JAOS* 83:20ff.

FALKENSTEIN, A.

1959 *Sumerische Goetterlieder* I, Abhandlungen der Heidelberger Akademie der Wissenschaften, philosophisch-historische Klasse, Heidelberg: Carl Winter.

1963 "Zu den Inschriftfunden der Grabung in Uruk-Warka, 1960-61," *BaghMitt* 2:1-83

1965 "Die Ur- und Fruehgeschichte des alten Vorderasien," Fischer Weltgeschichte, vol. II, *Die altorientalischen Reiche* I, pp. 13ff. Frankfurt: Fischer Buecherei.

FEIGIN, S.

n.d. *YOS* 12, unpublished, cited by permission of W. W. Hallo.

FERNEA, R.

1970 *Shaykh and Effendi.* Cambridge: Harvard University Press.

FIGULLA, H.
1914 *Altbabylonische Vertraege,* VS 13. Leipzig.
1958 "Fifty Old Babylonian Letters from Harmal," *Sumer* 14:3ff.
1965 "Tavern Keepers and the Like in Ancient Babylonia," in *Studies in Honor of Benno Landsberger on his Seventy-fifth Birthday,* AS 16:211ff.

FINKELSTEIN, J.
1955 "Subartu and Subarians," *JCS* 9:1ff.
1961 "Ammiṣaduqa's Edict and the Babylonian 'Law Codes'," *JCS* 15:91ff..
1962 "Mesopotamia," *JNES* 21:73ff..
1963 "Mesopotamian Historiography," *Proceedings of the American Philosophical Society,* vol. 107, pp. 461-72.
1968 *Old Babylonian Legal Documents,* CT 48. London.
1969a "The Edict of Ammiṣaduqa: A New Text," *RA* 63:45ff.
1969b "The Edict of Ammiṣaduqa" (translation), in *ANET Supplement,* ed. J. Pritchard, pp. 527f. Princeton.
1970 "On Some Recent Studies in Cuneiform Law," *JAOS* 90:243ff..
1972 *Late Old Babylonian Documents and Letters,* YOS 13. New Haven.

FISH, T.
1936 *Letters of the First Babylonian Dynasty.* Manchester.

FLANNERY, K.
1972 "The Cultural Evolution of Civilizations," *Annual Review of Ecology and Systematics,* vol. III, pp. 399ff..

FRANKENA, R.
1966 *Briefe aus dem British Museum (LIH and CT 2-33),* AbB II. Leiden: Brill.
1968 *Briefe aus der Leidener Sammlung (TLB IV),* AbB III. Leiden: Brill.

GADD, C.
1965 "Hammurabi and the End of His Dynasty," ch. 5, vol. II, part 1 (= fasc. 35), *Cambridge Ancient History,* third edition.

GAUTHIER, J-E.
1908 *Archives d'une famille de Dilbat au temps de la première dynastie de Babylone.* Le Caire.

GELB, I.
1969 "On the Alleged Temple and State Economies in Ancient Mesopotamia," in *Studi in Onore di Edoardo Volterra,* vol. VI, 137ff.
1967 "Approaches to the Study of Ancient Society," *JAOS* 87:1ff.

GIBSON, M.
1974 "Violation of Fallow and Engineered Disaster in Mesopotamian Civilization," in *Irrigation's Impact on Society,* eds. M. Gibson and T. Downing, pp. 7ff. Tucson: The University of Arizona Press.

GOETZE, A.
1948 "Thirty Tablets from the Reigns of Abi-ešuḫ and Ammi-ditana," *JCS* 2:73ff.
1956 *The Laws of Eshnunna,* Annual of the American Schools of Oriental Research 31. New Haven.
1957 "Old Babylonian Documents from Sippar in the Collection of the Catholic University of America," *JCS* 11:15ff.

GRANT, E.
1918 *Cuneiform Documents in the Smith College Library.* Haverford.

GURNEY, O. AND P. HULIN
1964 *The Sultantepe Tablets,* vol. II. London: The British Institute of Archaeology of Ankara.

HALLO, W.
1958 "Contributions to Neo-Sumerian," *HUCA* 29:69ff.
1972a "The House of Ur-Meme," *JNES* 31:87ff.
1972b *The Ancient Near East: A History.* New York:Harcourt, Brace, Jovanovich.

HARRIS, M.
1968 *The Rise of Anthropological Theory.* New York: Thomas Y. Crowell.

HARRIS, R.
1962 "Bibliographical Notes on *naditus*," *JCS* 16:1ff.
1963 "The Organization and Administration of the Cloister in Ancient Babylonia," *JESHO* 6:121ff.
1964 "The *nadītu*-woman," in *Studies Presented to A. Leo Oppenheim,* pp. 106ff. Chicago: University of Chicago Press.
1975 *Ancient Sippar. A Demographic Study of an Old Babylonian City 1894-1595 B.C.* Leiden: Nederlands Historisch-Archaeologisch Instituut te Istanbul.

HEICHELHEIM, F.
1960 Review of Polanyi, et. al., "Trade and Market in the Early Empires," *JESHO* 3:108ff.

HELBAEK, H.
1966 "Plant Remains," Appendix 1 in M. Mallowan, *Nimrud and Its Remains,* vol. II, pp. 613ff. London: Collins.

HIRSCH, H.
1967 Review of *CT* 45 in *ZANF* 24:330ff.

JACOBSEN, T.
1943 "Primitive Democracy in Ancient Mesopotamia," *JNES* 2:159ff.
1957 "Early Political Development in Mesopotamia," *ZA* 52:91ff.
1970 *Toward the Image of Tammuz,* (papers by Jacobsen) ed. W. Moran. Cambridge: Harvard University Press.

JONES, T.
1951 "By the Waters of Babylon Sat We Down," *Agricultural History* 25:1ff.

KANG, S.
1972 *Sumerian Economic Texts from the Drehem Archive.* Urbana: University of Illinois Press.

KING, L.
1912 *CT* 33. London.

KLENGEL, H.
1971 "Soziale Aspekte der altbabylonischen Dienstmiete," in *Beitraege zur sozialen Struktur des alten Vorderasien,* ed. H. Klengel. Schriften zur Geschichte und Kultur des Alten Orients 1, pp. 39ff. Berlin: Akademie Verlag.

KLENGEL, H., ed.
1971 *Beitraege zur sozialen Struktur des alten Vorderasien,* Schriften zur Geschichte und Kultur des alten Orients 1. Berlin: Akademie Verlag.

KOHLER, J.
(See Ungnad, A.)

KOSCHAKER, P.
1931 *Ueber einige griechische Rechtsurkunden aus den oestlichen Randgebieten des Hellenismus, mit Beitraegen zum Eigentums- und Pfandbegriff nach griechischen und orientalischen Rechten.* Leipzig: Abhandlungen der Saechsischen Akademie der Wissenschaften, philologisch-historische Klasse, 42/I.
1942 "Zur staatlichen Wirtschaftsverwaltung in altbabylonischer Zeit, insbesondere nach Urkunden aus Larsa," *ZA* 47:136-80.

KRAUS, F.
1947 "Die Istanbuler Tontafelsammlung," *JCS* 1:93ff.
1951 "Nippur und Isin nach altbabylonischen Rechtsurkunden," *JCS* 3:1-228.
1953 "Le rôle des temples depuis la troisième dynastie d'Ur jusqu'à la première dynastie de Babylone," *Cahiers d'histoire mondiale,* I:518ff. Paris.
1958 *Ein Edikt des Koenigs Ammiṣaduqa von Babylon,* Studia et Documenta ad Iura Orientis Antiqui Pertinentia, vol. 5. Leiden: Brill.
1964 *Briefe aus dem British Museum (CT 43-44),* AbB I. Leiden.
1966 *Staatliche Viehhaltung im altbabylonischen Lande Larsa,* Mededelingen der Koninklijke Nederlandse Akademie van Wetenschappen, Afd. Letterkunde, Nieuwe Reeks, Deel 29, No. 5. Amsterdam: North Holland Publishing Co.
1968a *Briefe aus dem Archive des Šamaš-ḫāzir in Paris und Oxford (TCL 7 und OECT 3),* AbB 4. Leiden: Brill.
1968b "Sesam im alten Mesopotamien," *JAOS* 88:112ff.
1970a "Akkadische Woerter und Ausdruecke I-III," *RA* 64:53ff.
1970b *Sumerer und Akkader,* Mededelingen der Koninklijke Nederlandse Akademie van Wetenschappen, Afd. Letterkunde, Nieuwe Reeks, Deel 33, No. 8. Amsterdam: North Holland Publishing Co.

KRAUS, F., M. ÇIĞ AND H. KIZILYAY
1952 *Altbabylonische Rechtsurkunden aus Nippur.* Istanbul.

KRAUS, P.
1932 *Altbabylonische Briefe* 2, MVAG 36/I. Leipzig.

KRUECKMANN, O.
1928 "Beamter," *RlA* I:44ff.

LABAT, R.
1963 *Manuel d'épigraphie akkadienne.* Paris: Imprimerie Nationale.

LANDSBERGER, B.
1915 "Bemerkungen zur altbabylonischen Briefliteratur," *ZDMG* 69:491ff.
1937 *Die Serie ana ittišu,* MSL I. Rome: Pontifical Biblical Institute.
1939 "Die babylonischen Termini fuer Gesetz und Recht," *Festschrift Koschaker,* Studia et Documenta ad Iura Orientis Antiqui Pertinentia, vol. 2, pp. 219ff. Leiden: Brill.
1954 "Babylonian Scribal Craft and its Terminology," *Proceedings of the 23rd Congress of Orientalists*, p. 103. Cambridge.
1955 "Remarks on the Archive of the Soldier Ubarum," *JCS* 9:121ff.
1957 *The Series ḪAR-ra = ḫubullu, tablets V-VII,* MSL VI. Rome: Pontifical Biblical Institute.

LANDSBERGER, B.
1960 "Scribal Concepts of Education," in *City Invincible,* ed. Kraeling and Adams, pp. 94-102. Chicago: University of Chicago Press.
1967 *The Date Palm and its By-products according to the Cuneiform Sources,* AfO Beiheft 17. Graz.
1968 "Jungfraeulichkeit: Ein Beitrag zum Thema 'Beilager und Eheschliessung' (mit einem Anhang: neue Lesungen und Deutungen im Gesetzbuch von Ešnunna)", *Festschrift David,* pp. 41ff. Leiden: Brill.
1969 *The Series lú = ša and Related Texts,* prepared by Landsberger, ed. M. Civil, MSL 12. Rome: Pontifical Biblical Institute.

LANDSBERGER, B., Ed.
1955 *Das Vokabular S^a,* MSL III. Rome: Pontifical Biblical Institute.
1956 *Emesal-vocabular,* MSL IV:121ff. Rome: Pontifical Biblical Institute.

LAUTNER, J.
1936 *Altbabylonische Personenmiete und Erntearbeitervertraege,* Studia et Documenta ad Iura Orientis Antiqui Pertinentia, vol. 1. Leiden: Brill.

LEEMANS, W.
1950 *The Old Babylonian Merchant,* Studia et Documenta ad Iura Antiqui Pertinentia, vol. 3. Leiden: Brill.
1954-64 *Old Babylonian Legal and Administrative Documents,* TLB I. Leiden: Brill.
1954 *Legal and Economic Records form the Kingdom of Larsa,* SLB I/2. Leiden: Brill.
1957 "Some Aspects of Theft and Robbery in Old-Babylonian Documents," *RSO* 32:66ff.
1959 "Quelques remarques au sujet des tablettes de l'époque vieux-babylonienne du musée de Genève," *JESHO* 2:324ff.
1960a *Legal and Administrative Documents of the Time of Hammurabi and Samsuiluna (mainly from Lagaba),* SLB I/3. Leiden: Brill.
1960b *Foreign Trade in the Old Babylonian Period,* Studia et Documenta ad Iura Orientis Antiqui Pertinentia, vol. 6. Leiden: Brill.
1966 "Cuneiform Texts in the Collection of Dr. Ugo Sissa," *JCS* 20:34ff.
1968a "Old Babylonian Letters and Economic History," *JESHO* 11:171ff.
1968b "King Hammurapi as Judge," *Festschrift David,* pp. 105-28. Leiden: Brill.
1972 "Quelques remarques à propos d'un texte concernant l'administration et des terres vieux-babylonienne," *Festschrift Boehl,* pp. 281ff.

LEES, S.
1974 "The State's Use of Irrigation in Changing Peasant Society," in *Irrigation's Impact on Society,* eds. M. Gibson and T. Downing, pp. 123ff. Tucson: The University of Arizona Press.

LIMET, H.
1960 *Le travail du métal au pays de Sumer au temps de la IIIe dynastie d'Ur,* Bibliotèque de la faculté de Philosophie et Lettres de l'Université de Liège, 155. Paris.

LINDL, E.
1913 *Das Priester- und Beamtentum der altbabylonischen Kontrakte.* Paderborn.

MICHAŁOWSKI, P.
1976 The Royal Correspondence of Ur. Ph.D Dissertation. Yale University.

MEISSNER, B.
1893 *Beitraege zum altbabylonischen Privatrecht,* Assyriologische Bibliothek II. Leipzig.
1936 *Warenpriese in Babylonien,* Abhandlungen der Preussische Akademie der Wissenschaften, philosophisch-historische Klasse, 1936, I. Berlin.
NETTING, R.
1974 "The System Nobody Knows: Village Irrigation in the Swiss Alps," in *Irrigation's Impact on Society,* eds. M. Gibson and T. Downing, pp. 67ff. Tucson: University of Arizona Press.
OPPENHEIM, A. L.
1948 *Catalogue of the Cuneiform Tablets of the Wilberforce Eames Babylonian Collection in the New York Public Library.* American Oriental Series 32. New Haven.
1957 "A Bird's-eye View of Mesopotamian Economic History," in *Trade and Market in the Early Empires,* eds. Polanyi, Arensberg, Perason, pp. 22ff. Glencoe: Free Press.
1964a "Assyriology–Why and How," *Current Anthropology* 1, (1960), reprinted as Ch. I in *Ancient Mesopotamia.* Chicago: University of Chicago Press.
1964b *Ancient Mesopotamia.* Chicago: University of Chicago Press.
1965 "A Note on the Scribes in Mesopotamia," in *Studies in Honor of Benno Landsberger on his Seventy-fifth Birthday,* AS 16, pp. 253-56. Chicago.
1967 "A New Look at the Structure of Mesopotamian Society," *JESHO* 10:1ff.
OPPENHEIM, A. L., Ed.
1956-73 *The Assyrian Dictionary of the University of Chicago,* vols. A/1, A/2, B, D, E, G, H, I/J, K, Ṣ, Z.
OWEN, D.
1972 "A Unique Letter-order in the University of North Carolina," *JCS* 24:133f.
PETTINATO, G.
1968 "Il binomio tempio-stato e l'economia della seconda dinastia di Lagaš," *Oriens Antiquus* 7:39ff.
PINCHES, T.
1896 *CT* 2. London.
1898a *CT* 4. London.
1898b *CT* 6. London.
1899a *CT* 8. London.
1899b "Early Babylonian Contracts," *JRAS* 103ff.
1964 *CT* 45. London.
POEBEL, A.
1909 *Babylonian Legal and Business Documents from the time of the First Dynasty of Babylon, chiefly from Nippur,* BE 6/2. Philadelphia.
POLANYI, K.
1957 "Marketless Trading in Hammurabi's Time," in *Trade and Market in the Early Empires,* eds. Polanyi, Arensberg, Pearson, pp. 12ff. Glencoe: Free Press.
1968a "The Semantics of Money-Uses," in *Primitive, Archaic and Modern Economies,* ed. G. Dalton, pp. 175ff. Boston: Beacon Press.
1968b "Ports of Trade in Early Societies," in *Primitive, Archaic and Modern Economies,* ed. G. Dalton, pp. 238ff. Boston: Beacon Press.

PRITCHARD, J., Ed.
1969 *Ancient Near Eastern Texts Relating to the Old Testament,* 2nd edition, 1965, Supplement. Princeton: Princeton University Press.
PRITSCH, E.
1950 "Zur juristischen Bedeutung der šubanti-Formel," *Bonner Biblische Beitraege* I:172ff.
RANKE, H.
1906 *Babylonian Legal and Business Documents from the Time of the First Dynasty of Babylon, chiefly from Sippar,* 6/1. Philadelphia.
REINER, E.
1961 "The Year Dates of Sumu-jamūtbāl," *JCS* 15:121ff.
RENGER, J.
1966 "*ṭēmam panam šuršûm* und verwandte Ausdruecke," *JNES* 27:136ff.
1967 "Untersuchungen zum Priestertum in der altbabylonischen Zeit," *ZANF* 24:110ff.
RIFTIN, A.
1937 *Starovavilonskie juridičeskie i administrativnie dokumenti v sobranijach SSSR.* Moscow.
ROELLIG, W.
1970 *Das Bier im Alten Mesopotamien.* Berlin.
SALONEN, A.
1968 *Agricultura Mesopotamica,* Annales Academiae Scientiarum Fennicae, Ser. B, vol. 149. Helsinki.
SAN NICOLÒ, M.
1931 *Beitraege zur Rechtsgeschichte im Bereiche des keilschriftlichen Rechtsquellen.* Oslo.
SCHEIL, V.
1902 *Une saison de fouilles à Sippar.* Le Caire.
1915 "Les Ḫabiru au temps de Rim-Sin," *RA* 12:114ff.
SCHORR, M.
1913 *Urkunden des altbabylonischen Zivil- und Prozessrechts,* Vorderasiatische Bibliothek 5. Leipzig.
SCHROEDER, O.
1917 *Altbabylonische Briefe,* VS 16. Leipzig.
SCHWENZNER, W.
1915 *Zum altbabylonischen Wirtschaftsleben,* MVAG 19/III. Leipzig.
SJOEBERG, Å.
1969a *The Collection of the Sumerian Temple Hymns.* TCS III, Locust Valley.
1969b "Contributions to the Sumerian Lexicon," *JCS* 21:275-78.
VON SODEN, W.
1933 *Die lexikalischen Tafelserie der Babylonier und Assyrer in dem Berliner Museum II: Die akkadischen Synonymlisten.* Berlin.
1965-71 *Akkadisches Handwoerterbuch, a-ramû.* Wiesbaden: Otto Harrassowitz.
VON SODEN, W. AND W. ROELLIG
1967 *Das Akkadische Syllabar,* 2nd ed., *An.Or.* 42. Rome.
SOLLBERGER, E.
1951 "Thirty-two dated Tablets from the Reign of Abī-ešuḫ," *JCS* 5:77ff.
1965 "A Three-Column Silbenvokabular A," in *Studies in Honor of Benno Landsberger on His Seventy-fifth Birthday,* AS 16, pp. 21ff. Chicago.

STAMM, J.

1939 *Die akkadische Namengebung*, MVAG 44. Leipzig.

STOL, M.

1976 *Studies in Old Babylonian History*. Leiden: Nederlands Historisch-Archaeologisch Instituut te Istanbul.

SZLECHTER, E.

1953 "Les tablettes juridiques datées du règne d'Abī-ešuḫ conservées au Musée d'art et d'histoire de Genève," *JCS* 7:81ff.

1958 *Tablettes juridiques de la Ire dynastie de Babylone, conservées au Musée d'art et d'histoire de Genève*, Paris.

1963 *Tablettes juridiques et administratives de la IIIe dynastie d'Ur et la Ire dynastie de Babylone, conservées au Musée de l'Université de Manchester et à Cambridge, au Musée Fitzwilliam à l'Institut d'Etudes Orientales et à l'Institut d'Egyptologie*. Paris.

THUREAU-DANGIN, F.

1910 *Lettres et contrats de l'époque de la première dynastie babylonienne*, TCL I. Paris.

1924 *Lettres de Hammurapi a Šamaš-hâṣir*, TCL 7. Paris.

UNGER, E.

1931 "Topographie der Stadt Dilbat," *ArOr* 3:21ff.

1938 "Dilbat," in *RlA* II. Berlin.

UNGNAD, A.

1909a *Altbabylonische Privaturkunden*, VS 7-9. Leipzig.

1909b "Untersuchungen zu den im VII. Hefte der Vorderasiatischen Schriftdenkmaeler veroeffentlichten Urkunden aus Dilbat," *BA* 6/5. Leipzig.

1914 *Babylonische Briefe aus der Zeit der Hammurapi-Dynastie*, Leipzig.

1915 *Babylonian Letters of the Hammurapi Period*, PBS 7. Philadelphia.

1920 *Altbabylonische Briefe aus dem Museum zu Philadelphia*, reprinted from the *Zeitschrift fuer vergleichende Rechtswissenschaft* 36:214ff.

UNGNAD, A. AND J. KOHLER

1909 *Hammurabi's Gesetz*, vol. III. Leipzig.

1910 *Hammurabi's Gesetz*, vol. IV. Leipzig.

1911 *Hammurabi's Gesetz*, vol. V. Leipzig.

UNGNAD, A. AND P. KOSCHAKER

1923 *Hammurabi's Gesetz*, vol. VI. Leipzig.

VEENHOF, K.

1972 *Aspects of Old Assyrian Trade and its Terminology*, Studia et Documenta ad Iura Orientis Pertinentia, vol. 10. Leiden: Brill.

WAETZOLDT, H.

1972 *Untersuchung zur neusumerischen Textilindustrie*. Centro per le antichità e la storia dell'arte del Vicino Oriente, Studi economici e technologici, vol. 1: Rome.

WALTERS, S.

1970 *Water for Larsa*, Yale Near Eastern Researches 4. New Haven.

WALTHER, A.

1917 *Das altbabylonische Gerichtswesen*, Leipziger Semitische Studien VI/4-6. Leipzig.

WATERMAN, L.

1916 *Business Documents of the Hammurapi Period from the British Museum*. London. (pp. 41-92 = *AJSL* 29:149-200; pp. 93-107 = *AJSL* 29:289-303; pp. 108-33 = *AJSL* 30:48-73; pp. 134-37 = *AJSL* 29:201-04.)

YOFFEE, N.

1976 Review of Veenhof, K., "Aspects of Old Assyrian Trade and Its Terminology," *JNES* 35:62-65.

1977 "The Old Babylonian Texts from Kish: A First Report," to appear in *Ancient Near Eastern Studies in Memory of Prof. J. J. Finkelstein*. Memoirs of the Connecticut Academy of Arts and Sciences, vol. 19, in press.

Addenda

To p. 22, Table I add — A-ṣ 15 *RA* 69, p. 112
Date lost *TIM* 5 48

To p. 26 add — *RA* 69, p. 112 and *TIM* 5 48 also depict Utul-Ishtar renting property.

To p. 51, n. 120 add — Compare Civil, "Notes on Sumerian Lexicography III," *JCS* 28 (1976), pp. 183-87, who provides a welter of references to show the complex "morpholexical structure" of the term šu-kin--dab=*kamāsu* (that is, *kamāsu* B, "to kneel down," not *kamāsu* A, "to gather," p. 185, n. 5). When applied to agricultural implements, " ŠU.KIN is a graphic variation of túg-gur$_{10}$" (reading for túk-kin), according to Civil. The *YOS* 13 texts, however, are not cited, although *YOS* 13 72 and 73 in which ^{urudu}ŠU.KIN is used with *kamāsu*, "to gather," are pertinent for a critical evaluation of the different traditions of the lexical lists.

To the Bibliography add — ANBAR, M. "Textes d'époque babylonienne ancienne." *RA* 69: 109-36. 1975.
CIVIL, M. "Notes on Sumerian Lexicography III." *JCS* 28: 183-87. 1976.

To the Register of Cited Texts add
RA 69, p. 112 addenda
TIM 5 48 addenda